Northwestern University
STUDIES IN *Phenomenology &*
Existential Philosophy

Husserlian Meditations

Robert Sokolowski

Husserlian Meditations

How Words Present Things

NORTHWESTERN UNIVERSITY PRESS

EVANSTON   1974

Robert Sokolowski is Professor of Philosophy at The Catholic University of America, Washington, D.C.

Permission is gratefully acknowledged for quotations from the following works of Ezra Pound: Canto lxxiv, from *The Cantos* (*1–95*), copyright 1948 by Ezra Pound; Letter to H. L. Mencken, from *The Selected Letters of Ezra Pound, 1907–1941*, ed. D. D. Paige, copyright 1950 by Ezra Pound; Digest of the Analects, from *Guide to Kulchur,* all rights reserved, copyright © 1970 by Ezra Pound. These quotations are reprinted with permission from New Directions Publishing Co. and Faber and Faber Ltd., London.

First paperback printing 1980

TO
THOMAS PRUFER

Contents

Preface

THIS BOOK is an exposition of and a philosophical commentary on the work of Edmund Husserl. It presents his doctrines systematically, not chronologically, and interprets many of his texts. The exposition is not carried out for its own sake; through it I attempt to describe what it is to be truthful and to be human, and to show what philosophy is. In some respects what I say becomes a criticism of what Husserl has written, but obviously the differences exist only by virtue of the identity that supports them.

In writing the book I have tried to keep in mind issues of classical political philosophy, issues current in linguistic analysis, and concerns raised in the philosophy of being.

The manuscript of this book was composed in 1971–72, during a sabbatical granted by the Catholic University of America and under a Fellowship from the National Endowment for the Humanities. I wish to express my gratitude for these, as well as for help provided by the university toward preparation of the manuscript.

I wish to thank those who have helped me study Husserl and the issues discussed in this book, especially Hans-Georg Gadamer, William Rooney, Paul Weiss, John Brough, and the late Aron Gurwitsch. I am grateful to Jude P. Dougherty for his assistance and encouragement in the preparation of this volume, grateful also to the Husserl Archives at the New School for Social Research, and to its secretary Lloyd Carr. My old debt to the Husserl Archives at Louvain, and to H. L. Van Breda, Rudolf Boehm, and Iso Kern is still outstanding.

My book is dedicated to Thomas Prufer because so much of

it is a record of my conversation with him. His suggestions about details have removed blemishes, satisfied some deficiencies, and improved expression; the thoughts that support the book I have learned from or with him. As the Philosopher says, "with friends men are more able to think and to act."

I wish finally to express my thanks to Francis Slade, who has made clear to me several elementary distinctions on which all philosophical issues depend.

Robert Sokolowski
Washington, D.C.
June, 1973

List of Abbreviations

THE FOLLOWING is a list of the abbreviations of Husserl's works employed in the book. Where possible, the references will be made to the available English translations.

APS   *Analysen zur Passiven Synthesis.* Edited by M. Fleischer (*Husserliana XI*). The Hague: Nijhoff, 1966.

CM   *Cartesianische Meditationen und Pariser Vorträge.* Edited by S. Strasser (*Husserliana I*). The Hague: Nijhoff, 1959. *Cartesian Meditations.* Translated by D. Cairns. The Hague: Nijhoff, 1960.

Crisis   *Die Krisis der europäischen Wissenschaften und die transzendentale Phänomenologie.* Edited by W. Biemel (*Husserliana VI*). The Hague: Nijhoff, 1954. *The Crisis of European Sciences and Transcendental Phenomenology.* Translated by D. Carr. Evanston, Ill.: Northwestern University Press, 1970. Carr has not translated all the supplements included in the German; when quoting from or referring to sections he has not translated, we will mention them as available in the *Husserliana* edition.

EP II   *Erste Philosophie.* Volume II. Edited by R. Boehm. (*Husserliana VIII*). The Hague: Nijhoff, 1959.

[xvii]

EJ   *Erfahrung und Urteil.* Edited by L. Landgrebe. Hamburg: Claassen, 1954. *Experience and Judgment.* Translated by J. Churchill and K. Ameriks. Evanston, Ill.: Northwestern University Press, 1973.

FTL   *Formale und transzendentale Logik.* Halle: Niemeyer, 1929. *Formal and Transcendental Logic.* Translated by D. Cairns. The Hague: Nijhoff, 1969.

Ideas I   *Ideen zu einer reinen Phänomenologie und phänomenologischen Philosophie.* Volume I. Edited by W. Biemel (*Husserliana III*). This is a new and expanded edition based on Husserl's handwritten notes and includes supplements and critical remarks. W. R. Boyce Gibson's English translation, *Ideas: General Introduction to Pure Phenomenology* (New York: Macmillan, 1931), is based on the first edition, published at Halle: Niemeyer, 1913.

Ideen II   *Ideen zu einer reinen Phänomenologie und phänomenologischen Philosophie.* Volume II. Edited by M. Biemel (*Husserliana IV*). The Hague: Nijhoff, 1952.

Ideen III   *Ideen zu einer reinen Phänomenologie und phänomenologischen Philosophie.* Volume III. Edited by M. Biemel (*Husserliana V*). The Hague: Nijhoff, 1952.

LI   *Logische Untersuchungen.* 2 vols. Halle: Niemeyer, 1900–1901. A second, revised edition was printed by the same publisher in two parts: first in 1913, when everything but the Sixth Investigation was published, and second in 1921, when the Sixth Investigation appeared. *Logical Investigations.* 2 vols. Translated by J. N. Findlay. New York: Humanities Press, 1970. Findlay's translation is based on the second, revised edition. In giving references we will cite the Investigation (there are six) by roman numeral.

PP   *Phänomenologische Psychologie.* Edited by W. Biemel (*Husserliana IX*). The Hague: Nijhoff, 1962.

ZB   *Zur Phänomenologie des inneren Zeitbewusstseins.*
      Edited by R. Boehm (*Husserliana* X). The Hague:
      Nijhoff, 1966. This contains the *Vorlesungen zur*
      Phänomenologie des inneren Zeitbewusstseins,
      originally edited by M. Heidegger (Halle: Nie-
      meyer, 1928), the English translation of which by
      J. Churchill is entitled *The Phenomenology of*
      Internal Time Consciousness (Bloomington, Ind.:
      Indiana University Press, 1964). However, Boehm's
      edition also contains many supplementary texts,
      and our analysis will be mostly concerned with
      them, so we will usually be quoting pages in his
      edition. On occasion we use Churchill's translation,
      but the context should make it clear when we are
      citing pages from him and not from Boehm.

References to unedited manuscripts from the Husserl Archives
employ the abbreviation Ms and the standard numbering system as used by the Archives.

Husserlian Meditations

Introduction

IF I MAKE A STATEMENT and you say you agree, you and
I have used our ability to be truthful. What other people say, and
what we ourselves later experience and state, may confirm our
truth or force us to reappraise it; but some truth has been
achieved and its claims cannot be disregarded. Even rebuttals
take place only because an episode of verification, of "making
truth," has occurred.

Being truthful distinguishes human being, not just because
men bring about truth in ways other things cannot, but also
because to fail to be truthful is to fail to be human in a decisive
respect, and to excel in being truthful is to be human in an excellent degree.

We cannot be truthful without at least some implicit thought
about being truthful. We cannot be truthful indeliberately. But
there is a difference between obscure, inchoate thinking about
truthfulness and an explicit effort to think as systematically and
as distinctly as possible about being truthful in all its forms. To
think about being truthful is itself an exercise in being truthful,
but in a way different from making and confirming judgments
about things. It is to do phenomenology.

Edmund Husserl has carried out such study with extraordi-
nary rigor and insight, and our effort to think about truth will
be inspired by what he has written.

He is a good guide in these matters for two reasons. First, he
reflects systematically not just about being truthful, but also
about what it is to think about being truthful. He does this in
discussing the transcendental reduction, where he explains
what phenomenological description is and how it is possible.

Husserl can clarify what happens when you and I agree that "S is *p*," but he can also show what happens when you and I, as philosophers, think about such truthfulness. With his help we can come to see the kind of verification that takes place within philosophy.

Second, Husserl is comprehensive. He is able to accommodate the truth at work in mathematics and the deductive sciences, in ordinary statements, in perception, memory, anticipation, and imagination, in pictures and universals, in knowing other minds, and in reflection. When giving an account of these and other forms of truthfulness he describes the kind of presence, and also the kinds of absence and obscurity, which function in each. But his range does not extend far enough to cover the truth involved in virtuous action and the attainment of human goods other than speculative knowledge. These deficiencies stem from his emphasis on science as the dominant human achievement and from dispositions he inherited from the Enlightenment.

To think about being truthful is to display the parts it involves: we must distinguish components like judgment, concepts, expression, sensibility, repetition, presence and absence, registration and reporting. To do so properly we need to be shown the nature of such parts and how they fit into the whole of bringing about truth; and we ought to be warned about the mistakes that can occur when we distinguish parts. This is done here in Chapter 1, "Parts and Wholes."

The elementary parts involved in being truthful are three: empty anticipation of what we are concerned with, intuitive possession (fulfillment), and recognition of it as the same in both states (identity synthesis). This formal structure is at work on all levels of experience, from inner time-consciousness to the confirmation of scientific hypotheses. We discuss it in Chapter 2, and use it to answer two philosophical questions: What is a fact? and, How are judgments verified by facts?

The themes of Chapter 2 are continued in the Appendix, where we examine the place of logic and mathematics in the process of verification. This essay has its natural place right after Chapter 2, but it goes into such technical and textual detail that if so situated it would distort the general argument of the book. It has important things to say about the issues raised in Chapter 2 and should be read in connection with that chapter.

Intuition of essences is a special case of identity synthesis and is treated in Chapter 3.

The structure of parts and wholes and that of empty and filled intentions are two formal structures explored in earlier chapters. Chapter 4 examines another structure which runs through Husserl's work, that of unity within a manifold. This chapter is a short tour of Husserlian phenomenology. It illustrates his method by exploring with him a few areas of experience; it examines some forms of sensible perception and studies the ambiguity of sensations. But its main purpose is to show the force exercised by the structure of unity and manifold in Husserl's thinking. Many of his difficult passages can be simplified if one looks for the kind of manifold and the kind of unity he is trying to articulate. Chapter 4 also explains how phenomenological thinking can distinguish manifolds of appearance in the objects it wishes to describe; this is a special case of the more general issue of how philosophy articulates parts in what it analyzes.

In Chapter 5, "Signs and Sensibility," we treat the following progression: signs and what they indicate; expression and the exprimend; impression and the thing perceived; sensing and sensation. These are elements in being truthful; distinguishing them, and showing their relatedness, is an exercise in phenomenology. The analysis of expression provides an occasion to examine phenomenological discourse and its expression, and to show why it cannot be reduced to the dimension of the discourse and expression of natural experience. The problem of philosophical language is introduced at this point.

In *Logical Investigations* Husserl believed that phenomenological analysis finds the final elements of consciousness in sensibility. His thoughts on time gradually forced him to revise this view. Beyond sensibility he uncovers a dimension of experiencing, inner time-consciousness, that allows sensibility to take place and accounts for the possibility of philosophical reflection. Toward the end of Chapter 5 we describe Husserl's discovery of this new region, and we explore its structure in Chapter 6, "The Inside of Time." Husserl's original thoughts on remembering and on the complexities of the immediate present are discussed here. There is no easy way to talk about these matters, especially since they are best understood by showing how Husserl was led to them by obscurities in his earlier positions. And much of our anaylsis must be based on his working manuscripts, not on texts prepared for publication. However, the formal structures of whole and part, the empty and the filled, and unity within manifold are at work in the constitution taking place in inner time; by paying attention explicitly to them we may, perhaps, have diminished the difficulty of the material treated in this chapter.

Chapter 7 discusses the transcendental reduction, the move from mundane experience and thought about things to phenomenological experience and thought about truthfulness. The chapter is structured around the triad of world, thing, and consciousness. We examine Husserl's notion of world as the setting for natural experience and thought; we examine the perception of things as the fundamental kind of experience in the world; and we find that consciousness experiences itself in a way different from its perception of things, and so permits a new kind of reflective, phenomenological thinking to arise. Exploring the concepts of world, thing, and consciousness is not grandiose speculation; every attempt to think about being truthful must take a position about them, and by raising such questions Husserl faces explicitly what is often taken for granted, even by philosophers. Phenomenology takes place in a focus different from our experience of things in the world; to illuminate this difference we compare Husserl's transcendental reflection with Socrates' examination of the Athenian way of life. The dominant question in this chapter is: How does philosophy distinguish itself from nonphilosophical experience and discourse, and yet include the nonphilosophical within itself as the subject of its inquiry?

We also find that the "fact" of being truthful is not like ordinary facts in the world, and the peculiarity of being truthful is what makes discourse about it—phenomenological discourse —different from mundane speaking and thinking.

Chapter 7 has asked what philosophy is; Chapter 8 backs off from this issue and discusses language and thinking in their nonphilosophical forms. With these materials in hand we will be able, in Chapter 9, to make another approach to the problem, What is philosophy?

In Chapter 8 we discuss judgment. Judgment is contrasted with perception, from which it arises, and several dimensions of judgment are distinguished: expression and grammar, the morphology of judgmental forms, formal consistency of several judgments fused into one, the coherence of judgmental cores. These dimensions are examined in regard to the function of judgment as being true or false; after treating them, therefore, we discuss the return of judgment to perceptual intuition. Another theme developed in this chapter is the establishment of a distinct voice out of the anonymity of general opinion. A voiced self arises when judgments are framed with distinctness and with logical consistency; formal logic is tied to the actualization of a truthful speaker.

Toward the end of Chapter 8 we discuss two kinds of discourse which seem to violate judgmental coherence: judgments using metaphor, and "wrong" philosophical judgments. The problem of incoherent philosophical judgment leads to the subject of Chapter 9.

The truth of a judgment cannot be examined apart from reference to the time when the judgment is framed. Verification of a judgment is an episode in time, and we must know whether the judgment is being framed before, during, or after verification. We can then ask what happens to a judgment in each of these states, and determine the kind and degree of the judgment's truth. After these issues are clarified, in Chapter 9, for nonphilosophical judgments, we turn to philosophical judgments and attempt to show their special characteristics. The most important feature of philosophical judgments is that their truthfulness is obscured by failures of clarity and distinctness in the judgments themselves, not by obstacles which prevent verification of judgments that have been clearly and distinctly framed. We discuss the nature of this obscurity, its relationship to time, and what it means to say that the obscurity is overcome when we become truthful philosophically.

There is no judgment without a judger, so in Chapter 9 we also discuss the establishment of a distinct philosophical voice. It is contrasted with the emergence of a speaker of ordinary discourse and the emergence of the speakers of modern science. The ineradicable obscurity in philosophical judgment allows us to account for the plurality of philosophical voices through history. The chapter closes with some remarks on the public function of philosophy.

1 / Parts and Wholes

τὸ γὰρ καλὸν ἐν μεγέθει καὶ τάξει ἐστίν.
—Aristotle, Poetics 7. 1450b36–37

ὃ γὰρ προσὸν ἢ μὴ προσὸν μηδὲν ποιεῖ
ἐπίδηλον, οὐδὲ μόριον τοῦ ὅλου ἐστίν.
—Poetics 8. 1451a34–35

TWO FORMAL STRUCTURES are everywhere present in Husserl's philosophy: the contrast between empty and filled intentions, or between absence and presence, and the relationships between wholes and parts. Other formal structures, like that of an identity within a manifold, or the more specialized relationship of sign and the signified, are defined with the help of the first two. They in turn are not defined through any more fundamental formal structures, but are made clear in terms of one another. Parts come to be in a whole when certain presences can persist while other presences turn into absences, that is, when certain filled intentions remain filled while others become empty (Ms F I 13 IV, 1907, p. 224). Parts in wholes are correlative to empty and filled intentions. But empty and filled intentions themselves are parts within the whole of consciousness. Parts and wholes are not just correlative to consciousness; they are at work, as formal structures, within consciousness itself.

The two formal structures condition each other: there are empty and filled intentions because objects have parts, and parts arise within wholes because empty and filled intentions blend with one another. In both cases we have to do with formal structures which need material supplements to exist concretely.

[8]

Each structure will be realized in many different ways depending, respectively, on the kind of object that is to be a whole to its parts, and on the kind of consciousness that is to be engendered in a mixture of empty and filled awareness.

This chapter will discuss the logic of wholes and parts, and Chapter 2 will discuss empty and filled intentions.

§ 1. THE KINDS OF PARTS

THE LOGIC of wholes and parts is treated in the third of the *Logical Investigations,* and centers on the difference between pieces and moments. A number of terms are defined which retain their technical meaning throughout Husserl's development.

"Pieces," or independent parts, are parts that can be presented separately from their wholes. A tree is a whole whose parts are the trunk, roots, branches, leaves, bark, and wood, and any one of these parts is "separately presentable" (*LI*, III, § 3). Each can be perceived or imagined by itself, apart from the tree as a whole. "Moments," nonindependent parts, are parts that cannot be separately presented, like the hue, saturation, and brightness of color, or the pitch, timbre, and loudness of sound (§ 4). Color in turn is a moment which cannot be presented apart from extension.

A "mediate" part is one which is a part of a whole only by being part of another moment which in turn is a part of the whole; brightness is mediately a part of extension because it inheres in it only through color. An "immediate" part is one which needs no such intermediaries to be united to its proximate whole. Depending on how many intermediaries are needed, a given moment may be *nearer to* or *more remote from* its whole than another moment (§§ 16, 18).

Since certain moments require other moments as supplements in order to be presentable or to exist themselves, they are said to be "founded" on such supplements (§ 14). This notion of "foundation" is used incessantly in Husserl's writings, and he even tries to define the concept of "whole" by using it; that is, foundation can be considered as logically more basic than whole (§ 21).

Another name for a moment is an "abstractum," while a "concretum" is that of which a particular abstractum is a moment; color is a concretum for brightness. The concretum in turn may, like color, be a moment in another respect, but eventually we come to "absolute" concreta or independent wholes, like persons or things (§ 17). After Husserl makes the turn into transcendental phenomenology, the final concretum turns out to be transcendental subjectivity because, speaking phenomenologically, it is the only whole which has no reference to anything beyond itself, while all other wholes are to be taken as constituted by subjectivity.[1] In the natural attitude, however, the world is taken as the absolute concretum and consciousness is a part within it. The natural attitude and the phenomenological attitude are defined by what each takes to be the final concrete whole: the world or transcendental subjectivity.

The search for the final whole does not end with transcendental subjectivity, however, for as Husserl burrows deeper he finds that the living present must be taken as the final absolute or the ultimate concretum, since all of subjectivity exists and is constituted within it.[2]

Because pieces can be presented apart from their wholes, we might suspect that their wholes are just aggregates of independent individuals: a tree might seem to be a collection of roots, trunk, and branches. This is not the case. The unity of an aggregate comes about in consequence of an act of collecting; it is correlated to an act of thinking in which several independent things are gathered into a categorial whole (III, § 23). But a whole which gives rise to pieces is originally given as a perceptual and continuous whole; its parts—the roots, trunk, and branches—are contained in it and only subsequently separated out. In an aggregate the members are first perceptually given as independent wholes and then gathered together by thinking.

§ 2. PRESENTING PARTS AND TALKING ABOUT PARTS

MOMENTS CANNOT BE SEPARATELY PRESENTED to perception or imagination, but this does not prevent us from considering them apart in our thinking or speech. We can mean only brightness or hue and think or say nothing about color or

1. See EP II, § 31, p. 27, ll. 12–21; § 53b, p. 176, ll. 11–15. Also Ideen III, § 12, pp. 71–72.

2. See EP II, p. 470, ll. 29–42. The living present is the "total horizon" reached when phenomenology reflects on the conditions of its own possibility. See Crisis, § 71, p. 247.

extension, but then we are thinking or speaking abstractly. If we were to bring what we mean to intuitive presence in perception or imagination, we should have to bring along the supplementary parts that round it out into an independent whole. We could not hear pitch except as the pitch of some sound, but we can talk about pitch without mentioning sound.

We are not surprised to find that brightness and pitch need supplements, but there may be other objects we talk about without remembering that they are abstracta. We discuss them as if they were concrete and independent, and may be surprised to find that they need supplements if they are to be intuited according to their appropriate manner. For example, in Husserl's analysis a material thing must be subject to and capable of material causality if it is to be what it is. A thing described as impervious to causes would be what Husserl calls a "phantom," which is a moment in the physical object but needs the further level of capacity for causal interaction if it is to realize the sense of material thing. One would take an abstractum for a concretum if one were to eliminate causality from the material object. Again, a judgment may appear to be separable and presentable by itself, but concretely no judgment exists apart from an act of judging, and so none exists apart from someone who judges. Moreover, within the judgment itself Husserl distinguishes between judgmental form and judgmental stuff as two moments which we, in an unguarded thought, might suppose to be separable from each other: "That would presuppose the countersense, that one could have stuffs by themselves beforehand—as though they were concrete objects, instead of being abstract moments in significations." [3] Again, the subject and the predicate of a judgment are moments to one another: "Naturally then articulation [into subject and predicate] does not signify division into pieces; since the word 'pieces' indicates parts, each of which can also be detached as something self-sufficient. Now it is obvious that at least the predicate-member is not detachable as something self-sufficient. That the same is true of the subject-member will soon become apparent" (*FTL*, app. I, § 1, pp. 294–95).

Taking an example from Austin, there can be no perlocutionary act without an illocutionary act, and no illocutionary act

___

3. *FTL*, app. I, § 3, p. 298. In contrast, a complex proposition can be fragmented into the independent pieces that make it up; see § 9, p. 305. This appendix makes effective use of the logic of parts and wholes. See also app. II, § 2, p. 315; and § 5, p. 325.

without a locutionary act. In Saussurean issues, *parole* is a moment "founded" on *langue*. Likewise, to suppose that propositions can be presented independently is to take an abstract moment for a concrete whole, because propositions are only moments in concrete speech acts and also require some expression as a supplement and foundation. Strawson tries to persuade us he is talking about moments and not pieces or independent wholes when he writes, "Then I am not saying that there are sentences and expressions (types), *and* uses of them, *and* utterances of them, as there are ships *and* shoes *and* sealing-wax. I am saying that we cannot say *the same things* about types, uses of types, and utterances of types." [4] Moments are not separable in their presence or existence, but they can be isolated in thought and in speech, and we cannot say the same things about different moments.

Very often the surprising and disturbing element in Husserl's doctrine is the fact that certain things we have become accustomed to take as independent turn out to be dependent moments when they are considered from a new viewpoint. A material thing, for instance, is naturally taken as concrete and independent, but phenomenologically it is considered as dependent and founded on consciousness; the world itself, which is taken as the most encompassing whole in the natural attitude, turns out phenomenologically to be enclosed within a still wider totality, that of the consciousness which has a world: "Now the world is reached within pure subjectivity, as a moment within it (although not as a lived experience within it)" (*EP II*, p. 448).

On the other hand, things that we have taken as nonindependent may turn out to be independent; the stream of experiences, which we naturally take to be dependent as a part of the world, turns out in the phenomenological attitude to be detachable from it. After the phenomenological reduction in *Ideas I*, Husserl says, "If conscious experiences were not thinkable apart from their interlacing with nature in the very way in which colors are not thinkable apart from extension, we could not look on consciousness as a region for itself and absolutely its own, in the sense in which we must do so." [5] If consciousness were a

---

4. "On Referring," in *Logico-Linguistic Papers* (London: Methuen, 1971), pp. 8–9 (italics original).

5. *Ideas I*, § 51, p. 156. I have had to modify the translation of this passage and of most of the other passages in *Ideas I* that I quote later on; I will not repeat this observation each time. See also *Ideen II*, § 49b, p. 178.

moment in the world as colors are a moment of extension, the transcendental reduction would not be possible and we could not focus on consciousness as an absolute sphere. The argument leading to the reduction is supposed to show that the sense of consciousness is such that it is not a part dependent on the world; it is not an abstract moment in the concreteness of the world.

The argument for the reduction also shows that consciousness and the world are not two independent wholes gathered into an aggregate, and that consciousness is not an independent part externally related to the world. Consciousness turns out to be a wider whole that encompasses the world as phenomenon.

The sense of all these claims and the change of focus that makes them possible remain to be clarified, but the strategic role played by the logic of parts and wholes in the transcendental reduction is apparent from these general remarks.

§ 3. Unthinkable Separation of Moments

Although we can think or speak abstractly about certain moments, and simply not consider their necessary supplements and founding parts, we cannot think about such moments as capable of independent existence or presentation. Such thinking would be unfaithful to the way things are. Husserl's maxim, "To the things themselves," can be understood in these terms.[6] In his phenomenology he does not wish to analyze the meaning of words used when we intend something signitively and abstractly, but to describe how what is meant appears concretely in its actual presence, when all its moments must be taken into account. His phenomenological descriptions analyze concreta,

6. See *LI*, Introduction to (German) Volume Two, p. 252: "Otherwise put: we can absolutely not rest content with 'mere words,' i.e. with a merely symbolic understanding of words, such as we first have when we reflect on the sense of the laws for 'concepts,' 'judgements,' 'truths' etc. (together with their manifold specifications) which are set up in pure logic. Meanings inspired only by remote, confused, inauthentic intuitions—if by any intuitions at all—are not enough: we must go back to the 'things themselves.' We desire to render self-evident in fully-fledged intuitions that what is here given in actually performed abstractions is what the word-meanings in our expression of the law really and truly stand for." See also *Ideen III*, § 6, pp. 23–24.

not abstract parts. His frequent claim that such and such a combination is "unthinkable" (*undenkbar*) means that what has been proposed as concrete and real by an opponent is in truth only a nonindependent moment and not thinkable as independently real: "What we here express by the word 'present,' could be better expressed by the word 'think.' An attribute, a form of association and the like, cannot be *thought of* as self-existent, as isolated from all else, as being all that exists: this only can happen with 'thinglike' contents" (*LI*, III § 6; see V § 20, p. 589). We discuss the thinkability of certain combinations of moments when we treat the problem of judgmental clarity (see below, § 74).

The cardinal philosophical mistake, phenomenologically speaking, is to force an abstractum into being a pseudo phenomenon, and so to base philosophy on the abstract meaning of words and not on things as they actually appear. Phenomena are constructed, instead of being taken for what they are.[7] A faithful analysis of a phenomenon will list the moments at work in it when it is present to thoughtful perception.

Each moment requires a nest of supplements to exist and to be presented. The series of supplements and the order of mediation in them are fixed by the nature of the parts in question, and so the phenomenological description which enumerates these parts is guided by essential necessities. The essential connections make up an a priori law; it is founded not on the customs of language, nor on the psychological dispositions of men, nor on matters of fact we generally experience, but on what the parts and wholes are (*LI*, III, §§ 4, 7, 10, 23).

A positive expression of such a law ("Pitch is a moment of sound") states an essential necessity, while a negative formulation ("Pitch cannot exist without sound") states an essential impossibility. Expression of the law presumes insight into the necessity or impossibility of the states of affairs. In practice the negative formulation is often more appropriate. It is easier to recognize or intuit an essential connection by realizing the impossibility of its being otherwise than by appreciating the necessity of its being the way it is. Husserl's method of imaginative variation as a way of reaching pure essences involves negative insight into the limits or boundaries at which the given eidos becomes impossible (see below, § 29).

7. See Rudolf Boehm, "Die Philosophie als strenge Wissenschaft," in his *Vom Gesichtspunkt der Phänomenologie* (The Hague: Nijhoff, 1968), pp. 10–11.

The apodicticity Husserl claims for his phenomenological descriptions is based on insight into necessary connections among moments which become articulated in reflective thinking.

Although the sequence and mediation of moments are governed by essential law—brightness can be a part of extension only through color—pieces are not arranged into their wholes in necessary order. A finger is as immediately a part of the body as it is part of the hand; it is not necessarily mediated by the hand. Therefore the organization of pieces into their wholes, or the fragmentation of wholes into pieces, need not follow a systematic, necessary, and a priori rule. It can be done according to our convenience or custom, for we need not be guided by the nature of the parts. "There are diverse possible divisions in which the same part comes up, sometimes earlier, sometimes later, so that we have no temptation to accord any privilege to one part over another as regards the way in which it is contained in the whole. . . . The parts in any case also owe their serial order to the serial order of our divisions, and these latter have no objective foundation" (*LI*, III, § 19).

Consequently no apodictic, essential description can be given of the way pieces combine into their wholes, and no phenomenology of their structure is possible either, since phenomenology operates in the domain of the eidetically necessary, the domain of moments and their foundations. This lack of eidetic regulation between pieces and their wholes does not imply that pieces are not really parts, or that their wholes are only aggregates combined arbitrarily. An aggregate is a totality due entirely to our having collected it, but a whole has its pieces in itself, apart from anything we do to it, even though it does stand in our power to decide which pieces are to emerge, and in what order.

It is possible, furthermore, that what is a piece in respect to one whole may turn out to be a moment in respect to another (*LI*, III, § 7). A branch is a piece of a tree, but it is a moment when considered as a visual object since it appears only as a figure against a background, whether we actually perceive it or only imagine it. Qua visual object—but not qua branch—it must be founded on a field. And qua visual object it requires the copresence of extension, color, and other appropriate internal moments (§ 21). In respect to this particular totality, it is subject to an essential, a priori enumeration of parts.

§ 4. PHENOMENOLOGICAL MISTAKES, CONFUSION OF PARTS

A PHENOMENOLOGICAL ANALYSIS is concerned with eidetic necessities, and so deals in the currency of moments, not pieces. The actual and regular combinations of pieces in our experience are the concern of empirical sciences. Phenomenological science, besides enumerating the eidetic combinations of moments, must also describe the formal structure of parts and wholes that is realized in such moments and combinations, and it must account for the consciousness that can carry out such a narration and analysis. It has to account for its own activity. In doing so it displays the moments that are ingredient in conscious life. So on whatever level it functions—describing the structure of objects given to consciousness, describing the consciousness that constitutes objects, or describing the consciousness that does phenomenology—phenomenological analysis applies the logic of parts and wholes.

In regard to wholes and parts, phenomenological analysis goes awry essentially by taking a moment for an independent part or for the whole. It takes an abstractum for a concretum. It then forgets that its object by its very nature requires supplements; pointless dilemmas and paradoxes arise as to how the object is to be reconciled with other objects or dimensions—how thought is to be reconciled with sensibility, things with appearances, individuals with community—when they should never have been detached philosophically in the first place. Such a wayward procedure takes abstract signitive intentions as equivalent to intuitions of concrete things, and leads to controversies about words instead of analyses of what is given.

Taking the abstract for the concrete can occur as simply that, or in three more complicated guises. First, we may acknowledge that a certain object is a moment, but may not give a complete list of the supplements that lead to its concrete state. We may skip over causality in the constitution of material things, or omit the intersubjective dimension of judgment. This deficiency takes the abstract for the concrete "farther down the line," at one of the intermediate stages of the object's eidetic structure.

Second, we may give for one object the list of supplements that belong to another kind of object. A poem may be analyzed as a rhetorical speech, a rhetorical speech may be analyzed into parts appropriate to kinds of social compulsion, a human being may be analyzed in terms appropriate to an animal or a thing. Such deficient analysis can be persuasive because the dimension to which the object is reduced is indeed a dimension present in the object's structure, and there can be cases when the abstract dimension is realized as a concrete object. There can be rhetorical dimensions to a poem, and there are speeches that are simply rhetorical speeches, so philosophically we may be tempted to mistake a poem for an oration. There are animal dimensions to the human being, and there are some beings that are merely animal, so philosophically we may mistake man for an animal. We are led philosophically to take one object for another; in the object that we have distorted philosophically, we have taken an abstract dimension for the concrete whole.

The first and second forms of this philosophical "fallacy of misplaced concreteness" are not equivalent.[8] In the second, the error arises because there are sometimes concrete states of what is only abstract in the whole we wish to analyze. In the first, such concrete states may never be found; instead we are led by our confusion to postulate certain moments as concrete existents.

Third, we may provide an appropriate analysis of the object but fail to account for the kind of consciousness correlated to it. We may give a sufficient noematic analysis but fail to provide its noetic supplement. This is a deficiency not of distortion but of neglect. It omits discussion of the horizon within which the object acquires its sense; it also makes it impossible to handle problems of truth and verification associated with the kind of object in question, since truth and verification are the work of the consciousness correlated to the object. At this point we are led to the theme of Chapter 2, the distinction between empty and filled intentions.

8. Whitehead formulates this expression in *Science and the Modern World* (New York: Free Press, 1967), p. 51.

2 / Identity in Absence and Presence

> Was this taken
> By any understanding pate but
> thine?
> For thy conceit is soaking, will
> draw in
> More than the common blocks.
> —*The Winter's Tale,* I.ii

§ 5. THE EMPTY AND THE FILLED

A SERIES OF EXAMPLES will help us see the distinction between empty and filled intentions. (*a*) Empty: talking about something we are to visit, a lake, for example, and generally keeping our mind on it even apart from what we say; imagining it, thinking about it. Filled: seeing the lake, swimming in it, hearing the water, doing whatever constitutes the experiencing of lakes. (*b*) Empty: trying to remember what someone looks like. Filled: successfully remembering his appearance, having an image of him in our mind's eye. Remembering him is itself empty in contrast to perceiving him. (*c*) Empty: referring to the first two lines of Wallace Stevens' "Sunday Morning." Filled: reciting the two lines. (*d*) Empty: referring to the meaning of someone's expressions when he is speaking a language I do not understand; or referring to the meaning of a text when it is still undeciphered. Filled: being told the meaning of his utterances or the meaning of the text, or deciphering them myself after I have learned the language. (*e*) Empty: in the absence of the object discussed, stating facts about it. Filled: perceiving *that*

[18]

such and such is the case in regard to the object; actually seeing that the house is white. This is different from (*a*), where we merely perceive the lake; here we register facts, which is more than perceiving things. (*f*) Empty: making plans to learn to ride a bicycle or handle a scythe, these activities being taken as processes which we consciously experience. Filled: the experience of riding a bicycle or handling a scythe proficiently. (*g*) Empty: talking about moves in a game of chess or rules in a sport, like the rule that you must touch all the bases when you hit a home run. Filled: making the moves in an actual game of chess; touching all the bases after hitting a home run. (*h*) Empty: thinking about a decision that will have to be made in a critical situation; rehearsing the decision in imagination. Filled: the experience of making the decision. (*i*) Empty: hearing lectures about works of art and reading criticisms of them. Filled: enjoying the works of art that have been discussed.

All these examples are formally the same since each involves a contrast between empty and filled intending, but there is great variety in their concrete states. What fulfills the intention is different in each case; respectively, it is (*a*) a thing, (*b*) an image, in this case an image of memory, (*c*) words and sentences, (*d*) propositions, the meaning of what is said or written, (*e*) a fact or state of affairs, (*f*) the exercise of a skill, (*g*) behaving in accordance with a rule, (*h*) a decision, (*i*) works of art. Each kind of object dictates its own style of fulfillment and calls for its own phenomenological analysis of the moments involved. Each kind of object has its way of being meant absently, and its way of being intuitively given. We do not bring a sentence to intuition the same way we bring a material thing to direct presence, and both differ from intuiting an exercise of skill.

§ 6. The Vague and the Distinct

An object can become present and still need to be made more fully present.[1] The parts of the object may not be sufficiently distinguished from one another. In this case the object is said to be vague or confused and must be brought to

1. Our discussion of the empty and the filled, and the vague and the distinct, is taken from the perspective of *Formal and Transcendental Logic*, where Husserl's mature thought is expressed, but where

distinctness, which is done when the parts are sufficiently articulated.

(*a*) The lake may be seen in a fog, or I may be distracted or sick and unable to experience it appropriately, or it may be the first time I have seen one and I cannot take it all in. (*b*) I may have an image of memory of the person in question, but it keeps blending with the image of another friend of mine who looks like him, so that I cannot fix the image. (*c*) Someone may recite the sentences but mumble the words, so they are not acoustically distinct. (*d*) I may express the meaning by rote, not adequately framing the propositions or meanings. That is, the sentences may be distinct, but not their meanings. (*e*) I may register facts obscurely by not distinctly articulating, in my judgmental acts, the parts of what I perceive. Again, this is not the same as (*a*), which remains entirely on the level of perception; our present case is founded on perception but moves into categorial or judgmental consciousness and suffers an indistinctness appropriate to that higher level. (*f*) The first moves in riding a bicycle or handling a scythe are exercises of this skill, so they leave the empty intention and enter into actual presence, but they are clumsy and are vaguely and confusedly experienced. (*g*) I may make chess moves with hesitation while I am learning the game, or I may make a few practice moves outside the full context of a real game; they are not fully determined exercises of the rule. Small boys playing sandlot baseball may exercise the home run rule indistinctly. (*h*) I may make halfhearted decisions. (*i*) Looking at a painting or listening to music while I hardly know how to do so makes aesthetic objects present, but only vaguely.

Indistinctness of an object means that although the object is actually present, one might possibly take it for another object, or take another object for it. Not being distinct in itself, it is

---

the contrarieties are discussed primarily in relation to the judgmental consciousness; see *FTL*, § 16. The same themes are found in *Logical Investigations*, where they are applied to consciousness generally, but where they also contain some obscurities which Husserl managed to clear up later. See below, § 17. The concepts of empty and filled intentions are introduced systematically in Investigation VI, chs. 1 and 2 (see the Introduction, p. 668). The degree of fullness—the contrast between vague and distinct—is treated in chs. 3 and 5. On some ambiguities in the concepts of empty and filled intentions, and their relationship to the concept of objectifying act in the *Investigations*, see my study, "The Structure and Content of Husserl's *Logical Investigations*," *Inquiry*, XIV (1971), 327 and n. 34.

also not distinct from others which may appear, in the vague state, to be the same as the object in question. One thing can be taken for another—a river for a lake—or one image can be taken for another, one sentence for another, one judgment for another, one fact for another, one aesthetic object for another. So although the object "itself" is presented, in the sense that it is not meant emptily in its absence, nor pictorially through an image or representation, the object is not fully presented "itself" in the sense that its identity is sufficiently distinguished from the identity of other objects. The possibility of mistaking the object, even in its direct presence, still exists. The state of vagueness has this pernicious effect on consciousness and its work of identifying and knowing objects. Increase of distinctness diminishes the possibility of such mistakes.

Indistinctness is a kind of absence; but it must be distinguished from the pure absence in which the object is just signitively intended. When we intend an object in a signitive and purely empty way, the receptor set of our sensibility is not being affected at all by the object; when we intend it indistinctly, our sensibility is affected, but we are not responding with the appropriate articulation.[2]

§ 7. PRESENCE, ABSENCE, AND IDENTITY

THE PROPER WHOLE within which empty intentions and filled intentions can be understood is the recognition of identity.[3] The empty and the filled are two moments in the consciousness

2. In *LI* Husserl seems to think the only criterion for fullness of saturation is the degree to which the receptor set of sensibility is impressed by the object; see VI, §§ 22–23. The possibility of a more or less adequate articulation does not seem to be a problem for him. He seems to think categorial registration is automatic once sensible exposure to the object is achieved; is this position related to his failure to acknowledge a transcendental ego in *LI*? That sensible exposure does not guarantee adequate articulation is admitted in *FTL* and also in *Ideas I*. Also, in *LI* Husserl seems to think that total sensible presence, free of any perspectives, is conceivable as an ideal, even though it cannot be achieved in fact. In *Ideas I* he changes his view; the very notion of the thing given without perspectives is incoherent. See E. Tugendhat, *Der Wahrheitsbegriff bei Husserl und Heidegger* (Berlin: de Gruyter, 1967), pp. 76–79.

3. In *LI*, VI, ch. 1, Husserl develops the concepts of empty and filled intentions by isolating them from the act of recognition.

of identity. Correlatively, the presence and the absence of what is intended must be considered as moments in the whole which is the identity of the object presented.

Husserl's notion of *intentionality* includes both the empty and the filled consciousness; intentionality is not, as the terms might prompt us to think, equated with empty intention.[4] It encompasses both empty and filled intending. It is a whole which contains them as moments, and they in turn are mutually dependent on each other, for empty intending is what it is only in contrast to and in conjunction with its corresponding filled consciousness, while the filled requires the supplement of empty awareness to be what it is.

Correlatively, the *same object* is meant in both an empty and a filled way. We do not mean two distinct objects that are subsequently related to each other. The lake I think and talk about is the same lake in which I swim, but it is meant in different ways. I can intend it emptily and I can intend it intuitively, but "the lake" is the identity common to both modes. The object is a whole with the two moments of being meant in presence and being meant in absence. The present object is what it is only in contrast to and in conjunction with the same object as absent, and vice versa.

The object's identity comes to be presented only within the differences of presence and absence. It is founded on these differences and is a third dimension to them. Only when we are able to experience the object in its presence and in its absence do we encounter its identity. Identity is not a simple datum; it presents itself as a constant within the alternatives and the mixture of presence and absence. And, noetically, recognition of identity is founded on the blend of empty and filled intentions. Consciousness is the process of experiencing such identities; it takes place in different ways for different kinds of objects.

In describing how a certain kind of object is intended by consciousness, we may discuss how the object is present and how it is meant in absence, without emphasizing that the same object is meant in both cases. The object's identity may remain an unmentioned assumption, but it is an assumption and a necessary one, for unless the object is identical in both intend-

4. In *LI*, V, § 13, Husserl speaks of the "ambiguity" between intention as empty intention and intention in the wider sense, which includes the empty and the filled. He says, "This ambiguity, once recognized, becomes harmless."

ings, neither the presence nor the absence retains its proper sense (*FTL*, app. II, § 2a).

To put this formally: being meant in presence and being meant in absence are founded on identity. This tightens the mutual implications of all three elements and shows that they are each moments to one another. In the technical sense of "foundation," identity is founded on presence and absence, presence and absence are founded on each other, and both are founded on identity. Transposing this into the noetic key: recognition of identity is founded on filled and empty intentions, filled and empty intentions are founded on each other, and both are founded on recognition of identity.

We will have more to say about presence, absence, and identity when we discuss what Husserl calls the identity synthesis (see below, § 9).

§ 8. SIGNITIVE, PICTORIAL, AND PERCEPTUAL INTENTIONS

EVERY INTENTION involves sensibility. There is no "pure thinking" that might take place without the copresence of a sensuous dimension, and the attempt to postulate such thought is the typical philosophical mistake of separating a moment from its necessary foundation.[5] But the way sensibility functions as a base for intentions allows us to distinguish three kinds of intending: perceptual, pictorial, and signitive (*LI*, VI, § 14a).

In the perceptual consciousness sensibility enjoys impressions made by the object itself. Pictorial consciousness is based on sensible impressions like those made by the object, but not identical with them. Signitive consciousness is founded on impressions that can be totally unlike those given by the object. Perceiving the White House involves having the views and other

5. *LI*, VI, § 60, pp. 817–18: "It lies in the nature of the case that everything categorial ultimately rests upon sensuous intuition, that a 'categorial intuition,' an intellectual insight, a case of thought in the highest sense, without any foundation of sense, is a piece of nonsense. The idea of a pure intellect, interpreted as a faculty of pure thinking (categorial action), quite cut off from a 'faculty of sensibility,' could only be conceived before there had been an elementary analysis of knowledge." See also VI, § 25, pp. 738–40.

impressions the building makes in my sensibility; intending it pictorially involves having the views and other impressions a copy or model of the house makes on me, which are like those made by the house itself and could perhaps be correlated to the corresponding impressions of the building—"the view of the southern side"; intending it signitively involves impressions made by words, spoken or written, or by other signs, like a flag or emblem, that may conventionally stand for the house. In all these intentions the house itself is meant. Even in pictorial consciousness we intend the image as an image, that is, we intend something beyond and represented by the image.

In the *Logical Investigations* Husserl considers imagination as a kind of pictorial consciousness. In *Ideas I* he no longer does so, since an image in fantasy is not a thing in itself, as a picture or statue must be. Imagination is then taken as a modification of perception, like memory; it is a reproductive consciousness.[6] This change in doctrine between the *Investigations* and *Ideas I* is associated with a different understanding of sensations and images forced on Husserl by his new thoughts about inner time-consciousness (see below, § 58).

Although the way sensibility functions can be used as an index in classifying perceptual, pictorial, and signitive consciousness, sensibility does not bring about these kinds of awareness. They are different kinds of intentional acts, different ways of apprehending or interpreting what is sensibly present. The same datum can be the basis for all three kinds of intentions: a small statue of Napoleon can be perceived as a physical thing, or taken as an image of Bonaparte, or interpreted as a sign in a conventional code; for example, after agreement with someone else, I may put the statue outside my house to indicate that I have won an argument (*LI*, VI, §§ 26–27). These differences are not brought about by differences in sensible impressions; they are constituted by the kind of intentional act at work in each case.

Because the intention and not sensibility determines whether an object is taken perceptually, pictorially, or signitively, an object which is truly an image of another can sometimes be taken as a sign, and not as a picture of it: "For the sign, too, can be like what it signifies, even entirely like it. . . . A photograph of the sign A is immediately taken to be a picture of the

---

6. *Ideas I*, § 43; *EP II*, § 44, pp. 112–13; Tugendhat, *Wahrheitsbegriff*, p. 67.

sign. But when we use the sign *A* as a sign of the sign *A*, as when we write '*A* is a letter of the Latin written alphabet,' we treat *A*, despite its representational similarity, as a sign, and not as a likeness" (*LI*, VI, § 14a).

Now the major contrast, philosophically, within this trio of acts is to be drawn between signitive consciousness on the one side and the pictorial and perceptual on the other.[7] In a paradigmatic way, signitive intending is empty intending, while both pictorial (including the imaginative) and perceptual intentions are intuitive. This is where the axis is to be placed, even though the pictorial does differ from the perceptual as empty to full in an analogous way. The crucial distinction is between meaning the object on the basis of signs or expressions, which is empty intending, and directly meaning it either in its own presence or in its image. This difference is reflected in the fact that we say, "That is Napoleon," in an identifying way, whether we are looking at him, his portrait or statue, or imagining him in our mind's eye; but we could not say this about his name or any of the words used to talk about him. He "isn't there" in any way to a signitive intention, although he is presented or represented in the others.

The affinity of perception and picturing is further demonstrated by the similar patterns of sensibility in both. Whether in direct presence or in image, the object presents a flow of aspects and sides and profiles, and presents itself as the identity within this continuum. In contrast, the object of signitive consciousness is not meant in a series of profiles.

Since a thing can be intuited only as an identity within a continuum of profiles, the intuition of such an object encompasses a blend of empty and filled intendings, and the intuited object encloses a blend of presences and absences. We must distinguish two sorts of presence and absence: one in the contrast of sheer signitive and empty intention with perceptual intuition—talking about the White House while we are a hundred miles away from it versus seeing the house and walking around and through it; the other within the perceptual intuition of things, as the various profiles come and go and the various partial intentions change from empty to filled and back again.

---

7. *LI*, VI, §14b, p. 714; Husserl says his analysis shows "the mutual affinity of percepts and imaginations, and their common opposition to 'signitive' intentions."

The blend of present and absent profiles is at work in the perception and the imagination of an object, but does not function for the object meant in signitive intentions; however, the expressive wholes used in signification—the strings of words—do appear through such a mixture.

An interesting fourth to the trio of perceptual, pictorial, and signitive intentions is the consciousness appropriate to maps. At first glance maps seem to be a form of picture, but second thoughts make us hesitate: a map is quite different from a panorama. The essential in a map is not the depiction of parts, but the conventional relationships arranged between parts of the map and parts of what is mapped, and between the map as a whole and the whole which is mapped.[8] A picture can be recognized as an image of an original without the use of words, but maps need words to be interpreted. A map is intermediate between signitive intentions and perception. The status of maps is similar, of course, to that of models; and still other provocative questions can be raised about the intentional status of graphs.

The Austin-Strawson discussion of truth makes use of categories similar to Husserl's signitive, pictorial, and perceptual intentions, and the concept of maps stands out there as well. Austin writes:

> For example, maps: these may be called pictures, yet they are highly conventionalized pictures. If a map can be clear or accurate or misleading, like a statement, why can it not be true or exaggerated? How do the "symbols" used in map-making differ from those used in statement-making? On the other hand, if an air-mosaic is not a map, why is it not? And when does a map become a diagram? These are the really illuminating questions.[9]

The issues raised in the debate between Austin and Strawson, both central and peripheral, are exactly the questions that Husserl raises in his phenomenology. In particular, the issue of the nature and correspondence of statements and facts, which is the major concern in the debate, is the issue we shall handle in the rest of this chapter.

The much abused term "intuition" loses its suspicious overtones in the use Husserl makes of it. Intuition is simply con-

8. *LI*, VI, § 20, pp. 727–28; see also VI, § 52, p. 801, on the consciousness appropriate to models.

9. J. L. Austin, "Truth," in *Philosophical Papers*, ed. J. O. Urmson and G. J. Warnock, 2d ed. (London: Oxford University Press, 1970), p. 126.

sciousness of an object in its direct presence; it is the opposite of intending the object absently. Intuiting a lake is swimming in it, seeing it, riding a boat on it, all as opposed to talking about the lake when we are nowhere near it. There is nothing solipsistic or mysterious about intuitions, and in principle they can be publicly manifest and confirmed. A thing or a mathematical proposition is intuited by everybody in the same way, according to the style of presentation dictated by its kind of being. Some intuitions can be achieved only by several people working together; a complicated experiment requires several experts and many assistants to register the fact they are all looking for. We can, of course, choose to keep some intuitions secret, but we can do the same with murders, gold-hoards, and short cuts.

Husserl talks about our intuiting an object and about an object's being intuited, but he does not mention the case when we are fulfillers of someone else's empty intention. Practically everybody enjoys being actualized or recognized in this way; it must account for much of the pleasure people get in being public figures.[10] Even when pain is involved—a great spy is finally caught—there is a grim satisfaction in being appreciated as the one who was conspicuously absent and vigorously, though emptily, intended. It is one thing to be introduced to someone who has never met you before, but it is another and more enjoyable thing to be recognized by someone else as the person they have heard and read about or seen in image on television, in the movies, or in the papers. Something quite different happens and more than your sheer presence is actualized. Your identity is appreciated, for you are recognized as the same one that the others have meant in absence or in pictures. Identity is the invariant within presence and absence, not just a datum attached to perceptual presence.

A star's fans are valued only for the pleasure and status their recognition affords him; they are anonymous conditions for his actuality as a phenomenon and are not recognized by him in return, unless he happens to be a considerate man besides being

10. Dick Cavett, reminiscing, says: "And I thought, 'If I ever become famous, I'll talk to everybody who wants to talk to me, I'll be nice to people, I'll drop in at little houses on side streets where they don't expect me and dazzle and thrill them, and that'll be the fun of being famous. I'll stop in at drugstores and sit at counters and give the people a look at me and a little something to talk about'" (quoted by L. E. Sissman in "Profiles: Work, for the Night Is Coming," *New Yorker*, May 6, 1972, p. 49).

a public figure. And of course the inconvenience of being famous is that one can hardly go anywhere without being a phenomenon and having one's identity recognized.

Government could not occur without the capacity to intend something in its absence: representatives "stand for" the people, and emissaries of the sovereign have authority only because those to whom they are sent can intend the sovereign in his absence and recognize this man as his delegate. Political representation has many characteristics that mark it off from ordinary signitive or pictorial intention, but its possibility and the possibility of government rest ultimately on the capacity human being has for identity synthesis.

§ 9. IDENTITY SYNTHESIS

IDENTITY SYNTHESIS or the consciousness of fulfillment is the process of experiencing an identity in the transition from empty to filled intending. What Husserl calls a "dynamic" identity synthesis occurs when the empty intention is followed chronologically by an intuition; first the plain signitive intention, then the intuition (*LI*, VI, § 8). But an important distinction must be made.

While we have only the signitive consciousness, there is no intuition of the intended object at all, although there are foundational intuitions of the words or signs. But when the intuition comes about, the object now present is experienced *as fulfilling* the empty intention. The signitive intending remains around when the fulfillment is performed. "We must, therefore, maintain that the same act of meaning-intention which occurs in an empty symbolic presentation is also part of the complex act of recognition, but that a meaning-intention that was 'free,' is now 'bound' and 'neutralized' in the stage of coincidence" (VI, § 9). The fulfilled consciousness is a laminated consciousness, involving the presence as presence and the signitive awareness as filled by the presence. The object is present as filling an absence. What is expressed in words when we express what we intend is the meaning of the empty intention, not the fulfillment as such. The expression is the same whether the intention is purely empty or filled (see below, § 46).

The laminated cohesion of signitive and intuitive intending requires in addition an "act of identification"—or "act of recognition," or "experience of identity"—as a skewer. The absence is correlative to the signitive act, the presence is correlative to the intuitive act, and the identity is correlative to this recognizing act. Another name for this third act is the "act of fulfillment." Husserl writes, "A more or less complete *identity* is the *objective datum which corresponds to the act of fulfillment,* which 'appears in it.' This means that, not only signification and intuition, but also their mutual adequation, their union of fulfillment, can be called an act, since it has its own peculiar intentional correlate, an objective something to which it is 'directed' " (*LI*, VI, § 8, p. 696; italics original).[11]

Why all this machinery? These parts must be distinguished because recognizing or knowing something is complex. It is not simply having an impression of the object; just to have the object present, without manifestation of its identity, is not to recognize or to know the object. It is not to have a thoughtful perception. To recognize the identity of the object is to have the object thoughtfully, the way a human being has objects—with the possibility of expressing what is present to him. This kind of presence makes it possible to be truthful, to fail to be truthful, and to be deceived. In his phenomenology Husserl attempts to think about such matters, and he finds it impossible to do justice to them without the distinctions we have made.

In dynamic fulfillment the signitive intention chronologically precedes the intuitive, and this temporal separation makes it easier to display the parts involved. A "static" fulfillment is "the lasting outcome of this temporal transaction" (VI, § 8, p. 695; see also § 6). It is a simple recognition without temporally prior anticipation. Most of our recognizing, identifying, or knowing is static. I recognize and know my friends, my chair, this book, this building, the lake, as soon as I see them and without necessarily having anticipated them emptily before they come into view. But even static recognition is laminated and skewered; it involves the moments of signitive intention as fulfilled, intuitive intention as fulfilling, and is itself the experience of identity.

Objects are present to mind only as mediated by their absence. Mind's capacity to intend its object signitively—usually in language but also with other signs and symbols—means that it

11. All of § 8 is important for this theme. On negation as the experience of noncoincidence or nonfulfillment, see VI, § 11. Husserl distinguishes empty intentions from fulfillments in Investigation I, where he treats them in the context of meaning and its expression in speech. See I, §§ 9, 12–14.

can dislodge itself from its objects and still "mean" or "have" them. It can think about them in their absence. Then it returns to the objects and its direct enjoyment of them in a distanced adhesion. The work of mind, consciousness, is the process of having these identities in the appropriate synthesis of presence and absence.

Even when we encounter an object for the first time, we appreciate it as something that can be meant in its absence, so we experience not only its presence but also its identity. Once we have actualized our potential to be human and have gotten the sense of using signs, and so long as we have not lost our humanity through delirium, panic, illness, and the like, we experience everything as recognizable or nameable. As William James says, "For things hitherto unnoticed or unfelt, [man] *desires* a sign before he has one." [12]

There are degrees of identification. Even when an object is identified or recognized, degrees of saturation are possible in its fulfilling presence. I have identified and recognized the Hudson River, but Robert H. Boyle, who is said to know more about it than anyone else, does so much more completely than I. [13] He achieves the whole known as "experiencing the Hudson River" in a much more saturated degree than I, even though I do manage an intuitive recognition which is better than what some other people might accomplish. How a certain object is to saturate recognition to a greater or lesser degree depends on what kind of object it is; the rules are different for people, animals, buildings, rivers, cars, plants, paintings, and symphonies, and the phenomenologies of such objects would explore the differences. In the *Logical Investigations* Husserl does pick out one common denominator: the extent to which the sensibility founding the intuition is presentative and impressional, and not a base for signitive intending, determines how fully the intuiton saturates

12. *The Principles of Psychology* (New York: Dover, 1950), II, 356. See also *LI*, VI, § 5, p. 685.

13. Boyle is the author of *The Hudson River* (New York: Norton, 1969). On the jacket is written: "It is his ambition to know everything about the Hudson—every fish, every bird, every plant—but even though this is impossible, he has provided the reader with an unforgettable account of the Hudson River based on his own observations." This sentence illustrates several phenomenological themes: the pull toward exhaustive knowledge as the telos that drives scientific inquiry, the realization that this ideal of fulfillment cannot be achieved, the primacy of registration, and the difference between registration and report.

(VI, § 25, p. 740). This principle, though valid as formulating a condition for intuition, was modified as Husserl became more aware of the variety of ways in which saturation can be intensified.

Robert H. Boyle's recognition of the Hudson River is more distinct than mine, and mine is more vague than his. He articulates the parts more completely. Both vagueness and distinctness, however, take place within an identity synthesis, within the intuitive recognition of the object.

When Robert H. Boyle thinks and talks about the Hudson River, and when he recognizes the river and its parts, he does more than mutely perceive the river and entertain images of it; he frames judgments and registers and reports facts. How does he do this?

§ 10. FACT AND REGISTRATION OF FACT

THE PRINCIPLES OF PRESENCE, absence, and identity work in the case of categorial consciousness (*LI*, VI, pt. 2). A categorial intention is one in which we intend not a simple perceptual object, but an object infected with syntax. A fact or state of affairs, a group, a relation with its relata, are categorial objects. The continuous experience of simple perception is broken into discrete parts, and these parts are recognized as parts in the categorial consciousness: "It is clear . . . that the apprehension of a moment and of a part generally *as* a part of the whole in question, and, in particular, the apprehension of a sensuous feature *as* a feature, or of a sensuous form *as* a form, point to acts which are all founded. . . . This means that the sphere of 'sensibility' has been left, and that of 'understanding' entered" (VI, § 47, p. 792). "The single-rayed acts are not articulate, the many-rayed acts are articulate" (V, § 38, p. 640). We do not merely undergo the continuous presence of a cube; we explicitly distinguish parts. We intend not just the cube or its blue color, but the fact that the cube is blue.

As regards formal structure, we will use the term "fact" in a very general way. A fact is any categorial arrangement articulated in objects. An attributional arrangement—the fact that John is sick—and a relation—the fact that John is near Paul—both qualify structurally as facts. So does a collection. The arrangement of an object with its attribute—that "S is *p*"— is the normal meaning of "fact" in European languages, and we will continue to respect this as the primary instance of facts, but we will not exclude relations and other arrangements.[14] After all, it is conceivable that a particular language family may not use attribution as the primary way of articulating its objects.

Often the term "state of affairs" is used in contrast to "fact." States of affairs are taken as possible arrangements of things and attributes, and facts are taken as actualized instances of these possibilities. We will not follow this terminology; if the distinction is necessary, we can speak of possible facts and real facts. This is a more convenient terminology, and more in keeping with ordinary usage. If we ever use "state of affairs," it will be taken as synonymous with "fact" and used only for variety in expression.

The fact that Paul is awake, and the fact that John is beneath the sycamore tree, are categorial objects. It is possible to isolate from categorial objects the categorial form operative in them, such as the attributive form "S is p" or the relational form $a \, R \, b$. Still further categorial forms can be built on the basis of such first-level forms, like "(S is p) implies (S is not non-p)." This brings us into the realm of formal systems. But the problem of identity synthesis or fulfillment is not to be treated in terms of categorial forms; it is to be discussed for unformalized categorial objects like the fact that John is singing or that the cat is on the mat.

We can intend a categorial object signitively or intuitively, and the categorial object—the fact, the group, the relation—is the identity meant in both ways, just as the lake is the identity we can intend in absence and in presence.

Let us call "registration" the intuitive presentation of a categorial object. To register a fact, register a group, or register a relation is a different thing than to think about each of these emptily or signitively. But the fact, or group, or relation is never just what is intuitive, nor just what is emptily meant; it is that which is the same in both states.

Whether we intend a fact in presence or in absence, we do

14. In doing this we conform to the wide meaning Husserl prescribes for "judgment" in *FTL*, § 39; see below, § 71. Judgment is correlative to fact, and in both cases we have the ambiguous "judgment" and "fact" naming (1) all categorial articulations, and also (2) the paradigmatic articulation: the predicational or attributional **kind** of fact or judgment.

not turn our attention to our judgments. Judgments are operative while we intend facts, but we do not focus on them. That calls for a wholly new orientation of mind: we would have to reflect. Judgments are in the domain of meanings; facts are in the domain intended through meanings. Facts are "in the world," though in a way different from the way perceptual objects are there—for facts arise in response to thinking about things.[15] Facts are things in their articulated intelligibility. Even intending facts emptily in their absence is not reflecting on judgments.

How can we describe the transition from an empty categorial intention to a fulfilled one? There is no difficulty in describing the fulfillment of perceptual ingredients in the categorial object: "house" and "brown" are saturated by the usual perceptual intuitions. But if we intend the whole fact, "The house is brown," what is to saturate the formal element expressed by "is"? Formal components of meaning such as "is," "and," "next to," etc., do not find their fulfillment in perceptual moments given in the thing or its image: "What intuitively corresponds to the words 'and' and 'or', to 'both' or 'either', is not anything, as we rather roughly put it above, that can be grasped with one's hands, or apprehended with some sense, as it can also not really be represented in an image, e.g., in a painting. I can paint *A* and I can paint *B*, and I can paint them both on the same canvas: I cannot, however, paint the *both*, nor paint the *A and* the *B*" (*LI*, VI, § 51, p. 798).

When we ask whether we can sensuously present "*A* and *B*," therefore, we find we can depict *A*, depict *B*, and that we must begin to *think* in order to register the collection "*A* and *B*": "Here we have only the one possibility which is always open to us: to perform a new act of conjunction or collection on the basis of our two single acts of intuition, and so *mean* the *aggregate* of the objects *A* and *B*" (VI, § 51, p. 798).

"Is," "and," and "next to," as syncategorematic components of categorial wholes, are the deposit left by various categorial,

15. Our usage is similar in some respects to that of Strawson in his essay, "Truth," reprinted in *Logico-Linguistic Papers* (London: Methuen, 1971), § 2, pp. 193–202. Of "fact" Strawson says it is "the only possible candidate for the desired nonlinguistic correlate of 'statement'" (p. 195). The major apparent difference between Husserl and Strawson is that Husserl admits facts are in the world while Strawson does not; he seems to say that only unarticulated objects are parts of the world. And yet he admits it is not objects but the condition of objects that make statements true (p. 195); is not the condition of an object a fact?

"intellectual" acts of consciousness. They are not read off things as attributes, but originate in the acts by which consciousness articulates discrete parts within what it intends, and simultaneously composes a whole out of these parts. "Is" is the deposit of a predicative act, "and" is the deposit of an act of collecting, and "next to" is left by an act of relating. These are all acts of the intellect at work.

The formal syncategorematicals are distinct but not separable from the acts that constitute them; they are also distinct but not separable from the cores that they arrange. As so doubly distinguished, they are capable of being either present or absent, and can exist on the continuum of greater or lesser presence.

But how are syncategorematicals to be present and how are they to be absent? They are not saturated by any sensible feature in things. How are they to be saturated?

§ 11. CATEGORIAL INTENTIONS: EMPTY AND FILLED

WE CAN APPRECIATE the saturation of categorial intentions by contrasting it to the corresponding empty intentions, of which several must be distinguished.

1. The simplest case is an empty intention executed in the perceptual absence of the things and features ingredient in the categorial object. If I am behind the house and say, because someone told me so, "The front door is open," I emptily intend the fact that the front door is open. If I go to the front and look, and execute the judgment again in the presence of the front door, I register the fact intuitively. Without the perceptual presence of the object and attributes ingredient in the fact, the fact itself cannot be intuitively present.

When I am still behind the house and say that the front door is open, I frame a judgment distinctly but I am not concerned with my judgment; I intend the fact, which is absent at the time. I would have to reflect to become concerned with my judgment.

Let us introduce the term "to report" as a name for the act of explicitly intending a fact in the absence of its perceptual ingredients. When I am behind the house, I report the fact that the front door is open. When I go to the front and see, I register the same fact. The term "reporting" is appropriate because of its etymological overtone of carrying something away. We do not report a fact where it is registered—the "where" involving not just spatial affinity, but concentration of the mind as well.

Registration saturates what is said in a report.

The fact is the identity that can be registered and also reported. It cannot be limited to being just one or the other. It exists in these two profiles—and in others as well, as we shall see—and cannot be reduced to either.

Neither registration nor reporting thematizes the judgment. Both intend the fact, one in the sensible presence of the fact's ingredients, the other in their absence.

We must not be narrow-minded about what constitutes the perceptual presence of objects and qualities. Seeing whether the front door is open need not be confined to the very seconds during which the door is in my field of vision. Because of the retentional and protentional form of perceptual awareness, I may still be seeing whether the front door is open even though my eyes close for an instant or I turn away momentarily. The presence of the door is still at work in my sensibility; it is still making an impression on me, because the kind of impression it makes is not atomic: it is temporally stretched. It is an identity through time. It ceases only when I stop seeing if the door is open, and start doing something else or lapse into doing nothing in particular.

If I meet an impressive person, the aura of his presence may be still around in my sensibility for a while after he leaves. This is not remembering what he was like; it is the reverberation of his presence, which is still retained. If I make observations about him while the aura is still there, I am registering facts in his presence. The same is true if I turn away from the door to someone at my side and say the door is open; I am still registering that fact. In an overwhelming presence I may be unable to take the initiative to register a fact until the presence moves to the retentional state. The pressure on my sensibility may be so great as to make me all passive and unable to think. Most perceptive judgments are made in the reverberation of a presence, not face to face.

Of course other registrations can be made on the basis of memory, whose presence is still more distant to us, or on the basis of imagination. Memory and imagination are, in contrast to signitive thinking, kinds of intuitions, and so allow authentic registration of facts. Such registrations are different from those made on the real presence of an object. They are a kind of absentee registration. They may be more insightful because of the greater distance they allow for the activity of thinking and the testing of options, and because they allow us to examine the same thing over and over again. But they are not much good for confirming a judgment because we cannot trust them not to decay.

A man is thinking back over a meeting he had with some others. He lets the meeting take place over and over again in his memory; suddenly he realizes, "Those two were in collusion! They were signaling to one another. Perhaps they plan to exploit the disagreements that exist among the rest of us!" He has just registered this complex fact, and will report it to his friends. They will accept it as a report and attempt to register it in their own memory. Like all facts registered in natural experience, it is subject to further confirmation and refinement, so all the parties will try to confirm it, perhaps many times, by talking to the suspected plotters and seeing how they behave. The original registration of the fact was carried out not by inference but intuitively through memory, by allowing the meaning and all the subtle parts of the events to sink in. The man actually came to see the suspects signaling to one another and making devious moves; he did not conclude inferentially that they were doing so. Subsequent attempts at confirmation may allow him to see their moves more distinctly and let the reality of their action manifest itself more thoroughly; or they may show that he mistook what was going on, that the men were innocent after all.

There are other examples of belated registrations based on memory, which do not involve the complexity of other minds; while remembering, a man may think of a possible route up a difficult mountain, or see a new functional connection between two parts of a disease he is treating, or come to realize that he is acting out of jealousy in doing certain things. And sometimes we can register through inference in memory: a detective is brooding alone, in the middle of the night, over the facts or clues he has. He suddenly says, "Smith did the murder!" as everything falls into place. He is registering and not reporting the fact, because he has been dwelling on the imaginative and memorial presence of the clues, facts, and their ingredients. He reports the fact later when he tells it to his colleagues. The detective registers the fact as an inference or a possible fact; he does not see or even picture Smith committing the murder. A fact registered inferentially is registered with the support of

other facts, some of which must be noninferentially registered—
the "hard" facts or the clues in the case.

A similar inferred registration of fact is performed by an
anthropologist who finds artifacts, ruins, and burial sites, and
tries to reconstruct what things were like in a lost civilization.
His task is made infinitely easier if he finds written records and
can appropriate the reports of those who lived in that civilization.
Reading the records is appropriating the reports, not inferentially
registering facts, but it is more reliable than such registration
in finding out what happened—what was registered and actualized as a phenomenon—in those days.

An overwhelming presence may remain intellectually un-
digested for a long time, perhaps through one's entire life. We
may not have the categoriality to register it. A traumatic experience may persist as such in our sensibility. It may endure
retentionally and never really be forgotten; it may take on new
tones in imagination and memory. Subsequently we may succeed
in registering it, either by our own thoughtful achievement or
with the therapeutic help of others. We become capable of reporting it and are freed from its sensible weight. Until this occurs we may be painfully and helplessly aware that it needs a
name and an articulation, but unable to give it any; we do our
best to handle it with images, symbols, and gestures. Such
eventual registration takes place in regard to political matters as
well as personal experiences. A riot or a defeat in warfare—
think of *Trojan Women*—may find its sense only well after it
happens.

And lest these lugubrious examples depress us, we must
remember that good things can also be hard to articulate—falling
in love, winning a prize, meeting an old friend, climbing a
mountain, being a hit in a play. We may not want to bother
articulating them, since we don't want to escape into reports,
but thinking can register the presence more intensely; why else
do people write about their love?

Our first case of empty and filled categorial intention is
based on the presence and absence of the material ingredients of
a categorial object. It does not tell us much about the syncategorematicals; it does not illuminate the work of "is" in "The
front door is open." Our second example will help in that regard.

2. We intend a categorial object emptily when we fail to
execute the appropriate categorial act: we mean the object
signitively. When we say "and" but do not assemble "this and
that" explicitly and distinctly, we mean the categorial object

emptily—this time because we intend the syncategorematic element in the object emptily. Then when we actually do collect the two items, we have the "and" given intuitively.

Consider the case of a difficult mathematical proof. In step fifteen I am told to combine A and B. If I have been confused by the argument so far, I cannot as a mathematician authentically combine the two; I can emptily assert, "Yes, now 'A and B,'" but the "and" is not really at work here. The conjunction is only emptily, signitively, verbally meant. But if I learn the first fourteen steps, it will be possible for me to register the new categorial object, "A and B," in step fifteen. The categorial object "A and B" is now intuitively meant; the act that constitutes "and" has been able to go to work energetically; the conjunction is intuitively given.

This example illustrates the difference between the confused or languid intention of a syncategorematic component and the intuitive presentation of it. The mathematical fact or relation is absent to the first intention, although it is intended by it, and present to the second. In *Ideas I* Husserl writes: "We can . . . predicate in a 'blind' way that $2 + 1 = 1 + 2$; we can, however, carry out the same judgment with insight. The state of affairs, the synthetic objectivity which corresponds to the synthesis of judgment, is then primordially given, grasped in a primordial way" (§ 136, pp. 379–80).

Such examples are inappropriate, however, because they are mathematical and deal with formal states of affairs, not with concrete categorial objects. Also as mathematical they enjoy a peculiar kind of truth interest.[16] Let us turn to analogous examples in which concrete facts are intended.

3. A visitor rushes through the National Gallery of Art in a few minutes and, on his way out, says, "There are magnificent paintings in this museum; the colors in the Rembrandts are particularly subtle." He does not authentically register the facts that are there—the paintings as beautiful and the Rembrandts as subtle in color—even though he uses the appropriate words. He has not truly articulated his perceptions; he is not capable of predicating. He voices certain words but does not think or register facts; he emptily intends the facts. He uses his syncategorematicals languidly.

16. Husserl acknowledges the difference between purely arithmetical judgments and judgments involving perceivable things in *LI*, VI, § 56. On the special truth interest of mathematics, see below, App. § 4.

A poor dentist examines someone's teeth carelessly and says, "Your teeth are all right." He articulates the fact languidly. He emptily intends what is before him, not because of an absence of the objects ingredient in the fact, but because of his languid use of syncategorematicals in their presence. The failure is one of thinking, for the fact is given to thoughtful perception, not just to sensible absorption.

Someone is asked how many trees there are in a particular grove. He counts carelessly and fails to register the collection; the "ands" are used languidly. He intends the group only emptily.

In all these cases, the speakers may be correct in what they say; the paintings are magnificent, the man's teeth may be all right, the number of trees may be accurate. But the correctness is only coincidental; the speakers have not registered what is there.

These cases are not examples of reports. The people involved are all in the perceptual presence of the ingredients of the fact, and the mind is bent on registration, but it does not come off. It is a registration that misfires and does not bring about the actual presence of the facts. A report may be languid, as these cases are, but a report may also not be languid. It may authentically articulate the fact which is absently meant.

Another way of saying that the syncategorematicals are languidly used is to say that the fact has not been articulated. Its parts have not been put together explicitly. We can also say that the appropriate judgment has not been "framed" during the registration—but this is a slippery way of talking and can be used with safety only after we have clarified in what sense there is a judgment here as well as a fact (see below, §§ 13–14).

Of course the syncategorematicals include not just the copula and conjunctives, but all the formal components in an expression: words or inflections expressing implication, disjunction, possession, alternation, the dative or ablative sense, forms of punctuation, and so on. An expert writer will shape his sentences with great precision, and each formal element, separately noticeable, will modulate its part of the state of affairs he wishes to register. No inflection can be overlooked in Thucydides or Hobbes. But a poor writer or speaker, impressed by such complexities but unable to master them, will clutter the formal linkage of his phrases, piling up "therefores," "indeeds," "perhapses," "buts," and the rest, hacking again and again at what he wants to say but never saying it. His categorial objects are languidly performed through and through; there is no distinct identification of the fact he wishes to register or report; there are "no phrases bringing fact into the open." [17]

The difference between a confused or languid intention and an authentic registration is not a tangible difference; it is not displayed in the words that are uttered or in the sensible behavior of the speaker. We must focus on the domain of acts and the differences that arise within it. If we do not acknowledge this domain, we must admit we see no qualitative difference between an observation made by an expert and one made by a novice or duffer, so long as they all utter the same sentence.

The presence or absence of registration is partly dependent on the intellectual character of the speaker. We acknowledge some people as qualified to register certain facts, collections, and relations, provided the appropriate perceptual conditions exist, both objectively and in the person's own sensibility, and provided special motivations do not intrude. We do not argue with the plumber about his work unless we think he is sick or suspect that he wants to cheat us. Other people we judge as not qualified to register. And there are some facts that are quite ordinary, so that anyone who knows a certain language—and this presumes he has come to live a certain way of life—is able to register them.

If we meet a person whose intellectual habits we do not know, we do not take his word on an important matter right away; we test his qualifications to register by getting him to say more and by seeing how he reacts and responds to things we and others say. He in turn is not bound to answer us or to reveal his mind. Because authentic judging is not perceptually visible—it is not like racial or national features, physical deformities or strengths, lisps, twitches, or a steady gaze—it is possible for a man to keep his judgments and registrations to himself and remain unknown to us. He may go further and require us to assent to what he reports, but conceal the registrations which we demand as explanations for what he says; we are asked to trust him, which is not what we do when we accept what he says because we already know the registered reasons for it. When we take it on his word the underlying domain of registration is opaque to us. We may take his word for it; or try to coax or trick the reasons out of him; or force them out; or give up and

17. Geoffrey Grigson, "The Writer and His Territory," *Times Literary Supplement,* July 28, 1972, p. 860.

stop talking to him. Registrations are normally displayed in public, but they can be kept private too.[18]

It is more laudable to be able to register than merely to be able to report again what others have registered and reported to us. The registrar is the custodian of the truth which is handed about in reportage; he is not limited to what has been said, but can go on saying more about the object and can explain why what has been said is true. Often enough someone may wish to give the impression of having registered what he tells us, when all he is doing is reporting things he never could have articulated on his own, and which he may not truly understand.

4. One way of emptily intending a collection arises when one uses the word "and" languidly, without the energetic performance of collecting. There is another way, in which words do not play a part. I can perceive a gaggle of geese, a grove of trees, a bevy of girls. Each group, as a group of this particular kind of thing, has certain sensible characteristics—Husserl calls them "figural moments"—which attach not to the individuals but to the collection as a whole.[19] These sensible moments serve as the basis for emptily intending the group, even when the group is there before us. The group, as a categorial object, is not actually collected. It is not intellected or registered, but is meant emptily.

What has been stated for groups is true of all categorial objects: facts, relations, universals, disjunctions, and so on. Each can be emptily meant either by a languid use of the words that express formal components, or by allowing sensuous, figural moments to present the categorial object, instead of registering it by the act of thinking. There is nothing wrong with such

18. Henry James, *Washington Square*, ch. 4: "Catherine hesitated a moment; and then, looking away, 'I am rather tired,' she murmured. I have said that this entertainment was the beginning of something important for Catherine. For the second time in her life she made an indirect answer; and the beginning of a period of dissimulation is certainly a significant date." *The Turn of the Screw*, ch. 5: "Mrs. Grose's large face showed me, at this, for the first time, the far-away faint glimmer of a consciousness more acute: I somehow made out in it the delayed dawn of an idea I myself had not given her and that was as yet quite obscure to me. It comes back to me that I thought instantly of this as something I could get from her; and I felt it to be connected with the desire she presently showed to know more."

19. *LI*, VI, § 51, p. 799; *Philosophie der Arithmetik*, ed. L. Eley (The Hague: Nijhoff, 1970), pp. 203–10. See also *Ideen II*, § 4, pp. 10–11.

empty intentions in themselves, but they open the door to two degenerate surrogates for thinking, verbal and sensuous association.

5. There is still another kind of empty intending. After having registered a categorial object, I can "nominalize" it, change it from the object of an articulated, many-rayed act, to the object of a compressed, one-rayed act.[20] For instance, I register the fact that "Walter has come home," then I nominalize this categorial object and make it an ingredient of a further fact built on it: "It is good that Walter has come home," or "Because Walter has come home, Peter has left." The fact is folded up, the accordion is closed. The higher-level fact in turn can be nominalized and made an ingredient of a still higher categorial object, and so on: "S is p," "(S is p) is q," "[(S is p) is q] R [S' is p']," etc. In such a case we mention a fact or other categorial object, but do not register it. We are registering higher-level categorial objects.

This too opens a door to degenerate substitutes for thinking. We can take for granted the registrations that underly the higher-level categorial objects we deal with, and gradually forget how they are to be achieved. We stop thinking about them. In his later works Husserl claims this has happened to modern science, which has forgotten its origins. The remedy is to trace the series of registrations back to the elemental ones: to open the accordion and play its tune.

In sum, we have so far elaborated these possibilities: (1) reporting a fact; (2) registering a fact; (3) emptily intending a fact in one of three ways: (i) by a languid or confused use of syncategorematicals; (ii) by letting figural moments stand for registrands; (iii) by nominalizing the fact instead of articulating it. We can inauthentically report a fact by (i) languid or confused use of syncategorematicals and by (iii) nominalizing instead of articulating, but not by (ii), which is a surrogate only for registration, for the actual presence of the figural moments means we must be in the perceptual presence of the ingredients of the fact, and so cannot be just reporting.

20. *LI*, V, §§ 33, 36. In *Ideas I* Husserl says a polythetic act becomes monothetic; see §§ 118–119.

§ 12. JUDGMENT VERSUS FACT: PROBLEMS

WE DISTINGUISH between a fact as absent and as present on the basis of the absence or presence of the perceptual ingredients of the fact.

1. I am behind the house and say, "The front door is open." I say it with conviction because someone told me it was so, or because it is always left open at this time of day. I am concerned with the state of affairs or fact in which the front door is involved. I am thinking about an absent fact. I report that absent fact.

The temptation is to say I am thinking about my judgment, not about the fact. This is not so. I do frame a judgment when I intend the absent fact, but I am not concerned with the judgment. I am other-directed; I am concerned with the door as involved in a particular state of affairs, not with my judgment. But what is the place of the judgment then? How is it different from the absent fact?

2. When I go to the front of the house and register the fact that the door is open, a judgment is at work once again. I do have to frame a judgment to register a fact. How is the judgment different from the registered fact?

There is a misleading picture we must guard against at all costs. It would describe our situation in these terms: (*a*) There is a fact as an arrangement of things and attributes. (*b*) There is a judgment as another arrangement of words or meanings. (*c*) There is an act or complex of acts in the mind of the speaker. In this picture, the judgment is taken as a third element over against (*a*) and (*c*). Its domain is like the bubble of discourse in comic strips, the white—colorless—patch in which the words of the characters are printed. Our misleading picture would take the bubble of discourse as a mundane part of the world of the comic-strip characters: if they were to look around, they would see not only other characters, buildings, streets, etc., but also these bubbles and the judgments in them. Then, according to this misleading theory, the comic-strip people would sometimes carry out the enterprise of comparing—in some very special sense—what is in the bubbles of discourse with what are the arrangements of things and attributes. This would be the work of verification.

This theory claims that judgments are arrangements of

mundane objects which are to be matched against arrangements of other objects, which we call facts. When we are perceptually absent from facts, we still have this thing called a judgment which we generate and can concern ourselves with. When we are perceptually in the presence of facts, we also generate a judgment when we register the fact, and because the judgment is a subsistent thing, we have a judgment laminated against the fact—like a transparent plastic design laminated against a mosaic.

The perversity of this theory comes not from its urge to distinguish a judgment from (a) facts and (c) acts of consciousness, but from its desire to distinguish judgments from facts within the same level of being and within the same attitude of conscious awareness. The theory believes that while we are concerned with objects and their arrangements, we can, without a change of focus, also run into judgments.

But a judgment arises only in response to a change of focus from concern with objects and facts. We have to reflect to bring about the presence of a judgment. To appeal to the comic strip again, if the characters are to become aware of the bubbles of discourse and what is in them, they must adopt a focus different from the one in which they look at buildings and trees and their arrangements. They have to reflect, and when they do so they are no longer in a focus appropriate to seeing buildings and trees or registering, reporting, and generally intending facts. For this reason, comic strips or cartoons that put their discourse outside the picture box are less misleading philosophically; still, those that use bubbles acknowledge the problem by making their bubbles colorless and so presumably invisible to characters in the strip. This is their way of showing that one must reflect to notice a judgment.[21]

Of course, there is a sense in which the words in the bubbles are a part of the comic-strip world; persons in the strip would hear the sounds of the words. Analogously, the sensuosity of words is an ordinary part of our own world. But words taken this way are not being taken in the way that a philosopher concerned with the problem of truth wishes to take them, nor in the way in

---

21. Many interesting questions arise in the philosophy of comic strips. How do we interpret those that use no words at all? How is the owner of a given speech identified, particularly if the bubbles of discourse don't have strings? What sort of pictorial consciousness is at work in following a comic strip? How can characters be differentiated from one another?

which someone talking normally to someone else takes them. They are being treated as ordinary material things. The judgments expressed in them are not being recognized. Recognition of judgments as such means taking them as somehow not a part of the world in the way things and their arrangements are.

This peculiar status of a working judgment is recognized by Austin: "There must also be something other than the words, which the words are to be used to communicate about: this may be called the 'world.' There is no reason why the world should not include the words, in every sense except the sense of the actual statement itself which on any particular occasion is being made about the world." [22]

To anticipate a further doctrine in Husserl's philosophy, the way in which judgments are not part of the world gives us a hint about the way the transcendental ego is not part of the world. The transcendental ego is the one who makes judgments, who recognizes their special status over against the world, who is able to talk about this status, and, finally, who is able to describe himself as the one capable of such reflective judgments and descriptions. The transcendental ego is not separated from the world in the way a pure spirit or angelic mind might be, but after the fashion of a working judgment. And just as a judgment can also be taken as an ordinary part of the world, so the ego can become implicated in ordinary mundane connections; but when he does that, he is not exercising his function of making truth.

In trying to unmask the misleading picture about the place of judgments in the world, we have not done much to resolve our initial problem about the place of judgment in intending and registering facts.

§ 13. JUDGMENT VERSUS FACT: ELEMENTS OF A RESOLUTION OF THE PROBLEM

THE ELEMENTS for treating this problem are provided in Husserl's *Formal and Transcendental Logic*. In that book there is a subtle change in the way judgments are treated.[23]

1. In his first approach (§§ 23–25), Husserl simply places

22. "Truth," p. 121. See also Strawson, "Truth," p. 199 n. 1.
23. Some of these steps will have to be repeated, in a new context and in greater detail, in the Appendix, § 3.

the domain of judgments and meanings over against the domain of facts and things. The former is the apophantic domain; it is reached by reflective consciousness—reflective on our judgments and meanings, not on our acts—and it aims at a fulfillment in which its judgments and meanings are matched against facts and things. The domain of facts and things is attained in the straightforward, nonreflective consciousness. The formal structures of the apophantic domain are explored by apophantic logic, which is closely allied with classical Aristotelian logic. The formal structures of the objective domain are explored by what Husserl calls formal ontology.

In this initial presentation, Husserl simply presents two distinct domains—here the apophantic, there the objective—and tries to describe some relations between them, especially the "relationship" of fulfillment of the apophantic by the objective. He stresses that the domain of judgments is reached by reflective awareness, and clearly distinguishes reflection from straightforward intending.

But the two domains and the two attitudes, straightforward and reflective, are merely positioned next to one another. The peculiar status of the judgment and of reflection is not brought out. This first presentation is susceptible to the misleading interpretation we described above.

2. In a second approach to this problem (§ § 42–45), Husserl phenomenologically derives the apophantic or judgmental domain from the objective. He begins with the straightforward awareness we have of things. We perceive objects and register facts involving them. We can go further and register facts involving facts. All this takes place without reflection on judgment. We sustain the straightforward, thing-directed or world-directed attitude throughout. The registered facts belong to the same world as the things we perceive.

But then our procedure may suffer disturbance when some of the facts we have articulated begin to conflict with other registrations. They become doubtful, questionable, or just probable facts. Finally things may come to such a pass that we find that certain facts are not facts at all. They are not the case; they were merely our opinion—the facts *as supposed*. At this point a new domain emerges, the domain of the supposed as supposed, the apophantic sphere. Our focus on this domain is not the same as our focus on the objective, worldly, thing-domain where facts dwell. The two domains become differentiated; we now have "my judgments" as opposed to "the facts." And "my judgment" is simply "the supposed fact as supposed." As the two domains become differentiated, the two kinds of awareness become differentiated as well: reflection on the supposed as supposed becomes differentiated from the straightforward consciousness of things, facts, and world.

We have used "rejected" facts as a device to distinguish the apophantic from the objective. Once we have these two domains, there is no need to limit the apophantic to abandoned facts or mere opinions. Any fact, even one we legitimately register, can be considered as merely supposed; this is what happens in critical thinking. We turn our facts into suppositions and then match them against things, to register them again and thus confirm them. We interrupt our straightforward concern with things and facts, become reflective about our suppositions—this is not yet to become reflective on our acts, nor is it to become phenomenologically reflective—and look again to what is, in order to verify what we have come to believe.

Husserl's second approach to the status of judgments shows most vividly that there are judgments only for a reflective consciousness. We can talk about judgments philosophically only if we are willing to acknowledge the special focus of mind that brings them about.

§ 14. JUDGMENTS ARE NOT ABSENT FACTS

A JUDGMENT, a supposed fact as supposed, is not the same thing as a fact intended in the absence of its perceptual ingredients. It is not the same thing as a reported fact. If I say the front door is open while I am behind the house, I intend the fact whose ingredients are not perceptually present to me; but I do not intend my judgment. I must reflect on my opinion to bring about the presence of the supposed fact as supposed.

Two people are behind the house:

John: The front door is open.
Peter: Paul left it open.
John: If it starts to rain, since the door is open the rug may
    get wet.

The speakers so far intend the door and some facts to which it is ingredient. No reflection takes place; there is no focus on meaning. But then the conversation continues:

John: What did you say before?
Peter: I said Paul left the door open.
John: But you said earlier that Paul wasn't here today.
Peter: So I did; and I'm sure of that. I must have been wrong about who left the door open. Perhaps it isn't open after all.

In this second exchange, the focus turns on the judgment Peter made. It is treated as a supposed fact and its inconsistency with another supposed fact—the judgment that Paul isn't here today —is noticed. This exchange does not concern itself directly with facts, but with judgments. The shift of focus that makes present the judgment, the fact as supposed, is called reflection.

We can reflect on judgments during our report of facts in the absence of their perceptual ingredients, as in the exchange we have described. We can also reflect on judgments during the registration of facts in the presence of the material ingredients —while we are looking at the front door and seeing that it is open. We must interrupt the report and interrupt the registration in order to focus on the judgment. The same judgment or fact as supposed is reached in both cases. There are not two kinds of facts as supposed, appropriate to the two situations. The same one is reached in both situations, even though the situations are different and defined against one another.

Interesting possibilities arise when we consider the public nature of framing judgments. I may frame judgments in registration or reporting, while you accept them simply as supposed facts; or I may entertain a judgment as a supposition while you, gullibly, take it as a report or a registration. Still more complexities arise when more than two interlocutors enter the picture. And of course, although you may take my reports as mere suppositions—you are more critical than I—it is very important that you know whether I am taking them as reports or not; it is also important for me to know if you are appropriating my reports as reports—are you turning to my way of thinking?—or as mere suppositions. Small skirmishes and great battles in words are won or lost because the combatants know or do not know what the true position of their enemy is.

Two notes on terminology. Judgments are facts as supposed. We have stipulated that "fact" is to be taken in a very broad sense—applied not just to attributive arrangements like "X is y," but to all arrangements of objects, including relations and collections. "Judgment" must be taken in a correspondingly wide sense. It does not name only predicative arrangements like "S is p," but any kind of categorial articulation which is taken as supposed. True, the predicative arrangement is primary and "judgment" usually means that, but it can mean other categorials as well. Husserl takes judgment in this wide sense, and so do we (*FTL*, § 39).

Also, we have quite inconspicuously used the term "to frame" a judgment. Framing means to judge explicitly and authentically, as opposed to languid, vague, and confused judging. In framing, the parts are explicitly put together. We will discuss this more thoroughly when we treat the distinctness of judgment in Chapter 8 (see below, § 73).

§ 15. The Shift between Registered or Reported Facts and Judgments

It still seems hard to wash away the misleading theory we described above. When we register a fact, don't we frame a judgment as well? Don't we have a judgment stuck against the fact, like a plastic design against a mosaic?

No, we do not. The twoness is not in judgment versus registered fact as two separate elements; it is in the incipient split of our thinking. The mind is always incipiently reflective. When it registers a fact, it is always on the verge of reflecting on what it has done and making it into a fact as supposed. This shiftiness of mind is what makes us believe that there are two things, a judgment pasted against a fact. We overlook, philosophically, the mind and the two different attitudes it has. It is therefore correct to say that we frame a judgment while we register a fact. But the judgment, the fact as supposed, is different from the fact registered only by virtue of the kind of focus the mind exercises.

If we are enraptured by a certain object, we may almost lose ourselves as we go on registering facts involving it. We may almost eliminate the reflective propensity of mind and practically let the object speak in us; but no matter how rhapsodic we get, we do settle down sooner or later and become capable of reflecting on what we have said. We can then consider the facts as supposed, and recognize them as the same facts we registered in our enthusiasm. This shows that we were, all along, at least slightly reflective. At the other extreme we may plunge into reflection and almost become impotent to register facts. We stay with those we have framed, brood over them, and frame no more. But no matter how thorough our reflection, we always remain about to register once again. Reflection keeps this inclination back to what is the case. Neither of these two extremes is ever realized in its pure form. Each of the two attitudes is around marginally while the other dominates. Mind is the capacity to shift from one to the other.

We have described the shift from registered fact to judgment; the same shift is possible in reporting facts. While we report we are marginally reflective, and we can tend toward the extremes of enthusiastic reporting with almost no reflection, and overwhelming reflection with practically no reporting. Neither state can be free of the other's presence.

In the concrete, registration and reporting interweave, and reflection is always bouncing against both. We will, for instance, register a fact, reflect on it as supposed, and then report it if we are satisfied; or we will report a fact, reflect, and register it. Or we will slip from reporting to registering, or vice versa, with no full reflection intervening.

Some people are very good at shifting from facts to judgments and back again. They are critical thinkers. Some may be proficient in certain regions of facts and judgments—the experts —and others are just good at it generally. Some people are not so good at this; they find it hard to focus on a fact as supposed. They tend to take every judgment as a reported fact. Even they must have some sense of the difference and on occasion they may use it extremely well, but it is not habitual with them.

One may be good at making these shifts and not be able to talk about what the shift is and what its components are. To talk about such matters requires philosophical reflection, which is different from reflection on facts as supposed.

Everyone who speaks a language is able to manage the shift to some degree. Language is used to register or to report a fact. But as the fact is being registered or reported, the string of words also appears on the scene. We can repeat the stream of words, and this is the sensuous support for our focus on the judgment. The words and the sentence express the judgment, the fact as supposed.

When we register a fact we marginally listen to ourselves

speak. There is not only the sensuous presence of the ingredients of the fact; there is also the sensuous presence of the words used to register or report the fact. The sensuous presence of the words can be repeated—not to register or report the fact again, but to sustain sensuously the presence of the fact as supposed.[24] If we could not hear ourselves speak, we could not frame judgments. Even in using sign language, we must see the signs we make and—or at least—enjoy the kinesthesia of making them.

I can then use language to talk about my judgments and their fitness to what is the case. I could not do this with pictures. I may appreciate a picture of my friend, but I cannot register pictorially the resemblance or nonresemblance between the picture and him, nor can I picture what it is to be a picture of him. That is why philosophy can be done only in language, not in pictures, for with language we can register or report resemblances, identities, and differences, and register or report what it is to be a picture. Language allows us to be reflective, and on many levels, whereas pictures apart from language do not.

Judgments, registered or reported facts, and the shift of mind among these are some of the components that make a truthful character possible.

We have stressed the shift of mind between facts which I register or report and my own judgments. This approach is abstract; I also work in a similar way with the registrations, reports, and judgments of others. I can be carried along by what someone registers and passively register along with him. I can be carried along by what someone reports and passively

24. I can repeat the sensuousness of the words without actually registering their meaning, but keep the words around until the meaning can be articulated. For instance, I am told a telephone number; I keep repeating it "musically," without actually registering the number; I can hold on to it this way for a while until I manage to write it down or actually think the number through. On the sensuousness of signs, see J. Derrida, *Speech and Phenomena*, trans. David Allison (Evanston, Ill.: Northwestern University Press, 1973), esp. ch. 6, "The Voice That Keeps Silence." On p. 76 he says, "The voice is heard. Phonic signs . . . are heard by the subject who proffers them in the absolute proximity of their present. The subject does not have to pass forth beyond himself to be immediately affected by his expressive activity." On p. 77: "When I speak, it belongs to the phenomenological essence of this operation that I hear myself at the same time that I speak." On p. 79: "For the voice meets no obstacle to its emission in the world precisely because it is produced as pure auto-affection." On the place of the voice in constitution of the self, see Husserl's important remark in *Ideen II*, § 21 n.

report along with him. Or I can stop short and shift my mind to what he says, to the facts as supposed by him, to his judgments. I can entertain his judgments critically and saturate them, positively or negatively, by my own registrations. My capacity to be critical of my own thinking depends on my capacity to do the same with others, and on their capacity to be critical of me. I become something of another mind to myself when I think critically about what I say, and another becomes something of my own mind when I entertain or appropriate what he has to say. This is the most intimate way in which friends can have things in common. It also makes toleration of adversaries possible, since one can entertain a judgment without ascribing assent to it and making it one's own report or registration.

§ 16. FACT AS THE IDENTITY WITHIN A MANIFOLD

WE HAVE DISTINGUISHED the fact as registered, the fact as reported, and the fact as supposed. "The fact" is the identity within these three states. It would be misplacing concreteness to say the fact was just any one or any two of these moments.

Besides reporting and supposition, other ways the same fact can be meant absently are through a languid or confused exercise of syncategorematics, through sensible association of figural moments, or by being mentioned in a nominalized way but not articulated. The same fact can appear in all these guises. It is the identity within the manifold of these appearances. The appearances are structurally related to one another. We can move from the registered fact to the fact as languidly articulated; from there we can nominalize it; from there we can report it authentically; from there we can reflect on it as supposed, as a judgment. All kinds of transition are possible, and we still have the same fact.

There is no access to the fact except under some such appearance. There is no privileged view of the naked fact which might serve to measure the accuracy of these dressed versions of it. There are only these appearances. Among them, of course, the fact as registered is primary since it rules the adequacy of the others, but it is only one way of being a fact, and would not be what it is as a moment if it were not for the others. A registered fact must be able to slip into being a fact as supposed or a fact emptily meant; and a registered fact must be able to serve as the saturation of the others. What it is depends on them.

Therefore, while we have the fact in one of these states, we realize its potential to fall into the other conditions. While we register a fact, we realize that we can, at another time, entertain this same fact as a supposition; and while we have it as a supposition we realize we are able to register it at another time. We could not hold the fact in different states at the same time, however, and this introduces an element of temporality into knowledge (see below, §§ 80, 82).

"The fact" is not to be found exclusively in any one or other of these various moments. It is the identity present in them all. All the moments are needed to constitute the fact; any one, even the registration, would not suffice. Further, it makes no sense to speak of one of these moments without the others, since they are dependent on one another as well as on the identity common to them all.

Of special concern are the states of the fact as being registered and the fact as being supposed. This is the contrast between registered fact and judgment. Epistemologies sometimes consider these two states as two independent wholes—as pieces instead of moments. Then they ask how one of these pieces can be made to match the other: how can propositions or judgments or opinions be made to fit facts or states of affairs or things? How can a whole "in the mind" be made to match a whole "in the world"? They cannot answer this question, and so the insoluble "problem of knowledge" arises.

But "the fact" is not to be found just in the one or in the other of these two moments; it is the identity in both and in other possible moments as well. The judgment or the proposition is the fact as supposed; the "real fact" is the fact as being registered. It then becomes obvious that judgments can fit things as they are; the two should never have been separated in the first place. They are moments to one another. It also becomes obvious that logical forms—the formal structures operative in judgments—can have "application" in the real world, the world of facts.

To be human involves living in the element of facts in some degree of distinctness and clarity, and so appreciating at least vaguely the various states in which facts exist. The works of mind and body which do not as such register, report, intend, or reflect on facts, like passion, action, choice, labor, craft, aesthetic, and what Aristotle calls *noûs*, are understood by being contrasted to the mind for facts.

Living in the element of facts is made possible by language, the governing part of a way of life. Styles of living with facts can differ; there are many world views or forms of *Lebenswelt*. But the world philosophy speaks of is always a world infected with registration and reportage. It is not the unspoken world of sheer things and masses, for if it were philosophy could not talk about it either, as Kant correctly saw. It is the world in which facts have come to be.

§ 17. A MISCONCEPTION IN HUSSERL'S EARLY THOUGHT

HUSSERL HAD SOME DIFFICULTY getting clear on what we have called registration of categorial objects. His initial description is in *Logical Investigations*, but he later abandoned it. Both the doctrine and the change are instructive.

We are dealing with first-level categorial objects, those whose immediate ingredients are perceptual things and qualities, as opposed to higher-level categorial objects, whose immediate ingredients may be other categorial objects.

Here is how Husserl describes the registration of a predicative categorial object—a fact or state of affairs—in the *Investigations*:[25] In the perceptual, founding act, we enjoy the undifferentiated presence of S as a whole. Another perceptual act emerges which has as its object one moment, a, within S. This moment a is already contained in the undifferentiated mass of S. Therefore the new act that intends a is felt to coincide with part of the original act that intends S, the part that intends a. The emergence of the two acts and their felt partial coincidence occur in one whole of consciousness; i.e., the act intending S stays at work while the act intending a comes to be. This allows the felt coincidence to take place.

Now the felt coincidence of the two acts serves as the sensuous presentation for the categorial act that intends the state of affairs "S is a" (*LI*, VI, § 56). The felt coincidence presents the predicational identity between S and a, and this identity is registered by the new categorial act. The categorial

25. *LI*, VI, § 48; see Tugendhat, *Wahrheitsbegriff*, pp. 118–23.

intention is over and above the act that intends S and the act that intends *a*. It is founded on these two. It registers an object over and above the perceptual objects of these two acts, for it registers a fact or categorial object.

The felt coincidence of the two founding acts works exactly as the sensuous impression works in the fulfillment of simple intentions: as the immanent sensuous presence which is interpreted or animated as the actual presence of an object in intuition (see below, § 49). The actual impressions made on my sensibility by the White House are ingredients of the intuitive perceptual presence of that building; the felt coincidence of the underlying acts is an ingredient of the intuitive, registering presence of the categorial object. When the categorial object is only signitively meant, this felt coincidence does not take place and the registration of the categorial object does not have a base on which to occur. In the languid use of formal terms, in sensuous association, and in mere mention, the underlying acts do not get to work and coincide, so registration does not take place. An empty intending of a state of affairs is fulfilled when the underlying acts do get to work, when the articulation and coincidence come to pass, and the actual registration occurs—when we begin to think about what is before us.

What we have developed for predicative objects can be worked out, with appropriate modifications, for other categorial objects.

The merit of Husserl's analysis is that it recognizes a distinction between meaning a categorial object emptily and intuiting it. It also succeeds in intimately relating the founding perceptual acts to the categorial intention founded on them: registration of a categorial object takes place while the mind is in active intercourse with the objects that become ingredient in the categorial object.

The disadvantage of his analysis is that it limits the authentic exercise of syncategorematicals to situations in which the mind is in the perceptual presence of the ingredients of the categorial object. It implies that a categorial intention can operate *only* when the mind is in active perceptual contact with the objects ingredient in the categorial object.[26] It would deny that there can be anything like an authentic and framed report. For in a report, if it is explicitly framed, the perceptual ingredients are not around and yet the syncategorematicals are at work.

26. See Tugendhat, *Wahrheitsbegriff*, p. 124.

This description also does not sufficiently distinguish between registration and framing a judgment. We can explicitly frame a judgment in a reflective attitude, when, for example, we insist that we really maintain a certain proposition; this involves turning away from perceptual enjoyment of the ingredient objects if they are immediately present, or it can even be done in the absence of the perceptual ingredients named in the judgment.

In sum, the *Investigations* imply that syncategorematicals can be put to work authentically only in registration; it overlooks their ability to work in reporting categorial objects and in framing judgments. These distinctions are better managed in *Formal and Transcendental Logic*. Even in that work, the contrasts between reporting a fact and framing a judgment, and between registering and reporting a fact, are not as vividly expressed as they might be. But the distinction between registering a fact and framing a judgment is very clearly formulated, and this allows Husserl to overcome the insufficiency of the *Investigations*.

In the second edition of the *Investigations* Husserl admits he no longer holds the doctrine of "categorial representation," the appeal to a felt coincidence of underlying acts (Foreword to VI, p. 663). He does not explain why he has changed his mind, nor do his other works published so far provide reasons. We may speculate that the change came from a clearer awareness of the distinctions between registering, reporting, and framing.

Although the analysis in the *Investigations* has flaws, it is one of Husserls' major philosophical accomplishments to have drawn the distinction between empty and saturated categorial intentions. And the insufficient analysis in his first attempt sets the stage for more adequate treatment in later works.

3 / How to Intuit an Essence

τὰ μὲν οὖν εἴδη τὸ νοητικὸν ἐν τοῖς
φαντάσμασι νοεῖ.
—Aristotle, *De anima* 3. 7. 431b2

And as imagination bodies forth
The forms of things unknown, the
    poet's pen
Turns them to shapes, and gives to
    airy nothing
A local habitation and a name.
—*A Midsummer Night's Dream*,
    V.i

§ 18. CORRELATION OF PARTS-WHOLES AND PRESENCE-ABSENCE

THE CONTRARIETY OF PARTS and wholes is founded on the contrariety of empty and filled intentions; and, reciprocally, the latter is founded on the former.

Empty and filled intentions and all the structural elements in them, as well as the sensibility they are based on, are parts within the whole which is consciousness of identity. They are moments, and phenomenological analysis has the job of showing how they supplement each other in the concrete life of consciousness. Empty and filled intentions are structured according to the logic of wholes and parts.

But parts themselves come to be in correlation to empty and filled intentions which are played off against one another. We have "parts" when, in perception or imagination, we can vary one element in an object while others remain unchanged; such variation amounts to bringing about successive absences—red disappears when green moves in, green disappears when brown arrives—while the permanence is a retention of presence—the spherical shape remains the same. Underlying both the changing and the permanent parts is the identity of the object or at least of the kind of object we experience; a recognition of identity supports the empty and filled intentions whose coming and going gives rise to parts.

We have "pieces" when we can perceive or imagine one of these parts in the total absence of certain others; these parts are independent of each other. We have "moments" when we cannot imagine the presence of one part in the total absence of certain others. But even moments are capable of being varied against one another—the color can change while the shape is fixed—and this shows that they are indeed parts. The impossibility of separating them shows they are moments. All these possibilities are different kinds of mixtures of presence and absence, filled and empty consciousness.

In the *Logical Investigations* Husserl indicates that there is a relationship between the logic of parts and wholes and the notion of essence. The Second Investigation tries to show that essence and the consciousness of essence are not reducible to anything else, and must not be eliminated from philosophical consideration; Husserl's argument makes use of the notion of moments (II, §§ 36–39).

These initial attempts are developed, in Husserl's later thought, into the doctrine of eidetic intuition, the process by which essences are brought to direct presence and registration. In describing this process Husserl incorporates both the logic of parts and wholes, as he arranges various levels of dependent or independent essences in relation to one another and to the individuals they inhabit, and the doctrine of empty and filled intentions, as he distinguishes between the intuitive registration of an essence and the various ways it can be emptily and confusedly intended.

§ 19. EMPIRICAL UNIVERSALS

THERE ARE SEVERAL STAGES in the constitution of an essence. Before we reach pure essences we must acquire empirical universals, in a process involving three steps.

1. On the most primitive level, we make judgments attributing similar features to various individuals. We say, "This

truck is red," "This house is red," "This book is red." In each
judgment an individual feature or moment is attributed to an
individual substrate. The same word "red" is used to show that
we recognize the likeness of one object to another, but the color
of each item is not taken as rigorously "the same" as the color
of the others. The objects are only like one another; they are
associatively similar, not identical in respect to the feature.[1] One
suggests the other. The judgments are surface judgments, based
on impressions and brought about by passive association.

Such judgments do not transcend the situation in which they
are used, nor the speaker who uses them; their truth and falsity,
and even their meaning—since individual substrates and individual features are meant in their concreteness, not as instances
of a species—are determined only in a situation (*EJ*, § 80,
p. 319). The attribute goes beyond its particular situation only
in being recognized as associatively like another individual we
have experienced, but this associative likeness does not disturb
the individuality of what we are experiencing. It does not turn
the feature into a universal. It also does not filter out private
associations. I may say this dog is like that, when the basis of
their similarity is that both suggest a pet I once had. Such an
association is idiosyncratic. My words tell more about me than
about the object of my judgments.

Associative judgments work among individuals. Presumably,
although Husserl does not mention this, particular individuals
could give way to a settled image into which similar cases
coalesce. A settled image is itself a particular, and new individuals could be found similar to it instead of similar to individual cases that we remember.

As we make more judgments of this kind we may enrich our
image of what we are expressing and develop anticipations of
future experience, but such enrichment and anticipation are not
very much different from the kind acquired by someone who has
been bitten several times by Great Danes; he reacts with fright
when he sees a Great Dane again, but the reaction is the work
of his sensibility, not necessarily his mind. Individual associative
judgments are largely the achievement of sensibility too, even
though they make use of words. Words and judgments on
this level may be only conditioned and settled responses to

---

1. See *EJ*, § 81a. Treatment of the intuition of universals can be
found in *EJ* § § 80–98, and in *PP*, § 9. See also Ms F I 29, 1922–23,
pp. 281–94.

stimulations. The judgments themselves are associatively, not logically, united (*EJ*, § 81a).

Such judgments are not merely the work of sensibility, because the explicit distinction of subject and individual feature, "This is that," is more than sensibility alone can achieve. It is the primitive and vague work of thinking as it first differentiates itself from sensibility. A judgment and discourse are being rudimentarily framed. But these judgments are so close to sensibility that they can easily slip back into being just sensible shouts or responses, even though they keep the verbal form of judgments.

2. We can use the same words but now mean something different when we take "red" in each case to mean "the same" color. Each judgment becomes the assertion that this case is an instance of a category.[2] We subsume individuals under a universal, and do not simply associate similar individuals with one another or with an image we have built up of "red things." Association may be the occasion for us to make this judgment, but the judgment is not based on association alone; it is based on what the thing is. The judgment is a public claim to state what the thing is, not just how it appears to me. In such judging a universal, a "one in many," is at work (*EJ* § 81b, pp. 325–26). Even though we may not yet have explicitly thematized the universal, we have experienced its identity at work in our conscious life. It has been constituted.[3]

Only with the emergence of universals does the individual as such emerge, since the latter is determined against the former, as an instance of whatever universal is being meant. Thus, although the associative consciousness is immersed in particulars, it does not have a sense of individual as opposed to universal.

In (1) we make judgments that identify an object with an individual moment that is part of it; in (2) we subsume an individual under a general attribute. In (1) we judge, "S' is p'," "S'' is p''," "S''' is p'''." In (2) we judge, "S' is p," "S'' is p," "S''' is p" (*EJ*, § 81b, pp. 323–24).

2. *EJ*, § 81b, p. 324: "There result the judgments S' is p, S'' is p, and so on, in which p no longer designates an individual predicative core but a general one, namely, the universal as that which is common to two or more S's successively apprehended."

3. See Alfred Schutz, "Type and Eidos in Husserl's Late Philosophy," *Philosophy and Phenomenological Research*, XX (1959), 154.

3. It is now possible for us to focus on the universal and make judgments about it. This requires a shift from thinking about individuals; we must intend that which is identically the same in many individuals. We now make judgments about "red," not about red things. As our experience grows we enrich our concept of "red" or any other empirical universal, like "dog" or "automobile." This is not an associative enrichment or the modification of a settled image; it provides us with more things that can be said about our universal, and more parts are registered within it. We are now able to anticipate future instances not just through sensible association but by expecting future cases of exactly the same essence we have so far determined.

Future instances may adjust and add to the content of our universal, but now we cannot passively absorb the new dimension as we do in the modification of a sensible image. We have to think how the new parts and deposits fit with the old, and either reject or adapt one or the other if conflicts arise. We operate with a distinct consciousness of parts and with an explicit consciousness of negation and contradiction. Associative judgments do not have this awareness, even though they do reach a sense of distinction or otherness between a substrate and its features and a sense of negation between dissimilar features—this is why they move across the threshold from sensibility to thought.

As opposed to associative awareness, distinct thinking and conceptualization make up what Ezra Pound calls "the act of dissociation." "The job of a serious writer is to dissociate the meaning of one word from that of some other which the poor boobs think means the same thing." [4] To dissociate is the work of writers and thinkers. Association has its proper excellence, but it is lost when it tries to masquerade as thinking; honest thinking is dissociation.

The state of a universal at any time in history, the sum of the parts it has in the collective knowledge of the community that thinks critically about it, is how Husserl defines the empirical "concept" of the thing in question: the concept of sodium, the concept of sound, the concept of virus, the concept of life. Such a concept is never closed in fact, although it aims

4. Letter to H. L. Mencken, January 24, 1937, in *The Selected Letters of Ezra Pound, 1907–1941*, ed. D. D. Paige (New York: New Directions, 1971), p. 286.

teleologically at the ideal of consistent, coherent, and exhaustive determination, at an ideal concept in which everything is said.[5] The ideal is never reached—there is always something more to say—but the direction toward the ideal defines scientific inquiry into the object.

§ 20. EIDOS

CONSCIOUSNESS OF AN EMPIRICAL UNIVERSAL is the kind of awareness that operates in empirical science. It is not yet consciousness of a pure essence or eidos. It does not register the a priori structure of the object in question. It cannot engender an a priori science. To acquire this sort of consciousness we must leave the domain of perceptual experience and move into the intentionality of imagination, where we perform the process Husserl calls free variation.

In free variation we start either with an object from our perceptual experience or with an imaginary object. We let our imagination run free. We contrive a series of variants of our paradigm, instances that are similar to the original. In fact, we run through only a finite number of variants or substitutions, but we have the insight that we could go on indefinitely, *ad libitum*. Our imagination takes us beyond the restrictions of actual experience; we contrive examples we have never and could never encounter in the world: "We stand then in a pure fantasy world, so to speak, a world of absolutely pure possibilities" (*PP*, § 9a, p. 74). And because of the *ad libitum* character of our substitutions, the example with which we began the process loses its paradigmatic status, for we see that we might

---

5. *FTL*, § 42e, p. 116: "All the various particular formations that [the judger] actively acquires in doing so have categorial coherence by virtue of the identity of the substrate-objectivity . . . ; and they progressively constitute for the substrate the determining concept accruing to it precisely from all these judicative performances—the current 'How it is, all told,' a concept always in progress, always being further fashioned, and also refashioned." In judging about nature, for example, Husserl says we aim toward " 'Nature as it simply is,' . . . the idea of the true being of Nature or, equivalently, the idea of the concept completely determining Nature, as the concept that would be yielded in a (to be sure, impossible) complete and harmonized judging about Nature."

have begun with any other instance and could have run into our original example as just another of the infinite possibilities (*EJ*, § 92, pp. 356–57).

In this process of free variation we become aware of an identity that persists in all the cases we can imagine. It is the invariant, the essence, which is the basis of the similarity of all the examples we can contrive. Only because this essence persists in them can they be "variants" of a paradigm and not random individuals. Since this essence is freed, through imagination, from the restrictions of actual experience, it is called a pure essence or eidos. It is one and the same eidos in all the examples we imagine, and so it does not matter which of the infinite possibilities we begin with or actually contrive; any one of them serves as well as any other to display the eidos.

As in the case of empirical universals, we can turn our attention from the individuals to the essence itself and ask what moments make it up. We can ask, "In such free variations of a paradigm, . . . what remains kept as the invariant, the necessary universal form, the essence-form, without which something of this sort . . . would be entirely unthinkable as an example of its kind?" (*PP*, § 9a, p. 72; see *EJ*, § 87a).

If we articulate this eidos by registering some moments that compose it, we have brought it to intuition. The pure a priori essence, which was at work in our thoughtful experience of individuals, is now brought to distinct and intuitive presence. "This universal essence is the eidos, the '*idea*' in the Platonic sense, but grasped purely, and free of all metaphysical interpretations; taken exactly as it becomes intuitively given to us, immediately, in the view of ideas [*Ideenschau*] that arises in such a way" (*PP*, § 9a, p. 73). Free variation is not just "our way" of getting to an eidos that exists in itself and could be enjoyed in a less laborious way by other kinds of mind—no more than perception through profiles and impressions is "our way" of getting at things that might be less imperfectly intuited by other beings. Rather, the eidos is just what comes to be through the process of free variation. This is where it is intuitively identified, where it presents itself in its own kind of unsurpassable presence. There is no eidos except for beings that possess mind, imagination, and the ingenuity to manipulate imagination. "The being of the universal in its different levels is essentially a being-constituted [*Konstituiert-sein*] in these processes" (*EJ*, § 82, p. 330).

There is also no eidos except for minds that have judged

conceptually and have registered empirical universals. We cannot jump from sheer perception or from associative judging to eidos. Nor could we jump from empirical conceptual judgments to eidos, without having isolated empirical universals.

Registering an eidos makes intuitive what is confusedly or emptily meant when we register an empirical universal. It makes intuitive what may be sensed and anticipated in the distinct judgments that attribute a category to individuals. When we make such judgments, we may feel the need to get clear about what we are saying, and may sense the force of a special kind of necessity in our discourse which is not the necessity and universality that our generalized experience supports. This is a pull to a shift in thinking, not just to more of what we have been doing. It is a pull toward the kind of process Husserl describes as the intuition of an eidos. But until the move to register eide has been made, it simply has not been made. We do not start the career of our minds with the presence of eide, only to become submerged into sensibility and forgetfulness of these forms; we must move forward to thinking about eide.

Learning a language puts us on the road to registration of pure essences, but the ordinary use of language does not need eidetic registrations. Associative judging, for instance, can barely suspect that there is such a thing as an eidos. Cultures in which empirical conceptualizations are only vaguely reached cannot appreciate an eidos, although some individuals may suspect that some such new move can be made.

Within a culture, judging conceptually would presumably first arise in regard to matters of justice and not in regard to speculative questions about the world. In judging about what is fair, we cannot give associative impressions. We have to conceptualize and attribute something as "the same" for several cases. Persons who are able to make such judgments, in keeping with the conventions and customs of the way of life in which they exist, are honored as intelligent; their judgments, once made, meet with the general approval of the people, not because of the prestige of those who made them, but because the judgment does identify something appropriately "the same" in the cases under question, and almost everyone can see it once it is done. A person who can, in addition, register—whether in poetic or literal language—some of the necessities which could not conceivably be otherwise, is honored as wise. Besides the intelligence of a good judger, he needs insight into what supports good judgment, and a fertile imagination to conceive the limits of what is possible, to acknowledge what must necessarily be.[6] He is capable of thinking about ultimates.

In our day we claim to separate eidetic necessities concerning justice from those concerning the cosmos, but it was not always so and perhaps it need not be so for us either. Indeed, despite what we claim, perhaps it is not so for us after all. Perhaps our conception of justice is in fact involved with what we conceive, in our science, to be the necessities of the cosmos; for example, our conception of the individual and his rights may be influenced by the mathematical conception of being that underlies modern natural science.

We should not be misled by the obviousness of such examples as "bodies are extended" to think that the registration of eidetic structures is a simple matter that anyone can do. This example is trivial and tired, although the first registration of extension as an attribute of body—and perhaps even a renewed registration now—is no mean achievement. Scientific eidetic insights can amount to scientific revolutions.[7] In matters of justice eidetic insight may help establish a way of life; but to achieve such registration, a suitable intellectual and ethical disposition must be acquired, not only by the man who frames it but also by the people among whom he lives.[8] The excellence of registrations is due not only to individual genius but to the vigor and goodness of the tradition within which they are formed.

A culture subsists on eidetic registrations that have in the past been made within its tradition. The "sayings of wise men" are preserved as expressions of what are conceived as the limits of human existence and the limits of the world. These traditions

6. Maimonides, with his strong sense of the public function of wisdom, says that the prophet must not only have gifts of speculation, but also power of imagination. See *The Guide of the Perplexed*, trans. S. Pines (Chicago: University of Chicago Press, 1963), pt. II, chs. 36–37.

7. See Rudolf Boehm, "Die Philosophie als strenge Wissenschaft," *Vom Gesichtspunkt der Phänomenologie* (The Hague: Nijhoff, 1968), pp. 12–13.

8. Aristotle, *Nicomachean Ethics* 10. 9; Maimonides, *Guide*, pt. II, ch. 11, p. 276: "For our community is a community that is full of knowledge and is perfect. . . . However, when the wicked from among the ignorant communities ruined our good qualities, destroyed our words of wisdom and our compilations, and caused our men of knowledge to perish, so that we again became ignorant . . . we grew up accustomed to the opinions of the ignorant, [and] these philosophic views appeared to be, as it were, foreign to our Law."

always drift into sedimentation, and there is forever a need to reawaken and reregister them.[9] What was once eidetically appreciated, and now remains as the settled power controlling a way of life, must continually be appropriated.

§ 21. Necessity and Universality in Eidos

FREE VARIATION is exercised in imagination and thus escapes the contingency and factualness of perceptual experience. In building up our empirical universal, the starting point and the actual series of experiences do make a difference; our material concept of animal would be different if we knew only reptiles and baboons. There is historicity in such universals, and we have no warrants for going beyond what experience has actually taught us. But since an eidos can be extracted from imaginative examples, and no instance has any priority or governing power over any other, the contingency of which specific instances we have actually encountered is overcome.

Is there contingency to the extent that we must have experienced at least one instance of the eidos in question, even though it does not matter which instance? Strictly speaking even this limitation does not exist, for it is enough if we can imagine an instance. We may be unable to contrive one, but then that limitation comes from within ourselves, and not from the destiny that decrees which beings we will encounter in the world. We may be too weak, not ingenious enough to use our freedom, but the issue has been moved from the control of fate to our own power of contrivance. All contingency is overcome in the world of ideas—as a matter of principle.

The world of Husserlian eide is a "separate" world, the modern *chōrismos*, but it is reached through the vehicle of imagination. An eidos remains a moment that can only be viewed in its instances; it is not a separable part, a spectacle for gods and separated souls (*Phaedrus* 247; Plato of course speaks in images). But since its instances can be members of an imagined world, it can exist and be given apart from the actual

9. See the title of bk. III, ch. 1 of Machiavelli's *Discourses on the First Ten Books of Titus Livius:* "That a sect or a republic live long, it is necessary to take it back frequently to its principle [to its beginning]." ("A volere che una setta o una republica viva lungamente, è necessario ritirarla spesso verso il suo principio.")

world of experience and perception. As an eidos it is just as real in the world of our contrivance as in the world of our experience.

A distinction must be made, of course, between eide that can be instanced only in fantasy, like dragon, mermaid, and troll, and those that can be instanced in actual experience, or whose instances we have reason to infer from the experience of other kinds of things (*Ideen III*, § 7, p. 26). But even eide whose instances have real existence are presented as eide through imagination.

An empirical universal is always open to determination by further actual experience. An eidos of a real object, such as the pure essence of a material thing, animal, or tool, is not open to correction by further experience once it has been distinctly registered. It is a priori; it sets boundaries within which experience takes place. No experience could ever change an eidos once it has been adequately acquired through imaginative free variation. All its moments, the eide that blend to make it up, are necessary parts.

§ 22. REGIONAL ESSENCES

EIDE ARE HIERARCHICALLY ARRANGED. Some are genera to others, like color to red, or animal to bird. Some eide are dependent or abstract, like red, quality, or extension; they require other eide as foundations in order to be concretized; they are essentially adjectival. Other eide are concrete or independent, like animal, man, or tool; they can be instanced without further eide as substrates; they are essentially nominal. Much of what Husserl says in his later works about eidetic relationships is a repetition of his theory of independent and nonindependent parts, in which the notions of abstracta and concreta were first introduced (*Ideas I*, § 15 n.).

A special place is held by what Husserl calls regional essences. In *Ideas I* he says a region is determined by a highest concrete genus: "Every concrete empirical objectivity is ordered, with its material essence, into a highest material genus, a 'region' of empirical objects" (§ 9, p. 64).[10] So color is not a regional essence because it is abstract and not concrete, while

10. See also *Ideen III*, § 7, p. 25: "A priori there must be as many ontologies as regional concepts."

mineral is also not one because, although concrete, it is not a highest genus. Man, animal, and material thing are examples of regional essences.

Husserl continues: "A regional eidetic science or, as we might also say, a regional ontology corresponds to the pure regional essence." This is an a priori, eidetic science which articulates all the eide, concrete or abstract, that are subordinated to the regional eidos; within the region of material thing, for instance, we would have the pure essences of color, hue, saturation, and brightness. Looked at in terms of parts and wholes, each regional essence, being a highest genus subordinate to no other, is an encompassing whole, independent, within which dependent and subordinate moments must be understood and located according to their proper arrangement. Synthetic or material a priori judgments would express the blends of eide that occur within a given region. The empirical sciences are dependent on regional eidetic science, which articulates their a priori structures and presuppositions and provides a basis for classifying them: "We have to distinguish, in principle, as many empirical sciences (or groups of disciplines) as ontologies" (*Ideen III*, § 7, p. 25).

§ 23. CONCEPT AND ESSENCE

IN DEVELOPING HIS THEORY of empirical universal and eidos, Husserl uses the terms "concept" (*Begriff*) and "essence" (*Wesen*). We can speak of the concept of animal or the concept of dog, and we can speak of the essence of animal or the essence of dog. What is the difference between concept and essence? It can be clarified in three ways.

1. A concept works among meanings and judgments and inhabits what *Formal and Transcendental Logic* calls the apophantic domain, while an essence works among objects and registered and reported facts, among what is intended through meanings. It inhabits the ontological domain.

In the *Investigations* Husserl distinguishes between formal "categories of meaning" (*Bedeutungskategorien*) and formal "categories of objects" (*Gegenstandskategorien*; "Prolegomena," § 67, p. 237). The first are formal categories that apply to the meanings of intentional acts. They are applied to the apophantic domain. Through them we refer to various kinds of parts and wholes that exist among meanings. Judgment or proposition, subject, predicate, judgmental form, *and concept* are among these categories. A concept works as part of a judgment. It is at home among meanings, not among things meant.[11] The second are formal categories applied to objects perceived and articulated. They are applied to the ontological domain. They refer to various kinds of parts and wholes operative in any object at all in its possible categorial articulations. Fact or state of affairs (registered or reported), object, attribute, group, number, relation, individual, *and essence* are among these categories. An essence works among objects and within facts.[12]

A concept is to an essence as a judgment is to a registered or reported fact; a concept is an essence as supposed.

An essence can be at work in a registered or reported fact without being itself thematized or registered or reported as an essence. If I register or report that "Albert's spaniel is black," the essence of living bodies as extended and hence colored is at work in this fact, but it is not registered thematically. Essences provide the "ontological space" within which facts can be registered and reported. Likewise, a concept can be at work in a framed judgment without itself being that which the judgment is about.

We can turn our attention from registered and reported facts to the essences operative within them. We do this when we abstract empirical essences, or when we abstract pure essences (eide) through free variation. Then we register or report the structure of the essence, as we articulate moments within it. Correlatively, we can turn our attention from judgments—facts as supposed—to the concepts operative within them. Then we can articulate the parts of the concept.

2. Each notion works in an appropriate focus. "Essence" works while we remain captivated by objects and their articulation. To become aware of an essence, empirical or pure, we need never leave our focus on objects; even the eidetic intuition is carried on in this attitude. "This is the essence and it contains

11. See *Ideen III*, p. 98, l. 1; p. 100, l. 39; p. 102, l. 32 to p. 103, l. 8; *Ideas I*, § 13, last sentence.

12. We perform an intuition of an essence while we remain focused on things; no reflection on meanings is needed. The citations in n. 11 contrast essence and concept in regard to the direction of focus.

the moments X, Y, and Z" is spoken in an attitude directed naturally toward objects in the world. "Concept" works when we leave off talking about objects and begin to talk about our meanings, our opinions, our suppositions. "This is the concept and it contains the moments X, Y, and Z" is spoken in an attitude reflective on meanings.

3. Granted this distinction between essence and concept in regard to focus, what sort of affinity is there between the two? It is the same affinity that exists between the ontological domain and the apophantic domain generally. The concept is the essence as supposed, and intentions which involve concepts aim, teleologically, at the registration of essences as their fulfillment. As regards terminology, we might say the concept "reflects" the essence, or that it "mirrors" or "pictures" the essence, or that the two are correlated.[13]

In some passages of *Ideas I* Husserl says the essence finds "expression" through its concept or meaning (§ 10, pp. 68–69). In his own critical comments (p. 385, l. 30 of the *Husserliana* edition) he shows his dissatisfaction with this way of speaking, but continues to use it in *Ideen III*. In § 7, for instance, he says concepts are the "expression in thought" of correlative essences (pp. 26, 28). "Expression" is not a suitable term because its proper sense is the relation between a meaning and its verbal manifestation, and it is dangerously confusing to begin applying it to the concept's relation to essence (see below, § 45).

A helpful passage is found in the critical notes to *Phänomenologische Psychologie*. Once we have brought an eidos to intuition, we can mean it signitively or emptily at times when we are not intuiting it. Once it has been registered, it can be reported. In the signitive act of reporting, the element of meaning which corresponds to the essence is the concept. Then, the word associated with the essence, the word which *names* the essence, *expresses* the concept. The signitive intention whose meaning is the concept finds its fulfillment in the actual registration of the essence.[14]

---

13. *Ideas I*, § 74, p. 208: "Exact concepts have their correlates in essences which have the character of 'Ideas' in the Kantian sense." See also § 124.

14. *PP*, p. 561 (marginal notes to p. 74): "For every intuited eidos we can fashion a word as its name, and confer this eidos on the name as its permanent meaning or 'concept,' i.e., a meaning-intention, like a bill of exchange which refers us to the process of ideation."

"CONCEPTUAL THINKING" begins when we become aware of universals and begin to take individuals as instances of universals. Then individuals are "conceived" as such and such, they are subsumed under concepts. Concepts are applied to experienced objects; that is, the signitive act containing a concept is fulfilled by an intuition of an individual which is taken as an instance of this universal. "Applying a concept" is the name given to this process of fulfillment. It is different from the process of fulfillment in which we try to determine or fashion a concept, in which we try to discover "what is the virus?" or "what is sound?" Then we are not intuiting individuals but the essence in them. We are not applying concepts, but elaborating them by registering the essence they reflect.

Just as there are empirical essences and pure essences or eide, so there are empirical concepts and pure concepts. In a marginal note Husserl mentions "the ambiguity of concept, pure concepts, and empirical concepts!" (*PP*, p. 561). The pure concept reflects the a priori material structure, the eidos of the thing we are thinking about. The empirical concept contains what has become known to the community that thinks critically about the kind of thing in question. An empirical concept aims teleologically at the ideal concept in which everything that can be articulated about this kind of thing has been registered.

We should not confuse an ideal concept with a pure concept, the reflection of an eidos. A pure concept is actually acquired; empirical concepts do not aim at it. Rather they are founded on it and contain it as part of themselves. An ideal concept is never actually acquired, but remains the ideal for empirical inquiry.

§ 24. REGIONAL CONCEPTS

THE DISTINCTION between concept and essence will help us handle a difficult but important passage, § 7 of *Ideen III*. We have seen that a regional eidos is the basis for a regional ontology. A regional essence is the highest concrete genus, the one subordinated to no other, in a hierarchically arranged series of essences (*PP*, § 9e, p. 82). The regional essence is, however, homogeneous with the essences ranged under it.

In *Ideen III*, § 7, we seem to find a different doctrine. There Husserl says a region is not a highest genus, and it is not homogeneous with the genera subordinated to it. Tugendhat considers this a rejection by Husserl of his earlier position.[15] But perhaps the difference of positions can be reconciled by noting that in *Ideen III* Husserl is talking about regional *concepts* versus generic concepts, while the earlier doctrine contrasted regional *essences* against subordinated generic or specific essences. We have moved from essences to concepts.

The problem that provides the context for this issue is: How do concepts, generic and regional, arise "out of experience"? (pp. 25–26). It is clear that generic concepts are built up from repeated experiences, and a concept like "mineral" is the summary of the parts we have registered as joined together regularly in the experience of this particular whole. Such a concept awaits new experience for further confirmation or adjustment; new observations or conditions may add to or modify the content, the parts that make up the concept. Is a regional concept like "material thing" essentially the same—apart from being higher on the scale of genera—as a concept like "mineral"?

It is not the same. "Mineral" is the summary of registrations of experience. "Material thing" does not summarize the content deposited by repeated experiences; it is "the regional form, the correlate to a basic kind of experience" (p. 34). The material thing is called a "form" which is correlated to a distinct kind of experiencing. The expression "material thing," says Husserl, "does not determine a content, but a form for all possible objects of this kind of possible experience" (p. 33; see also p. 35). The form of "thing" is a form for objects; these objects are not distinguished by any particular contents we have come to expect in them, but by being the objects of a special kind of experiencing. Husserl also says the idea "thing" is a "rule" prescribing the pattern of experience and a "frame" that determines the boundaries of an experience of this sort (p. 33). It sets a style for intuitions.[16] Specifically, the concept of material thing corresponds to a form of experience in which we encounter an identity persisting through causal interactions, through a manifold of spatial profiles, and through time. These formal directions of possible experience remain invariant while the actual

15. See E. Tugendhat, *Der Wahrheitsbegriff bei Husserl und Heidegger* (Berlin: de Gruyter, 1967), p. 179.

16. *Ideen III*, § 7, p. 31: "No matter how unknown the thing is, how little we might know so far of what future experience will teach us, one thing is clear a priori, that an absolutely fixed frame is marked out for the course of possible experience." See also p. 36; *Ideen II*, § 18g; Tugendhat, *Wahrheitsbegriff*, pp. 77–78.

content encountered in them—the basis for generic concepts—is totally variable.

Since a regional concept is a concept of a form, frame, or rule that defines the possibilities of a certain kind of experiencing, it is clear that such experiencing can never come up with anything that will count against or invalidate anything in that concept; it would be destroying its own self if it did that. All experience can do is determine contents within the frame prescribed for it; within that frame, changes and adjustments and development do take place. But the conditions that allow such changes and adjustment and development are not themselves subject to the same processes that they condition, allow, and govern (p. 34, ll. 14–20). These conditions are moments of the regional concept in question.

Sometimes we may find we have been exercising the wrong kind of experience; the object is not a human being but a beast, or not a beast but a rock. We have been anticipating the wrong form of experiencing. In such a case we do not make an adjustment within our attitude; we abandon it and undertake a new kind of experiencing. Everything in regional concepts is necessary and no changes can be made without shattering the whole. No identity persists through modifications. But if we simply have to make a change among generic concepts—we thought for a while it was a Great Dane, but it turns out to be a little horse—we do not change the form of our experiencing; we continue to experience an animal, but we anticipate a different content in what will be encountered.

Husserl concedes that a generic concept "also prescribes a rule for the course of experience. But in a totally different sense than the idea of a thing" (p. 33). A generic concept, he says, prescribes the way *thinking* prescribes: once granted a form of experiencing, thinking can anticipate certain contents (p. 33, ll. 35–38). But the anticipation of a kind of experience as such is not this sort of anticipation. Thinking does not set up ways of experiencing; it presupposes them and is parasitic on them. A way of experiencing is a fundamental way of being in intercourse with the world, of being at work as consciousness.[17] Thinking may register various arrangements within a way of experiencing and make the experience more varied, refined,

17. A generic concept, not being proper to a special way of experiencing, is not correlated to an ontology of its own. There is no canine ontology, but there are regional ontologies for the material thing, for animals, for society, works of art, sport, and so on.

critical, and perhaps more humane. But thinking cannot establish a new kind of experiencing, for it is essentially a founded activity.

It is true that while one is not exercising a way of experiencing, one can anticipate it conceptually. One can anticipate an art object, an animal, a human being, a material thing, as forms for experiencing. And there are correlative concepts for such objects, the regional concepts. Does not the possibility of conceptual anticipation make regional concepts the same as generic concepts? Not at all; a generic conceptual expectation, content-laden, always remains one option among many within a kind of experiencing, while the regional anticipation simply awaits the kind of experiencing itself.

Although thought cannot engender a new sensibility, it can appreciate and register the a priori elements of a regional concept and help us avoid confusing one region with another. If thinking is not clear, "the people won't know where to put their feet or what to lay hold of or to whom they should stretch out their hands. That is why an intelligent man cares for his terminology and gives instructions that fit." [18] Thinking also contributes to experiencing the way sketching a face helps us to perceive it better. The lines and parts of our sketch are like the parts we generate in our judgment. Thinking is parasitic on and dedicated to experiencing and cannot replace it, but experiencing without thought is opaque and dull.

This distinction between the generic and the regional does not come to light so long as we are focused directly on objects and concerned with essences. Talk about essences, regional or generic, does not let us speak about differences in the way we anticipate what is to come in experience. For that, we must turn to talk about concepts and the tendency of concepts "to be applied" by saturation in the experience of things. In *Ideen III*, § 7, Husserl does talk about concepts, while in other passages he talks chiefly about essence. This accounts for the apparent disparity of doctrine between *Ideen III* and other texts.

§ 25. FURTHER DISTINCTIONS

THE DIFFERENCE between regional concept and generic concept should not be confused with the difference between

18. Ezra Pound's Digest of the Analects, in *Guide to Kulchur* (New York: New Directions, 1970), p. 17.

eidetic or pure concept and empirical concept. Even what is meant through a generic concept can be turned into an eidos through free variation. Although Husserl usually employs regional essences like the material thing as examples of eidetic intuitions, he also uses such examples as red, green, or sound, whose concepts are obviously generic and not regional.[19]

Although a generic concept like "red" or "dog" is always open to the modifications of further experience, it is still possible to perform an eidetic transformation of it. There are a priori elements of red, even beyond those it has by virtue of being a color or a quality. A priori, red will never be green or yellow, and a dog will never be a cat or an elephant. Such eide may indeed be culture-bound; perhaps other traditions do not break up the color continuum or even the animal kingdom the way ours does. The eide are not taken metaphysically, but as moments that can come to be registered as phenomena, and some eide may arise only for a consciousness that articulates certain distinctions and not others. However, it would seem that regional concepts are not bound to culture and language, since they reflect basic ways of experiencing and not ways of thinking—thinking being the process of registering alternatives and distinctions and introducing systematic negations and types of otherness within these kinds of experience.

Some examples Husserl mentions of regional concepts in *Ideen III*, § 7, are material thing, esthesiological thing (by which he presumably means the phantom), man, psyche, and animal. Some examples of generic concepts are red, sound, mineral, the metal gold, reptile, sensible quality, and celestial body. It is interesting that he classes the plant as a generic concept, not a regional one (p. 33). This is in keeping with his neglect of plants in the material ontologies he sketches in *Ideen II*. Presumably plants are taken simply as kinds of material things. Although Husserl recognizes a place for psyche in animals, he seems to do so because of the consciousness attained by that kind of soul.[20] The work of soul as a principle of life, which is

19. *PP*, § 9a, pp. 73–74; § 9e, pp. 81–82; *EJ*, § 87a, pp. 341–42; § 89.

20. See *PP*, § 15, p. 104, ll. 20–33, and pp. 104–6 generally, where life is equated with being conscious. See also app. XXIII to *Crisis* (Husserliana ed., pp. 482–84, not translated by Carr), where biology is interpreted as part of self-understanding, with the need for a reference to an ego. Only by incorporation into self-consciousness does an organism acquire its true sense, claims Husserl. Finally see *Ideen III*, § 2, p. 10, ll. 7–14.

realized in isolation from consciousness in the case of plants, does not seem to be recognized by him. Plants do not constitute a distinct region of being, nor is the experience we have of them distinctive, in Husserl's view.

In its descriptive analysis, phenomenology is most interested in examining regional essences and concepts, the major forms of experiencing. The attempt to scrutinize all generic essences would tumble into infinite distinctions and triviality, like the phenomenology of petting dogs or eating yoghurt.

Husserl's contrast between regional and generic concepts leaves us with some problems outstanding. At what point do we draw the line between the generic and the regional? How many regions are there, and why are there that many? Should, for instance, the experience we have of domestic animals be considered regionally different from that of wild animals? Can one concept be generic in one respect and regional in another? Can a given culture lack a certain region? What does it mean to have an underdeveloped regional concept?

§ 26. EIDETIC INTUITION AND ALGEBRAIC FORMULAS

AT THE END of his description of free variation and eidetic intuition, Husserl remarks that mathematics works with concepts derived this way, and that anyone who knows even a little mathematics will be familiar with intuiting an a priori and carrying out ideation (*PP*, § 9f, p. 87; *EJ*, § 89, pp. 351–52). Following this hint, perhaps we can use mathematics to illustrate eidetic intuition.

An analogy can be drawn between an algebraic formula and an eidos as a rule or form for individual instances. Consider a function, $f(x) = y$. If we substitute values for the independent variable, we get the following values for the function as a whole: $f(1) = 3, f(2) = 5, f(3) = 7, f(4) = 9$. Any one of these can be considered the paradigm, and the rest can be considered variants. The process of free variation—free substitution—can go on indefinitely. However, in order to control the process we must turn our attention from the individual variants to the invariant form or rule that allows each instance to be a variant of the paradigm. This rule, of course, is the formula $2x + 1 = y$. This formula works like the eidos. It is that which allows an infinite number of cases or variants to be "the same." The formula itself is never given as one of the numerical instances it controls; likewise the eidos itself is never given as one of the variant individual cases. Both are disclosed only in a new focus of attention, away from individuals to the rule or form that governs them.

To carry our analogy further, Husserl would claim that in free variation we proceed as if we were given a series such as $f(1) = 3$, $f(2) = 5$, $f(3) = 7$, $f(4) = 9$, etc., and then were told that each of these is "the same" as the rest, that we could continue to add variants *ad libitum*, and finally that we could discover, by reflection on the series and by a kind of induction, that the invariant is $2x + 1 = y$.

While we experience the series of variants, we sense the necessity of the rule operating in them. We are not totally free in the substitutions we can make: when we insert a certain value for the independent variable, the dependent variable is necessarily determined for us. But only the turn to intuition of the formula shows us the cause of this necessity. In nonmathematical experience, as we keep substituting variants, we also feel the pressure of necessity coming from a dimension different from the one we are focusing on; we are not entirely free in contriving our variants, but must follow the rule which we will discover when we turn from the individuals to the eidos.

§ 27. Exact and Morphological Essences

ALL A PRIORI eidetic sciences achieve their fundamental concepts through imaginative variation; however, there is a difference between sciences based on exact eide, like geometry, optics, and Newtonian physics, and those based on what Husserl calls morphological eide.

An exact eidos is one which, besides being the invariant in free variation, is also an ideal limit toward which the variants are projected (*Ideas I*, § 74). A geometrical line, plane, circle, and cube are examples of exact eide. They are the result of "idealization"—not to be confused with ideation, the process of making an eidos intuited—and are never given to sensible experience. They are Kantian ideals and are constructed. They preclude all vagueness. Their correlatives in the domain of meaning are exact concepts.

One of the best examples of the formation of an exact

concept is Newton's definition of a ray of light in the *Optics*. He observes that light obviously has spatial parts, since "in the same time you may stop it at any one place, and let it pass in any other. For that part of Light which is stopp'd cannot be the same with that which is let pass." Then he goes on, "The least Light or part of Light, which may be stopp'd alone without the rest of the Light, or propagated alone, or do or suffer anything alone, which the rest of the Light doth not or suffers not, I call a Ray of Light." [21]

A ray of light is therefore a mixture of perception and thought. Newton begins with light, which is an element in our experience, refers to the familiar experience of interrupting a "part" of it, then projects this procedure of interruption to an ideal limit—the smallest part that can be interrupted. This ray is never perceived and yet it originates from what we do perceive. It is an exact essence and precludes all vagueness, even that which is appropriate to the morphological essence of light. But it has not been turned into a purely geometrical essence either, because it still is a ray of *light*. It contains within its concept that much of its origins, and so is differentiated from other exact essences like force, mass, velocity, lines, temperature, ideal gas, the sound wave, energy, and the frictionless machine. [22]

An exact essence is constructed as an ideal limit. In contrast, a morphological essence is not constructed or conceived as an ideal limit. It is a pure essence—it can be brought to eidetic intuition—but its vagueness, in whatever style is appropriate to the essence in question, is part of its a priori structure. Instances of morphological essences are given to direct, sensible perception, and although they are not ideally constructed, one can still speak of normal and abnormal cases of them. Examples are things like bench, house, horse, tree, dance, animal, and so on. [23]

21. *Opticks* (New York: Dover, 1952), p. 2.

22. See Talcott Parsons, *The Structure of Social Action* (New York: Free Press, 1968), I, 33. Parsons thinks it possible to conceive a "perfectly rational act." In a Husserlian perspective, this is counter-sensical; acts and their rationality are not subject to idealization. They have morphological essences. See *Ideas I*, §§ 73, 75. The structures of social life generally are morphological.

23. See *Ideas I*, § 73, pp. 206–7: "One condition for this is the exactness of the 'conceptual construction,' which is in no sense a matter of our arbitrary choice and of logical dexterity. . . . But to what extent 'exact' essences can be found in an essence-domain, and whether exact essences figure in the substructure of all essences apprehended in real intuition, and therefore also of all the components

Husserl observes that the essences he describes in his science of phenomenology are morphological, not exact, so further examples would be the essences of perception, expression, meaning, evidence, truth, sensation, and experience, all as they are revealed in phenomenological analysis.

Some morphological essences lend themselves to transmutation into exact essences, while others do not. There is no ideal toward which lamps or chairs can be made to converge, although there are morphological eide for them. And their inability to be made exact is not based on convention, but on the kind of things they are.

§ 28. INDIVIDUALS AND APODICTICITY

WE ACQUIRE empirical universals by working on perceived individuals. In free variation we also work with individuals—variants—but they are imaginatively contrived. We attempt to flush the eidos out of them. Neither procedure can work on the essence separately and by itself. Essence, whether empirical or pure, is registered as the invariant in many instances. It requires a two-dimensional consideration: of individuals as instances of an essence, or of an essence as the same in many individuals.

To stress this in the case of free variation, Husserl mentions that the variants we imagine must all be kept in mind when we move from one variant to the next. We do not just step from one to the other; if this were so we would reach only a sheer individual with each new variant. "We must keep conscious of the manifold as such, as a multiplicity, and never let it, as such, drop from the mind's grasp. Otherwise we do not acquire the eidos as an ideal identity, which it is only as the *hen epi pollōn*" (*PP*, § 9c, p. 78). The eidos is given in tandem with its possibly infinite class of instances.

Once some parts and limits of the eidos have been determined, two kinds of judgment are possible. We can speak about the eidos and its parts, as in the statement that the essence of material thing involves extension and causality, or we can talk about individuals in an essential way: this stone, or these

of the essence, these are matters that depend throughout on the peculiar nature of the domain." See also *Crisis*, § 9a–c, and pp. 376–77.

stones, or all stones, must be subject to causality and be extended (*Ideas I*, §§ 5–6). Such judgments about individuals are what Husserl calls apodictic judgments. They are not about the pure essence—that would be a definition or an axiom (*Ideas I*, § 16)—but about individuals as instances of an eidos. They state what could not be otherwise in certain individual objects; and these arrangements could not be otherwise because of the eidos the individuals exemplify.

Apodictic judgments are like compressed syllogisms which apply eidetic laws to individual instances. They incorporate both elements of free variation, the individual case and the eidos; they reflect the structure of imaginative variation, and are the institutionalized expression of what it achieves. Husserl often mentions that his own science of phenomenology works in the element of apodictic judgment.

§ 29. NEGATIVE NECESSITY

OUR ANALYSIS of eidetic intuition has stressed the recognition of invariant moments within individual variants. It has emphasized what we might call the positive aspect of free variation: the determination of which moments, a priori, make up the content of an essence. Most of Husserl's own approach to eidos is concerned with this positive effort.

There is another aspect to eidetic intuition which is only mentioned in passing in Husserl's texts, but is so important that without its presence eidetic intuition would not be what it is. This is the negative aspect of free variation: the insight that removal of certain moments in a variant, or the addition of certain moments to it, destroys the individual—either totally, as a being, or at least as an instance of the eidos we are trying to isolate.[24]

24. See Aron Gurwitsch, *The Field of Consciousness* (Pittsburgh, Pa.: Duquesne University Press, 1964), p. 192: "In the performance of the process of free variation, it appears that, as long as certain structures remain invariant, however thoroughgoing and deep-reaching the variation might otherwise be, the resulting products of our imagination are still conceivable as possible specimens of the class of the object chosen as the point of departure. When, however, these structures are altered, the process of free variation no longer yields possible specimens of this class. From the mere attempt and failure of this attempt to contrive in imagination an object of the considered class not exhibiting the structures under discussion, the

When we contrive variants, after all, we imagine new instances which are different from the paradigm and the other variants we have proposed, instances in which certain parts have been removed. In a material thing, we may imagine a case in which the red color is removed and replaced by green, or we may try to remove color entirely. As long as the removal leaves our imagined object intact as still a variant of our paradigm and still an instance of the eidos we are concerned with, we know we have not displaced anything essential. But if removal of a certain part destroys the imagined object as an instance of such a kind—or destroys it entirely as a being—we realize we have tried to separate something inseparable, a moment of the essence. If we try to imagine a material thing without causality or extension, we no longer have a material thing; these are parts of its pure essence. If we try to imagine a nontemporal melody the same would be true; temporality is of the essence of music. In contrast to our consciousness of being able to go on *ad libitum*, which is characteristic of successful free variation, we have here the insight that we cannot go on at all in this direction. We cannot contrive even one individual according to this recipe.

This is another reason why disclosure of an eidos must operate within imagination (the first reason being that a pure essence has to be freed of the factualness and contingency of perceptual experience). If our variation stayed within perception it would reach only an empirical generality and not eidetic necessity. In perception we could never try to present the test variations that turn out to be impossible and so mark the essential limits of the object; only imaginative consciousness has the freedom to try to trespass the boundaries of what the object is, in order to bring out the impossibility of violating them. In perception we would never know whether a certain arrangement of parts has never been encountered merely as a matter of fact, or as a matter of eidetic necessity; we have never in fact experienced color without extension, but how can we tell if it is necessarily so? Would it make sense to try to anticipate such an

---

impossibility of such an object to exist, whether at all or, at least, as an object of the class in question, becomes evident." The "negative necessity" in eidetic intuition is anticipated in *LI*, VI, §§ 31–33, where Husserl discusses the theme of "conflict" among certain contents of meaning, and the insight that certain contents cannot be combined into certain wholes. The logic of wholes and parts, as developed in Investigation III, is also an anticipation of eidetic intuition; see Gurwitsch, *The Field of Consciousness*, pp. 194–96.

experience? Only the freedom of imagination brings out the necessity—and correlatively the impossibility—of things.

Often a single crucial example, well placed, is enough to show that such-and-such a combination is eidetically impossible and that we cannot experience anything along the line prescribed by a certain combination of terms. This is where a fertile imagination helps in philosophical exposition. The charming examples we have enjoyed in the philosophical writing of the last few decades are more than decorations; their serious work is to reveal eidetic impossibilities or necessities, particularly in regard to speech acts.

§ 30. How Variants Are Contrived

IT MAY APPEAR that the role of imagination in free variation is passive, as though we simply let our power of association loose to fashion, by its own inertia, variants similar to our paradigm. Passive association is part of free variation, but there is also an active element. We do not daydream; we deliberately try to contrive imaginative variants, and in doing so we are led by recipes, by arrangements of moments which we first combine in thought. We organize a formula in thought or in words, then try to imagine a case according to such a pattern.

In this process imagination is put to the service of thinking. It tries to follow rules and patterns which thought sets up for it. The strange consciousness of "being unable to imagine" a certain case is the inability to let a rule formulated by thinking find instances in what we can picture in our mind's eye. But the rule to be tested comes before the picture is tried; we first set up the arrangement, "body with extension but without causality," before we appreciate the impossibility of being able to imagine it.

Does this not mean that the eidos or rule has to be achieved even before the variants are presented? This seems to be the opposite of the procedure Husserl describes, in which the eidos is read off as an invariant in many imagined instances.

It is true that a combination of moments, a formula, has to be achieved before the variants are contrived, but this combination is not yet registered as an eidos until we have run into the impossibility of separating the moments in this particular whole. It is this sense of negative necessity, of impossibility of separation, that solders the moments into an eidos and lets us claim we have reached an eidetic intuition. The sense of necessity and impossibility is reached when we realize that we cannot imagine an instance of the eidos in question if this or that moment is removed.

§ 31. Variants Are Indispensable in Registering an Eidos

WHY DO WE HAVE TO GO to imagination to get this sense of necessity and impossibility? Why can't we stay with the signitive arrangement of moments? Is it not sufficient to inspect the meanings of the terms involved to see the necessity of their combination or separation? In other words, why can't we register a pure essence by itself, entirely apart from its instances? There are two reasons.

1. We are able to express an essence, and the necessity that binds its parts together, only by playing it off against that which is not essential. The essential as such is not appreciated except in contrast to the nonessential.

Anatole Broyard, in remarks about Ezra Pound's comments on *The Waste Land,* makes the following assertion about Pound's tendency to eliminate unnecessary words: "While the poem does gain in intensity, it gains in obscurity as well. . . . Everything is essence, heard against what is not said, and must be surmised as well as the reader is able." [25]

When "everything is essence," even in the registration of eide, the force of a statement about essence is lost. It reaches such an intensity that its impact dissipates. Imaginative variants provide the needed context of the nonessential, for they include attributes beyond those that make up the essence. Free variation does not leave us to surmise about the nonessential, but concretely presents it in the imagined case.

Once an essence is established and settled, people who are familiar with it can talk about it in its purity and may find it easy to "hear it against what is not said," because they have no need to mention the contrasting context of nonessentials. But

25. "Tilling *The Waste Land*," *New York Times,* November 3, 1971, p. 45.

registration of an essence is its first emergence out of what is nonessential, so it is necessary to state what it is "heard against." The imagined variants achieve this.

If a pure essence is discussed by itself, someone who has not registered it through free variation may think, unless he is impressed by the authority of those who know, that the definition of the essence is arbitrary and nominal. If we just consider the terms alone, why should a material thing necessarily involve extension and causality, why should music involve time, and why should something past be incapable of being done over again? Couldn't we just define these things differently? But if we begin with instances of body, melody, and the passage of time, we can register the impossibility of these things being what they are unless such attributes belong to them.

2. Appealing to imaginative variants also locates properly where the determination of essences is to be made. An imaginative variant is given as an intuition of an object; in contrast to empty signitive intentions, both imagination and perception are intuitive. Since we have to turn our attention toward the variant, we are kept from trying to find essential connections by just examining the meanings in signitive intentions. We look to the things themselves, not to our words about them. We do not find essences by reflection on our meanings or concepts, but in the structure of the objects of conscious acts.

To discover an essence we must go out of the signitive meaning, toward what is meant by it. We do not determine an a priori inclusion, exclusion, or compatibility by a mere inspection of meanings or concepts or terms; we determine it by letting the combined meanings, concepts, and terms go to work in intuition. We let them loose to follow their teleology and see if they can find instances. We give a certain arrangement of moments a chance to work in intuition.

True, we always move back and forth between what the object is and the concepts and terms we use in thinking about it. The two domains are not separable. But they must be distinguished in principle, and we must be aware whether the force of what we say stems primarily from discovering what things are, or from signitive opinions about them.

§ 32. A NOTE ON IDEOGRAMS

HUSSERL'S DOCTRINE of free variation and eidos has interesting implications concerning the difference between ideographic and alphabetical languages.

In ideographic languages the ideogram presents a pictorial instance of what is being named. It presents, as it were, a variant of the eidos; perhaps it presents the paradigm case, of which all perceived or imagined cases are to be considered variants. In addition to the ideogram, such languages also have a spoken word which is the name of the type of thing instantiated in the picture; they combine a signitive intention with a pictorial representation in their writing. In alphabetical languages the written words stand for the spoken words, so we must turn from the language to imagination to find pictures or instances or variants. Both the spoken and written forms of the language are purely signitive; in ideographic languages, the spoken form is signitive but the written form is pictorially intuitive.

4 / Identity in Manifolds

τὸ δὲ ἓν ποιοῦν, τοῦτο ὁ νοῦς ἕκαστον.
—Aristotle, *De anima* 3.6. 430b6

BESIDES THE CONTRARIETIES of parts-wholes and presence-absence, another formal opposition that occurs throughout Husserl's thought is that of an identity within a manifold. This pattern makes use of the contrast between presences and absences, for it involves showing how a single object can remain itself, and continue to be perceived as itself, while its various dimensions and appearances come and go. It also uses the logic of parts and wholes, since the manifold of appearances and the identity within them are moments to each other.

§ 33. THE MATERIAL THING AS AN IDENTITY IN MANIFOLDS

IT IS A COMMONPLACE in phenomenology that a material thing is the identity within a continuous flow of profiles. But this mentions only one of the manifolds in which a thing appears. Many others must be listed if we are to be precise.

Part of the essential sense of a thing is its causal interconnection with other things and with its environment; a thing is

"what is identical in the bond of causal dependencies. It is something that can live only in the atmosphere of causal lawfulness"
(*Ideen III,* § 7, p. 30). The qualities and states of a thing
undergo changes in function of changes around it, and after due
attention we can predict which changes will follow which. A
thing is not just a synthesis of various characteristics, but is
ruled by certain causal laws that make predictions possible for
that particular kind of thing: "To be acquainted with a thing is
to know in advance how it is going to behave causally" (*PP,*
§ 13, p. 102).[1]

So one level of unity within a manifold is the thing as a subject of potentially infinite changes in function of what happens
around it; in a thing there is "no change without a cause, and no
change of state without identity of the thing" (*Ideen II,* § 16, p.
49). Even when something seems to change without an apparent
external cause, when a substance loses its elasticity or when
water evaporates, the change is due to commerce with the environment and could be expressed functionally if the appropriate
factors are determined.

If we abstract from the moment of causality we are left with
what Husserl calls a "phantom," something that fills space but is
impervious to causes and brings about no effects (*Ideen II,* § 10,
pp. 21–22; § 15b). Husserl claims there is a phantom level in the
object of each sense; let us consider the visual phantom.

One of the moments of the visual phantom is a "side," like
the front side of a book or the southern side of a building. A
phantom has, essentially, many sides, so it is a unity within
them. But each side is also a unity within many "aspects" or
views. If the front side of this book is rectangular, it still presents
many aspects that are of various shapes—trapezoidal from one
angle, square, rhomboid, or practically a line from others, distorted and irregular in certain mediums, like a point at a great
distance, and actually rectangular from one "normal" viewpoint
which presents it "optimally"—but all these are aspects of a
rectangular side (*PP,* § 28, pp. 157–59). We confuse an aspect
with a side if we say that a coin is not round because it looks like
an ellipse from some angles, or that a square tower is not square
because it looks round at a distance.

Between sides and phantom we have another moment which
Husserl calls an *Apparenz,* and which we can translate "apparition." A sequence of sides, and consequently a sequence of

---

1. See also *PP,* § 22; *Ideen II,* § 15e, p. 45; § 16, pp. 45–50.

aspects, that can actually be experienced is an apparition.[2] The apparition of the Empire State Building we are familiar with is the sequence of sides and aspects that one sees driving around Manhattan or walking up and down the avenues and streets. An apparition fewer of us have seen is that from a helicopter circling around the building. So in many aspects we have one side, in many sides and aspects one apparition, in many apparitions one phantom, and the phantom plus many possible and actual causal functions constitute the one material thing.

The Empire State Building exemplifies a visual phantom of intermediate size. Its apparitions are dependent on my immediate kinesthesia of walking or riding. A smaller object, like a lamp or a box, will present various apparitions to the kinesthesia of moving a part of my body, like my head or trunk, and may not require my going from one place to another; it will also present new aspects and sides in response to my turning it around, a process in which the kinesthesia of my arms, hands, and fingers is at work. At the other extreme there are enormous objects, like a huge mountain at a great distance, for which my own kinesthesia is helpless to bring about an apparition; no matter how I move my self, nothing changes. Husserl says that the very notion of aspect practically loses its sense in such cases. No visual differentiation of aspects enters into the experience of such durable things. In order to engender an apparition at all, to provoke any change in aspect and sides, I have to undertake a long journey; but a journey is brought together into a whole by thinking, not by sensible experiencing. There is no kinesthesia of the whole journey, only of its smaller parts. Through a journey, the distant object is not perceived to have aspects and sides, but is registered by thought as having them.[3]

The enormous object may be said to have aspects indirectly, for its smaller parts—the ridge of a mountain, a shallow part of the sea—may present apparitions to our kinesthesia. Beyond such objects are things like the sky, which has no spatial aspects at all in any sense (Ms D 13 I, 1921, pp. 33–34).

2. See Ms D 13 I, 1921, p. 3, and U. Claesges, *Edmund Husserls Theorie der Raumkonstitution* (The Hague: Nijhoff, 1964), § 11. A concise description of apparition, side, and aspect is found in Ms D 13 I, 1921, pp. 2–6.

3. See ZB, no. 1 of the supplementary texts, p. 142: "I cannot get an intuition of the road from Berlin to Rome, not even in the form of a process of intuition, *scil.* within one act; but I can do so for particular pieces of the road." This text dates from 1893.

The phantom itself is more than the apparitions that have actually taken place; it is the unity of all the possible apparitions, including those that will, as a matter of fact, never be enjoyed. The objectivity of the phantom, and hence of the thing as well, is more than what has been encountered; the thing we view could always have been viewed in an infinite number of other ways. The identity of the thing is, in addition, more than what has actually been manifested in causal actions and reactions: it is also the unity within an infinite number of causes and effects that are always possible.

In describing manifolds of appearance for the material thing, we have gotten as far as aspects; we can move still further down, for the aspect itself is a unity within many impressions it can make upon us. I can see a thing under one aspect now—the elliptical-looking coin—and experience the same aspect an hour later. The impressions are different, but the aspect is identical (*Ideen II*, § 32, p. 130). Furthermore, even during a single enjoyment of an aspect we can distinguish a manifold of impressions within the temporal continuity of the experience.[4]

§ 34. IMPRESSIONS AND PROFILES: *Abschattungen*

THE MOVE INTO IMPRESSIONS is a move into a new dimension. Although things, sides, and aspects are quite obviously perceived as objective, impressions are experienced as episodes in my sensibility. So besides being the manifold in which aspects and hence things are presented, they present my lived body as well. As episodes in my lived body they enjoy a lived spatiality—they are in my head and not in my stomach, in my hand and not in my ear—and help constitute a field for inner perception. The lived body is constituted as the domain where

4. Husserl also raises the intriguing problem of the identity of objects in fantasy. See Ms F 1 29, 1922–23, pp. 207–18, 320–23. In what sense do I imagine the "same" centaur again? How does his identity differ from that of perceived objects? What kind of changes can he undergo and still be the same individual? If I imagine two centaurs together, how is the identity of one differentiated from that of the other? What if I imagine one after the other? How are they different? In terms of more public images, there are two Katzenjammer Kids, and one never becomes the other; Uncle Sam never turns into Santa Claus except metaphorically. What sort of identity does each of these have?

such sensible episodes take place; it has an appropriate kind of localization and mobility, which is not simply continuous with the worldly place of the shapes and motions of things.

The field of inner spatiality and my own kinesthetic powers provide still another manifold within which a material thing can be constituted as identical. Besides changing in function of changes in its environment and in other things, the thing will appear differently in response to changes in my spatial condition; by turning my body or its parts, by moving from one place to another, or even by focusing my eyes, I bring about a new pattern of appearances in the object, a pattern correlated to the kinesthesia that accompanies my motions. Further, the thing appears as an identity not only in the motions and changes I have actually carried out, but also as potentially available for a whole field of possible motions that are never actuated; "If I were to move *there*," I can always say, "the object would still present some aspect or other to me." The manifold of possibilities is part of the presence of a thing.

Moving up another notch, we can abstract from the lived body presented in impressions and consider impressions as events in my sheer stream of consciousness. From the *res materialis* and *res extensa* we move to the *res temporalis* (*Ideas I*, § 149, p. 415).[5] In their temporal aspect, impressions involve no spatiality at all. However, they in turn also appear through a new kind of manifold, a manifold of temporal phases, which leads us to the problem of inner time-consciousness. Impressions do not need another layer of impressions to be presented to consciousness, but they do need the manifold of temporal phases.

The manifold of temporal phases, which keeps getting engendered in the living present and also keeps being gathered into the living present, is the last stop in this hierarchy of manifolds (*APS*, § 27, p. 125). The way it works demands special examination; its way of generating manifolds and identities is the condition for all the other manifolds we have run through, and it is not itself conditioned by any of them.

We have looked only at one part of the work impressions do. We have spoken of them as episodes in sensibility, and as constitutive for the body image and the stream of consciousness. This is the subjective part of their work. But impressions also serve to present the material thing; the "sensed redness" as a

5. See Claesges, *Raumkonstitution*, p. 42.

sensible condition is also a presentation of the redness of a thing. An impression is also a "profile" of an object being perceived. The manifold of impressions is equivalent to a manifold of profiles.

This is the difficult problem of *Abschattungen*.[6] What we have expressed in two distinct terms, "impressions" and "profiles," Husserl expresses under the single term *Abschattungen*. *Abschattungen* are ambiguous, functioning both as impressional episodes in sensibility and as sensible presences of objects. The English terms "profiles" and "shadings" are usually used to express them in their work of presenting objects. A study of these English words may help us to understand the roles of *Abschattungen*.

"Shading" deals with colors. If a color is identified as precisely as possible—not generically, like blue, but specifically and with no further precision possible, like a definite shade of sky blue, blood red, or beige—the same color can undergo a variety of shadings and still remain itself; beige in sunlight, beige in fluorescent light, beige in dusk, beige when I am wide awake, or sleepy, or have just gotten up, or am dizzy, or have jaundice. Beige makes different "impressions" on me in different mediums and when I am in different psychic states. It goes through different shadings.

"Profile" (or "silhouette") deals with shapes and sides, and is hard to distinguish, in its customary use, from what we have defined as aspects. But in our prescriptive usage we take it to mean the many "sketches" of a single aspect we can enjoy, at different times, in different mediums, and in different psychic states.

The German word *abschatten* means, after all, to sketch or to outline something; it includes the sense of the draftsman's activity. An *Abschattung* is the sketching of an aspect or quality of an object. It includes, in its ambiguity, both the process of sketching and the silhouette sketched. It is both an episode in sensibility and an immediate sensible presence.

We have used the term "impression" to express the sensible, episodic role of *Abschattungen*, and we have contrasted impression to "profile," which expresses the presentational role. We might have used "impression" alone as the translation, for it does have some of the ambiguity of the German word. Besides naming

6. *Ideas I*, § 41; *PP*, § 29, p. 163; E. Tugendhat, *Der Wahrheitsbegriff bei Husserl und Heidegger* (Berlin: de Gruyter, 1967), pp. 71–80.

the sensation, it could also refer to the kind of appearance or presence the sensible object makes: the impression it makes in this light, the impression it makes when you are ill, the impression it makes after you have been looking at it for a while. Still, it is helpful to use "profiles," "shadings," and "silhouettes" to bring out the full sense of the German word, and to comply with customary translations. But we must not think that the profiles, shadings, or silhouettes are something distinct inside the impressions or sensations; they are the impressions or sensations taken in their presentational role.

The ambiguity of impressions/shadings, the fact that they are presences of things and also states of sensibility, was recognized in antiquity. According to Aristotle, when we perceive red things we are said to be in a reddish condition ourselves, our eyes suffused with the form of redness: "That which sees has become colored, in a way; for each sense organ is receptive of the sensible without the matter" (*De anima* 3. 2. 425b22–24). This makes it possible for us to be aware of our sensations, as well as of what we perceive. We can be aware of a sense only when it is working, and it is put to work only by its own proper object; a sense cannot ignite itself (2. 5. 417a6–9). The scholastic *species sensibilis impressa* is also an actualized condition of sensibility, achieved only when the presence of the proper object of the sense is brought about: *sensibile in actu est sensus in actu.*

To be aware of sensations is analogous to focusing on working judgments. We focus on judgments by virtue of the marginal awareness we have of them when we register or report facts; we reflect on impressions by virtue of the marginal awareness we have of them, as activations of sensibility, while we enjoy the profiling presence of things.

To return to our hierarchy of manifolds, we now have a single aspect as an identity within a manifold of impressions/shadings. Variations in the impressions/shadings occur because of changes in time, changes in the disposition of the medium through which we perceive, and changes in our own psychic state. In contrast to apparitions, sides, and aspects, which are all "objective," the impressions/shadings are "subjective" and depend on factors not attributable to the thing itself, but to the medium or to the sensibility of the perceiver.

Impressions/shadings, being episodes within sensibility, are themselves unities within the manifold of inner temporal phases.

On every step of the way, from the fully objective thing to the phases of inner time, the formal structure of an identity within a manifold is at work.[7]

§ 35. QUALITIES OF THINGS

A SOUND IS A UNITY in manifold; when I hear a particular sound, such as a single piano note, I experience it as sounding thus and so from my place. If I move right or left, nearer or farther, it presents a different appearance. My perception of the sounding note brings with it the awareness of the possibility of all other appearances or profiles it would have if I were elsewhere. The note as an identity is the objectivity that could sound these unlimited different ways. I may in fact activate an apparition from this infinite matrix—I may walk around while the note is sounding and hear a sequence of profiles—but I could never exhaust all the possible appearances. This procedure, of course, involves the sound as a spatial phenomenon; if I abstract from this objective spatiality and also from my bodily space— the sound is in my ears and head, and not in my arm or stomach—I still have the sound as a temporal object within my pure consciousness, within a temporal manifold, and I can attempt to determine, as Husserl does in his lectures on inner time and as Strawson does in *Individuals*,[8] what constitutes its objectivity as a lived sound. On all levels, once again, the sound is the identity within appropriate differences.

Other secondary qualities are unities within multiplicity. The gray of this desk looks different in different illuminations and from different angles, but it is throughout the same shade of gray.[9] The taste of oranges may differ as a function of the climate, or my bodily state, or what I eat with the orange, but the taste of oranges is precisely that unity that manifests itself in these different appearances. The fact that in one of these situations it may have the same "taste-shading" as a lemon does not mean that it turns into a lemon taste, because the orange taste and the lemon taste are unities within two potentially infinite

7. See ZB, no. 39, p. 284; *Ideen II*, § 32, p. 130, ll. 9–16; *CM*, §§ 17–18.
8. P. Strawson, *Individuals* (London: Methuen, 1959), pp. 59–86.
9. *PP*, § 28, p. 158; *Ideen II*, § 15c, p. 42; *Ideas I*, § 41, pp. 130–31; § 97, p. 283.

series of appearances, and are never identified with any one of their profiles. In a certain light, gray and blue may look the same, but they are not the same because they are not identified exhaustively with this view.

In touch, a surface may appear in different tactile profiles to different parts of the body, or to the same part in different conditions: sandpaper may feel different to my fingers and to my shoulder, and to my fingers depending on whether they are calloused or not. Touch has a distinctive role in the constitution of the lived body, and in mediation of this body with the objective world. For one part of the body can touch other parts, and in this process the relationship of touched and touching is reciprocal; I can say my hand is touching my knee, or my knee touches my hand. No other sense has the capacity to perceive itself this way in its act of perception. The sense of touch is also more basic than any other in constituting other persons. Touch arranges the spatiality of my own body and lets me recognize it as my own, since what I touch here or there can become my own touching agency. If I touch a foreign body, I can never make it my own tactile agent. The tactile sense constitutes my bodily field, within which I can locate all my other sensations.

The process of touching, furthermore, is a spatial motion, as one part of the body moves to another, and thus kinesthesia and touch are essentially related. Both the touching and the touched parts of one's own body have a sense of being located somewhere, so when I experience the "here" of my touching hand, I also sense the "there" of my touched knee; and the "there" of the touched part can be taken as the "here" of a touching agency when the roles are reversed. What I touch in my own body is not only able to become a touching agent: it can also be put into motion when I wish; I am able to experience, from both the inside and the outside, my body as an object that can set itself into motion. The spatial body image constituted by touch, the field within which sensations occur, is the same lived body that is able to move its parts and go from one place to another.[10] Its motions allow manifolds of other sensible impressions and profiles, like those of vision, hearing, and smell, to come to pass. The body over which I hold sway is the same one that enters into

10. See *Ideen II*, § 18a; *Crisis*, § 60; *APS*, § 3, pp. 13–15. Claesges develops the role of touch in *Raumkonstitution*, §§ 19, 22–23.

perceptual and causal contacts with other bodies in the world.[11]

It is clear that even the lived body is an identity within complex manifolds, tactile and kinesthetic, actualized and potential; it is the field where sensations, moods and feelings take place.

§ 36. A REMARK ON PHANTOMS

THE PHANTOM is what is left of a material thing when its capacity to exercise or suffer causality is left out of consideration. Husserl mentions the sights we see in a stereoscope as an example of phantoms which we actually experience: we can describe the spatial and surface characteristics of the figures we see, but it makes no sense to talk about their weight, elasticity, or magnetism, which would demand interaction with other bodies. Other examples Husserl mentions are the rainbow, the blue sky, and the sun (*Ideen II*, § 15b, pp. 36–37). (Here the sun is considered the way all celestial bodies were conceived by Aristotle: in our direct experience of them, they appear impervious to causal interactions with the world in which we live.) Phantoms have lost materiality, but they retain spatiality and the capacity to change in space, both by changing shape and by moving from one place to another.[12]

Although objects like rainbows and the blue sky are concreta, most phantoms are conceived abstractly. Husserl claims that there is a phantom moment in the objects of each sense. We

11. See *Ideen II*, § 36; *Ideen III*, §§ 2–3; *Crisis*, §§ 47, 62; *PP*, § 15, p. 107. In constituting the lived body, consciousness makes room for itself as it brings itself about. The lived body is where sensibility is localized. Some kinds of sensibility are a base for intentional acts, but the intentional acts as such are not localized in the body and do not build up a new level of the lived body. See *Ideen II*, § 39. The lived body reacts to psychophysical causation from the "world" outside it, but episodes in its psyche are not capable of changing things in the world. Nothing reacts to them; they are purely "epiphenomenal." See *Ideen III*, § 3, pp. 17–19; *Ideen II*, §§ 40, 41; *Crisis*, § 62.

12. In the introduction to Ms D 13 XVIII, pre-1916, Husserl mentions some reservations about the sun as an example of a phantom, because it does work changes in the world: it makes things warm, for instance. But other heavenly bodies, like the stars or planets, appear without perceptible causal effects.

have talked mostly about the visual phantom, but there are tactile, auditory, gustative, and olfactory phantoms too.[13] In each the object of the sense is taken as a spatial phenomenon without causal connections. The phantom tone is a space-filling sound, but not the sound made by a violin or a barking dog; nor is it the sound that can break glass; nor, presumably, is it the sound that will hurt my ear when it gets shrill enough. The case of a perception which becomes a pain or a sheer state of sensibility—the loud noise that hurts my head, the bright color that pains or dazzles my eyes—is an interesting limit case; it marks the point at which the impression is no longer a presentation, but only an effect. The pain is not one of the profiles of the object or its qualities. If someone blows a high-pitched whistle which hurts my ears, the pain is an indication sign that the whistle is being blown, not one of the ways of hearing it.

The apparitions and phantoms given to each sense are correlated to that sense's kinesthesia. Each sense organ is also a movable part of the body, and must be moved about in order to engender apparitions; through its motions, sequences of profiles and aspects come to pass, and we experience the profiles as correlated to the kinesthesia that is our way of undergoing that motion. It is sometimes possible to suffer the kinesthesia while the organ moves, but undergo no experience of profiles; the receptor is shut off, either because we want it so or because there is nothing to encounter. This constitutes the "empty space" appropriate to that sense organ (Ms D 13 I, 1921, p. 12).

Kinesthesia is the "noetic" side correlated to the "noematic" manifold in apparitions. Both operate on the level of sensibility; they are the hyletic substrate underlying the constitution of objects as known by full-fledged acts of consciousness. In phenomenological analysis, the description of apparitions and profiles as noemata must be supplemented by a description of the kinesthesia and sensibility that are their noetic counterparts.

Kinesthesia is immediately subject to our wills.[14] It is a capacity we can actualize without intermediaries and without

13. See *Ideen II*, § 15b, p. 38, where Husserl explicitly says there is even a tactile phantom. It is difficult to isolate the phantom for the sense of touch, even in thought, because the experience of being touched is practically equivalent to undergoing causal effects. The sense of touch, as the ancients said, is the most material of all the senses.

14. Ms D 10 I, 1932, p. 25; *Ideen II*, § 38; §60, pp. 259–60; and § 62, p. 284.

internal conditions, except those of inner time-consciousness, which is the condition for everything. Even our capacity to perceive is not as basic as kinesthesia, for it depends on the latter for its own possibility.

§ 37. THE MANIFOLD OF MEMORY

A TEMPORAL OBJECT becomes objective because it appears under many different temporal perspectives, or at least because the possibility of its so appearing is recognized. One manifold of perspectives in the domain of time is provided by memory, which follows on an original, intuitive appearance that has once taken place. An object or event is once intuited and repeatedly remembered; it is the unity in this kind of manifold. Each remembering provides a new perspective on the remembered because the identity is brought back at a new moment in my conscious life, retrieved each time from a more distant past (*APS*, §§ 24–25).

Before I can remember an object or event, it must have left the scope of my present awareness. The interstices of temporal absence, forgetfulness, divide each of the units of this manifold from the others. The object or event must be out of mind between intuition and the first remembering, and between each remembering and its successor. This implies that something we are intuiting for the first time is not yet temporally objective; there is no distance between ourselves and what we are aware of in this immediate presence because what we enjoy has not yet presented itself in a manifold of remembered profiles. We are captivated by things in the immediate present; we recognize their otherness and objectivity in memory.[15] Memory drives a wedge between ourselves and what we experience by allowing us to have it once again, but under a different guise. Memory allows a greater transcendence than does immediate perception.

The structure of immediate presence, which is not yet interrupted by forgetfulness, will call for an analysis of its own manifold, that of temporal phases. The manifold within the living present is such as to make the manifold in remembering possible. The first sense of pastness and futurity is within the

15. *APS*, § 45, p. 204; also the supplementary text, "Bewusstsein und Sinn—Sinn und Noema," § 15, pp. 326–27. This text is very good on temporality.

lived present, but a fuller and more objective sense arises with remembering, in which something that is totally gone from the present is brought back again.

I can always go back to a thing I have once seen and see it again. My spatial absence can be overcome by spatial changes. But I can never go back to what I remember except in memory, because I remember the object in its occurrence at a certain time. I remember an object-event. If I go back spatially to something I have perceived before, I have the same thing again but I have a thing-event which is only "totally similar" to the one I had before, not identically the same (APS, § 30). Memory has a right of its own which can be corrected only by better memory, just as perception is corrected only by perception.

Remnants of an event or written records can allow signitive intendings of what is remembered, but they are not substitutes for memory. They can establish or modify public facts, but as regards remembering they can at best only make one try to perform it better and overcome the kinds of errors and illusions proper to memory (APS, § 25, pt. 2). Memory alone provides elements in the manifold we are concerned with here. Thus it is true that when all the witnesses of an event are no longer alive, the event passes out of existence a second time, like a sound that ceases to reverberate, for their memories kept it present as a temporal occurrence. Commemorative paintings and statues are an attempt to bring about a kind of public memory, but they cannot replace veterans, survivors, people who saw it happen. Images support a pictorial intention of the events, but memory keeps the actual perception alive.

§ 38. CATEGORIAL OBJECTS AND CULTURAL OBJECTS

WE HAVE SEEN that a fact is the identity within the manifold of many possible states, as registered, as reported, or as supposed; and as meant in a languid intention, as nominalized, or as intended through figural moments.

A judgment, one of the possible states of a fact, is in turn an identity within a constellation of manifolds of its own (see below, § 74). It is the unity of meaning that is variously expressed in paraphrase, repetition, and translation; it tolerates differences in expression. It can remain the same while vaguely executed, along a continuum of degrees of vagueness, and while explicitly

framed. It is the same when framed in one instance and only
named in another. It also withstands changes from explicit use
to indirect discourse, and retains its identity when framed or
mentioned by different speakers. This is a manifold not available
to all contents of consciousness; I cannot have someone else's
pain or feelings in a kind of "indirect sensibility." A judgment
may not actualize all these potentials—I may frame some that
never get repeated or quoted—but as judgments the potential
manifold is part of what they are.

A sentence, a particular expression of judgment, is itself an
identity within a manifold because it is the same in many utterances, actual and potential, and can be transferred to many
speakers.[16] It can also be used and mentioned. It has an appropriate sort of vagueness, different from that of judgment,
and remains the same in its vague and its distinct states. But it
loses its identity in paraphrase and translation. It does not enjoy
the same manifolds of appearance that the judgment does.

Husserl does not talk specifically about poems, but it is clear
that the identity of a poem is not the same as that of a judgment.
In a poem the sensuous color of the words, the rhythms of the
original language, and the harmonics of meaning associated
with each term are all at work in the presence of the aesthetic
object. The poem thrives on repetition, but cannot withstand
paraphrase and barely survives translation, where it is a ghost of
its former self. Its meaning and expression are fused, so the
manifold of paraphrase is not available as a series of profiles
through which it can present itself. A paraphrase is an explanation of the poem, not a new presentation of it. New and different
presentations would be original readings that stress certain
rhythms or patterns not previously noticed. They allow the poem
to be itself again in a new way, a new member of the manifold
of its appearances.

Every "cultural object" which requires a performance to be
actualized—a musical composition, a play, dance, or poem—appears through a manifold of interpretations. All of them present
the object itself, and the object is the identity within the interpretations. A Chopin nocturne is the same even though Moravec
and Rubinstein play it differently. Some interpretations may
conflict with others, but this is tolerable because they are

16. So is a word: "The word *Löwe* occurs only once in the German language; it is identical throughout its innumerable utterances
by any given persons" ("The Origin of Geometry," in *Crisis*, p. 357).

profiles and not the thing itself (*PP*, § 16, pp. 116–17). Even interpretations that distort can provide another appearance of the object, for they show how it appears when it is not properly served; we expect good wine to taste bad with the wrong food, when we are ill, or if we are not good judges of wine, and we expect a good piece of music to go bad in the wrong hands, in an unfavorable medium, or before an unsuitable receptor. If a performance is bad enough, it may become like a perception which turns into a pain, and no longer be an appearance of what it was supposed to present.

Essences are categorial objects and identities within manifolds. An empirical essence is an identity within a manifold of actual experiences, while an eidos is a unity within free imaginative variation.

A number is a unity that can appear under many guises. Every time I count five things, the number five is present intuitively as a form realized in different kinds of matter. When I take to determining the number five through arithmetical operations, I can define it in reference to an infinity of other numbers. The number five is never just one of these defined mathematical objects; it is the same one that is defined in all these ways. The five reached by adding four and one is the same as that produced by seven minus two. When I find an entirely new way of defining cardinal numbers, for example, by set theory, I have new presentations of the same old five.[17]

§ 39. THE LIFE-WORLD AND THE EGO

EVEN THE *Lebenswelt* is a unity in multiplicity, for it is experienced differently in different cultures. The life-world Husserl hopes to isolate philosophically is the network of a priori structures common to all concrete life-worlds. It is never ex-

17. *LI*, VI, § 16, p. 720. See "The Origin of Geometry," in *Crisis*, p. 357: "The Pythagorean theorem, [indeed] all of geometry, exists only once, no matter how often or even in what language it may be expressed. It is identically the same in the 'original language' of Euclid and in all 'translations'; and within each language it is again the same, no matter how many times it has been sensibly uttered, from the original expression and writing-down to the innumerable oral utterances or written and other documentations."

perienced purely by itself, because it is an abstractum; it is what it is only as capable of taking on many appearances.[18]

Finally, the ego is an identity within several manifolds, those of immediate self-awareness, explicit reflection, repeated reflections, iterated reflections, memory, reflections in memory and on memory, fantasy, reflections in and on fantasy, philosophical reflection, spatial localization, kinesthetic and attentive capacities, and the like. In all these manifolds we find, and we continually expect to find, the same self in different appearances; we know we will never run into somebody else at one of the stages or at some later time.[19] The ego is never presented by itself alone, any more than a judgment can be presented without some expression, or a dance without a performance. The only way of identifying the ego philosophically is to describe the manifolds that are appropriate to it, and in which it appears as an identity.[20]

§ 40.   ABNORMAL MANIFOLDS

VARIOUS LEVELS of profile manifolds must be distinguished in the object when it appears normally; other manifolds, or other possibilities in the same manifolds, may be appropriate to the object in response to abnormal situations. There may be interference from things that affect the object we are concerned with, there may be modifications of the environment or the medium through which the object appears, there may be disturbances in the psychic state of the perceiver (his moods, his alertness), in his psychosomatic state (his health, the condition of his senses, his age), and finally in his history (whether the object is new or familiar to him).[21] It is part of the sense of a

18. *Crisis*, §§ 36, 38; see also app. XXV, p. 498, ll. 34–47 in the *Husserliana* edition, not translated by Carr.

19. *Crisis*, § 50, ⁋ 2; *Ideen II*, §§ 22–29; *CM*, §§ 31–32.

20. See *EP II*, § 40, pp. 90–91; § 41, pp. 93–94; also app. XXVIII, p. 472: "I am objective—identical in manifold self-experiences; but this manifold itself belongs to my present and past life, to me myself. I am—and in my being I have self-experience—as pulse of my being. I am and I was—and am identical in the unity of my time, but that is: correlate of possible syntheses that take place in me myself."

21. *Ideen II*, § 18b. Although the normal and abnormal are generally constituted intersubjectively, there is a sense in which the

piece of music that it is disturbed by noise, and that it may not hold together if we are distracted by worry or especially tired; it is part of the sense of a mannequin that it can appear human in certain kinds of light, or if we are surprised by it. These manifolds are possible appearances of the object, but under abnormal circumstances, which must be mentioned to account for the distortion.

§ 41. TRANSCENDENCE OF IDENTITIES IN MANIFOLDS

THERE IS TRANSCENDENCE in the difference between an identity and the profiles in which it is presented. The transcendence of a given object means that the object itself is more than this presentation of it, and that it can be itself again in another appearance. When we intuit a transcendent object in one of its profiles, we are aware that it is not exhausted by this appearance; in sensing this distinction, we are aware of the object's transcendence (PP, § 34, pp. 175–80).

The object is also transcendent to the whole manifold of profiles; it is not just their sum. It is the identity within the manifold.

If an object were to be exhaustively presented in one appearance, it would not transcend that appearance and the appearance would not be a profile, i.e., it would not be only one member of a possible manifold. Husserl claims that this condition occurs in the immediate awareness we have of our own sensa and acts while they are going on. There is no "other view" of them while they occur, nothing besides what we actually undergo. Hence they are not transcendent or objective yet, although they become so when we remember experiencing them. While they occur there are no absent parts at any moment; there are only the parts present to our awareness.

Although the identity transcends each profile and even the entire manifold of possible profiles, it is not separable from them; it is a moment founded on them. There is no identity without synthesis. To separate the identity would be to demand

---

concepts can be applied to strictly private experience; the "abnormal" perception of one sense, for instance, can be corrected by the other senses, or perhaps by thought. So even on this private level, the distinction between appearance and reality can be appreciated. See *Ideen II*, § 18c; and § 18e, p. 78.

an appearance of it independent of its possible appearances, which is nonsensical. On the other hand, one cannot complain that the manifold "hides" the identity; and one cannot demand that the identity appear as one of the parts of the manifold. To ask that the object appear as one of its profiles is also to speak nonsensically (*PP*, § 28, p. 160, ll. 20–23).

The point of a phenomenological description is to show what kind of manifold is involved in bringing about the concrete and intuitive presence of the object we are concerned with, which is the identity within this manifold. There is no way of explaining why the object appears in such-and-such a manifold; the object simply is like that, and no more can be said. The submission of phenomenology to the way things are means that as philosophy it is content to describe these unities and manifolds without trying to explain why they are like this. Husserl would take any such attempt at explanation to be a metaphysical construction.

As regards unities in manifolds, the major philosophical mistake is to confuse members of one manifold with those of another, or to confuse the manifold of one identity with that of another. These errors are forms of misplaced concreteness. The moments appropriate to an object's appearance are not faithfully and completely given. The manifold appropriate to a psyche may be confused with that appropriate to a thing, appearances of propositions confused with those of sentences, aspects confused with sides, manifolds of abnormality may be equated with those of normal appearance, memorial appearances confused with inner perception, temporal profiles confused with imaginative ones, the moments of an aesthetic object may be exchanged with those of a rhetorical one, and so on. There is no way to correct such mistakes except by descriptions that distinguish the confused manifolds and perhaps show what associations led to the errors. Hence Husserl's philosophical descriptions are often done in opposition to descriptions given by other thinkers.

Only when we have made the turn into the phenomenological attitude do we become concerned with objects as identities in a manifold of profiles; only then do the profiles become thematic. Such concern with appearances defines the phenomenological attitude. In the natural attitude we are absorbed in the object, and its appearances and identity are lived through but not noticed. The identity itself is not recognized as an identity until the turn is made. In the natural attitude we take it for granted that we are dealing with an identical object, but we do not appreciate the differences within which this identity is preserved, nor therefore do we appreciate the identity as such. Husserl says, "In this straightforward focus I know nothing at all about this manifold. Only through a reflection do I gain the manifold in the new direction of my gaze. I also grasp with it the unity that goes through the continuity of this manifold" (*PP*, § 28, p. 152; see also pp. 153–56). In the natural attitude, consciousness "lives in 'infatuation,' so to speak, with the poles of unity" (*Crisis*, § 52, p. 176). When we enter the phenomenological focus, a multiplicity that was experienced but not thematized comes into view, and the difference between the manifold and the object appears. We become concerned not with the object, but with the object in its ways of being given. And we appreciate and understand the transcendence of the object to its appearances.

The manifold in which an identity appears is never limited to a sequence of appearances that has in fact taken place, nor to any finite series. In principle the manifold can be extended to infinity; the thing can always be seen in new profiles, the proposition can always be repeated or paraphrased one more time, the event can always be remembered again, the life-world can always be lived in a new way by a new culture. This unlimited potential of the manifold, within the limits set by the object's eidos, is part of the way the identity appears.[22] Moreover, the infinity does not extend only into the future; the identity is always presented as that which could have appeared in an infinity of other ways in the past and present. Its actual train of appearances is only one among the infinitely many it could have realized. When we are given an object in its actual appearance, the field of coexistent potentialities is also given as a marginally intended background against which the actual series comes to be. I could be seeing the thing from that side instead of this, I could be hearing the sound from elsewhere, I could be saying this same proposition another way. True, the potential is grasped only as peripheral to the actual,

22. *Crisis*, § 48, pp. 166–67: "No matter where we turn, every entity that is valid for me and every conceivable subject as existing in actuality is thus correlatively—and with essential necessity—an index of its systematic multiplicities. Each one indicates an ideal general set of actual and possible experiential manners of givenness, each of which is an appearance of this one entity. . . . The total multiplicity of manners of givenness, however, is a horizon of possibly realizable processes, as opposed to the actual process." See also § 46, p. 159; and *FTL*, § 104, p. 274: "Something Objective is nothing other than the synthetic unity of actual and potential intentionality."

but it does comprise a necessary moment in the appearance of the thing, for the actual itself is founded on the potential. The actual appearances are what they are only as presences that might not have been, with another train of appearances taking their place and the identical object still being presented. The actualities of appearance are nested in an infinite field of potential alternatives.

While we experience a particular kind of object, there is a prejudgmental anticipation of what would happen if we were to do something or other in regard to it. If we move there, then such-and-such a series of appearances should come about; if we do this or that, certain reactions should occur (*Ideen II*, § 18a, pp. 57–58). This sense of "if-then," concerning both the appearances of the thing and its causal interactions, is a prejudgmental experience of the hypothetical. And if we do actualize one of the sensible possibilities, the infinite range of other possibilities becomes the set of those that might have been realized, but are not. They enter into a prejudgmental "contrary-to-fact" status, and can be categorially articulated in contrary-to-fact conditional judgments.

The field of possibilities is an essential moment in the experience of identities in a manifold and has to be grasped phenomenologically for what it is, without being reduced to a pseudo actuality. The reality of the possible as such is acknowledged, with philosophical concepts appropriate to it, in Husserl's phenomenology as it is in Aristotle's metaphysics.

Husserl's process of free variation is an attempt to master this infinite potential. The free play of imagination can never run through all the possible variations in the appearance of the object—it can never ring all the changes—but it does produce the insight that we could go on infinitely in a certain direction without violating the integrity of the object. "To every variation-manifold there belongs, essentially, the remarkable and especially important consciousness of 'and so forth as you wish'" (*PP*, § 9c, p. 77; see also §§ 9a, 9d). This consciousness of being able to go on, even without actually going on, is an insight into the infinite potential; it is the consciousness correlative to an infinite field of possibilities. The noetic correlate to a thing as a rule for appearances is the consciousness of an ability, the awareness that "I can" recognize the thing as an identity in these infinite manifolds.

As Husserl says in the Introduction to *Ideas I*, the move into phenomenology requires a double reduction, the phenomenological and the eidetic (pp. 44–45; see also § 60). The first makes us turn from objects to objects as identities in manifolds of appearance; the second gives us rules to govern the infinities in the manifolds.

§ 42. BREAKING UP CONTINUOUS MANIFOLDS

IN SOME MANIFOLDS it is easy to distinguish one member of the manifold from another: one utterance of a sentence is neatly marked off from another, one remembering is distinct from another, one performance of a play does not blend with another. In such cases it is easy to count the number of actual elements in the manifold, and although one could not come to an end in enumerating all its possible members, one can foresee that each is numbered as different from the others.

Other manifolds, particularly those involved in sensibility, are continua; how can one member be distinguished from another in such cases? How is one aspect to be marked off from another, how are profiles to be enumerated? How many profiles are there in a single apparition? On the level of time-consciousness, how many phases are there in a single act or sensation? To ask these questions is like asking how many points there are in a line, and how one point is demarcated from the next.

Continuous manifolds are engendered in a prelogical state of consciousness. They come about in sensibility and constitute the identities that sensibility enjoys. The problem of differentiating one member of the manifold from another arises because, in phenomenological reflection (which is the only kind of reflection that discloses these manifolds for what they are), we bring the distinguishing power of thought to bear on this domain of sensible continua and try to mark off parts within it; and "trying to rationalize the prerational is poor fishing." [23]

Thinking is the power of distinctly recognizing otherness and sameness. It takes objects apart, in the various ways there can be parts, and states that one is not the other. Sensibility is not decisive, as thinking is. It feels otherness and sameness, and it senses the differences of parts, but it does not mark them off. The parts flow into one another in sensibility (Ms D 13 XVIII, pre-

23. E. Pound, *Guide to Kulchur* (New York: New Directions, 1970), p. 45.

1916, pp. 6–7). Without this sensing of parts there would be no thinking; but without thinking we would not appreciate that we are sensing parts. Thus it is legitimate to say, phenomenologically, that there is a multitude of profiles or aspects or sides, without being able to say how many individuals there are in the multitude, and without being able to answer where one comes to an end and the next one begins.

One way of identifying a member of a continuous manifold is by appealing to the next manifold, within which that member is itself constituted as an identity. There is an infinity of sides to a phantom, and they blend continuously into one another, but a single side can be identified as the one that is the same in many aspects. The continuum of sides is an infinity, but each side is itself constituted by another infinity, that of its aspects. The continuum of sides is therefore an infinity of infinities.

This can be repeated on several levels. Each aspect is an identity within a continuous infinity of impressions, and each impression is a continuous infinity of temporal segments; each temporal segment in turn is a continuous infinity of temporal parts, all collected into the living and present segment. Husserl often mentions these last two levels, and says that the temporal flow of consciousness is a continuum of continua (see below, § 62). Perhaps the many levels on which continuous manifolds can be distinguished themselves form a continuum.

A material object, which is a discrete identity, is constituted by overlaid continua or subordinated infinities. The natural perceptual consciousness is not aware of these multitudes, which it engenders in the perception of a thing; its interest is in the thing and it overlooks the constituting manifolds. They can be systematically unraveled only in a phenomenological focus, when our concern turns from the object to the ways in which the object is presented. The "ways" are the multitudes of appearance, stretching from temporal phases to the many facts that can be registered in the object. These multitudes are not subjective forms imposed on a distinction-free thing; they are what the object engenders when it is at work being intellected and perceived (Ms F I 13 IV, 1907, pp. 231–36). And it is this work of the object—being intellected and perceived—which phenomenology intends to register. Phenomenology wishes to describe what is engendered when thing and mind come together; it gives names to the appearances born in their intercourse. But to be complete and fully consistent, phenomenology has to account for the appearances engendered between itself and what it is registering; this is why Husserl feels obliged to work out a phenomenology of phenomenology, and a theory of reduction.

Although an appeal to the infinity next in line can help us identify a member of a continuous manifold, it does not turn that member into a discrete individual. It does not fragment the manifold of which the member is a part. It does not mean that, after all, we really experience discrete atoms in sensibility. For the member so identified is presented as an identity only to the phenomenologically focused mind, not to the sensibility that originally enjoyed it. The identity given in the original sensibility is the material thing, or whatever concrete unity we have been experiencing, and not the members of its manifolds.

To identify and isolate a member of a manifold by appealing to the manifold next in line—to isolate a side by appealing to aspects—is to think abstractly. Such a member of a manifold is a moment, and needs its companion members to be concretely experienced; but like all moments it can be isolated in thought and in speech. The concretum in ordinary perceptual experience is the material thing. When we isolate a member of one of its manifolds of appearance, we isolate something that cannot be experienced as a concretum. We make the pyramid of appearance manifolds come to a point in an artificial place; in itself, the pyramid of manifolds comes to its point in the thing. Any phenomenological analysis of such members of manifolds remains abstract and incomplete—and liable to the fallacy of misplaced concreteness—until the ultimate in the analysis is made to coincide with what is ultimate in itself. The concrete object is the knot that ties all the manifolds together.

The standard example for perception and sensibility in Husserl is the material thing, but there are other concrete objects perceived and sensed: an aesthetic object, a tool, a machine, a person, a speech, an animal, and an institution are all rules for special experience, being instances of regional concepts. In each of these there are appropriate continuous manifolds which make up the sensibility associated with that kind of object. Within the manifolds of appropriate sensibility, the identity of the thing is perceived.

The sensibility has to be acquired. If a pianist is to perceive the aesthetic identity of a sonata, he has to be adept at playing scales. At the beginning scales and simple melodies and harmonies are musical categorial objects for him, and their parts have to be distinctly articulated. Once they are achieved as dispositions, they can become the ingredient sensibility which allows the sonata itself to be perceived. Similar practice steps are needed for the sensibility ingredient in perceiving linguistic wholes, such as a speech or a poem, in a particular language. Another sensibility is required as a base for appreciating a farm or animals with the perceptions of a good farmer; another is required for understanding machines, still another for business, another for sport, another for mathematics—since even the formal structures of logic and mathematics become a sensibility when they settle down. Men in a hurry try to have the perceptions without developing the sensibility.

Husserl says:

> Sensible intuition has various levels. For each level we have the original mode of spontaneous production, and the later mode of something finished and granted. As such it enters into the process of a new spontaneous production, where it has the character of sensibility; i.e., we are given something that solicits us, something received in experience, but not reproduced. In contrast to it, the higher production is not sensibility, but it produces a new sensibility. For what is next to be taken for granted springs out of it. Taking it for granted is intuition, sensible intuition, and thinking arises over and against this (Ms D 13 XVIII, pre-1916, pp. 6–7).

Phenomenological analysis of each region involves unraveling the sensibility appropriate to it. It sheds light on what goes into perceiving each sort of object.

We bring about our own character by forcing ourselves to practice and execute the clumsy categorial objects that later settle into our dispositions, then make it possible for us to delight in perceiving what appears through the sensibility we have acquired. But behind the practice is an eros which we have not chosen; in its service we become what we are.

§ 43. MANIFOLDS AND OTHER MINDS

THE MANIFOLDS we have discussed are primarily those that appear to the single consciousness. Many more must be mentioned when other minds come into the picture. As a solitary subject, I can discuss the manifold of aspects a thing presents when I move from here to there; but if the thing is taken as that which others may be perceiving as well, I must consider the apparition I have as only one of many which can be actual at the same time; the others are not merely possible, waiting for me to actualize them, but can be actualized by other minds. The other sides of the thing are being seen, or can be seen, by someone else while I see these sides facing me. The thing is more objective, more transcendent to me, when other minds are considered, and indeed the true objectivity of nature is established only when intersubjectivity is included (*CM*, § 55).

A judgment subsists as objective in the tension engendered by many minds that can be appropriating, interpreting, mentioning, or emptily intending it at the same time.

The "here" of my body takes on a new dimension when it is considered as a "there" for another lived body, not just as something I can transport from my spatial here to another place without the parameters set by other minds. Moreover, manifolds of the normal and the abnormal require intersubjectivity (*PP*, § 20). Privacy as such acquires sense only in the context of other minds. Even the privacy of sense data and acts requires others: "a hyletic datum is alien to the ego, but this alienage is such that it can be the possession of just one single subject; and it is only present . . . as what is perceived in one perception of this one ego. The hyletic has this in common with every experience. An external object is not subjective in this way; it can be perceived by indefinitely many subjects" (Ms D 10 3, 1920, p. 11).

Husserl knows that we never exist as solitary minds, but wishes to analyze those manifolds that are not dependent on the copresence of other minds. The device that leads to this is the reduction to the "sphere of ownness," as described in *CM*, § 44. This reduction yields an abstractum, not a concrete way of existing. By first methodologically excluding them, it allows us to be more sensitive to those manifolds that are appropriate to our experience of the world and things in the context of other minds.

5 / Signs and Sensibility

in short shall we look for a deeper
or is this the bottom?
. . . .
This liquid is certainly a
property of the mind
nec accidens est   but an element
in the mind's make-up
. . . .
so light is the urging, so ordered
the dark petals of iron
we who have passed over Lethe.

—Ezra Pound, *Canto* lxxiv

HUSSERL DOES NOT merely postulate empty and filled intentions, nor does he accept them naïvely from ordinary experience. In *Logical Investigations,* where many of his fundamental concepts are first established, he brings intentions themselves to intuitive presence by a philosophical analysis of meaning. The analysis is based on the way signs work in consciousness.

The First Investigation begins with a distinction between two kinds of signs, indications (*Anzeichen*) and expressions (*Ausdrücke*).

§ 44.   INDICATION

INDICATION INVOLVES two independent objects or states of affairs, related by association or causality in such a way that the presence of one refers us to the existence of the other (I, § 2). When the one is intuited, it is not meant as an end in itself but leads us to intend the other, even though the latter is not present. There is transcendence in being aware of indication signs, in the very simple sense of *transcendere,* "climbing over and going beyond." In being aware of the sign we are aware of something other than the sign. However, we continue to hold in mind what we have climbed over and gone beyond—we stay aware of the sign when we intend what is meant through it—so the transcending consciousness of signs is bifurcated. There is only one "datum," but two objects are meant. The given is interpreted as a sign for the absent.

There is no mystery when we transcend indication signs, for what is meant absently is the same kind of object as what serves as the sign: another fact or another thing. Even this harmless kind of transcendence, however, shows the capacity of mind to intend something other than what is immediately given to it—a capacity exercised in many different ways.

The presence of the indication sign motivates us to believe in the existence of what is indicated. The other thing or fact is intended as real. Indication signs work in the element of belief and real existence, not in mere conceptions. The indicated may be present, past, or future, but the actual presence of the sign refers us to it in its reality; we are not just made to think of the sense of what is indicated. In this way smoke is a sign of fire, a badge the sign of an office, a flag the sign of a nation, ruins a sign that people once inhabited a certain place, fossils the sign of earlier animal life.

Both the indicating sign and what is indicated are independent things or facts, and each could be directly presented apart from the relationship of indication, which is external to them. The relationship arises in the way they are taken or used by consciousness; it is not a moment intrinsically present in them. In principle we can perceive separately as independent objects the smoke and the fire, the flag and the nation, the ruins and—were we around at the right time—the people once living there. We could perceive separately the fact that two lanterns are shining in the belfry, and the fact that the British are coming by sea.

The absence of what is indicated is necessary to indication; smoke is not a sign of fire when we see both the smoke and the fire. Indication is the paradigmatic case of something absent being intended by consciousness.

The motion of mind from indication to what is indicated is a species of inference. Some inferences move simply from one proposition, fact, or thing to another; the kind working in indication moves from a real and actually present fact or thing to another real fact or thing which happens not to be present.[1]

§ 45. EXPRESSION: THE SIGN OF MEANING

IN EXPRESSION (which Husserl discusses in *LI*, §§ 5–15) we do not have two independent objects. In speech, which is taken as the paradigm, an expression is a complex whole made up of words and meaning. The expression is always sense-informed, a whole which includes its meaning as well as its sound as parts. A "mere" expression is the residue left when no meaning is present, but this debris of sound is, as Aristotle would say, a heap, not identifiable in any way except accidentally —a loud or unusual noise. "The word 'expression' is normally understood—whenever, that is, we do not speak of a 'mere' expression—as the sense-informed expression" (I, § 9, p. 281). Even when we don't know what certain sounds mean, we experience them as expressions with a meaning that can be discovered. A meaningless expression is not an expression at all (I, § 15, p. 293). Verbal sound patterns, as verbal, are not independent pieces; they cannot be separated from what they express.

What they express is their meaning (*Bedeutung*). A meaning is an ideal entity that can be realized in many different expressions: it is repeated when different instances of the same words are used; it is defined or paraphrased when expressed by other words in the same language; it is translated when expressed in different languages. Moreover, the meaning is an ideal unity over against all the acts of meaning that realize it, whether they are performed by one person or by different persons.[2]

1. On the place of association in establishing indication signs, see *LI*, I, § 4; and *PP*, § 30, p. 166.

2. *LI*, I § 11, p. 285; § 30, p. 327; § 31, p. 329. What Husserl means by the identity of meanings in the *Investigations* is different from what he means by it in *Ideas I* and thereafter. In the *Investigations* a meaning is said to enjoy the unity of a species, and each time it is realized in an act, the species is instantiated; see I, § 31. In the later works, and especially in *FTL*, the identity of an ideal meaning like the Pythagorean theorem is the identity of an individual cultural object, and it is correlated to particular acts of consciousness which constitute it. This difference has been stressed by Th. de Boer, *De ontwikkelingsgang in het denken van Husserl* (Assen: Van Gorcum, 1966), pp. 306–7, 588.

Expressions do not express the acts that constitute meaning. They indicate such acts, as smoke indicates fire (I, § 7). When I express a judgment it is the judgment I express, not my act of judging; when someone hears me speak he understands and can repeat the judgment I have expressed; but he infers that I have judged, as one infers fire from smoke, and he cannot repeat my act of judging—although he can imitate it—because it is a particular episode in my life of thought. When my judgment is present to my interlocutor, my act of judging is absent and only indicated, because the style of presence and absence at issue here is the kind enjoyed by judgments. However, that same act of judging is present to my interlocutor in contrast to the absence that would occur if he were not around and listening while I framed the judgment, but were only told I had done so by someone else (I, § 7, pp. 277–78). That would be another kind of presence and absence. The many senses of presence and absence must always be kept in mind.

Expressions also do not express the object, the referent of an act of meaning (I, § 12). We do not express Babe Ruth when we make several statements about him. We express what we think, our meanings, and through them we refer to Babe Ruth, but he is the object of reference and not the meaning expressed.

It is easy to confuse reference with expressed meaning because the meaning, as part of a signitive act, is teleologically geared toward fulfillment in the intuitive presence of the object of reference (I, §§ 9–10, 13–14). The meaning is meant to be laminated against the object of reference in the actual presence of the latter. It is tempting to overlook the mediation of signitive meaning, to skip from the expression to the object, and to consider the object of reference as that which is expressed. But this would be to overlook some of the moments necessary in the sequence of parts which make up meaning and knowing.

The act that constitutes meaning in an expression is the empty, signitive act which, we have found, stands opposed to perceptual intuitions and to the pictorial consciousness (see above, § 8). More precisely, in the language of *Logical Investigations,* when a signitive intention functions in an expression— when its meaning is actually expressed in speech—it is called a "significative" act, in order to stress the expressibility of its sense.[3] In the course of *Logical Investigations,* Husserl treats

3. The German terms are *signitive* and *signifikative;* see LI, VI, § 8, p. 695, n. 1; § 14a, p. 710; § 15, p. 715.

both terms as synonymous until very late in his analyses: "The terms 'signification' and 'signitive intention' were for us synonymous. It is now time to ask ourselves whether the same acts, or acts essentially similar to those found to function in meaning, may not occur quite divorced from this function and from all expressions" (*LI*, VI, § 15, p. 715). That is, he develops his analysis of meaning on the basis of expressive speech; only very late in the game does he turn to meanings or senses as they might function in acts not tied to expression. He isolates the notion of meanings, empty intentions, and all the other moments that go into the recognition of identity, on the basis of linguistic expression. The use of speech furnishes the concrete examples on which he performs his eidetic intuitions.

The answer to the question we have just quoted from Husserl is affirmative; he admits that there can be signitive acts apart from language and expression. Many signitive acts are not significative, although in principle all can be made significative by finding appropriate expression (VI, § 15, pp. 715–18). But philosophically we reach signitive acts and meaning not by inward looks, nor by postulation, but by reflecting on and structurally analyzing the moments involved in linguistic expression.

The distinction between linguistic and nonlinguistic meaningfulness is also recognized in *Ideas I*, where Husserl distinguishes prescriptively between *Bedeutung* and *Sinn*, meaning and sense (§ 124). The first term is to be used for meanings expressed in speech, the second for sense whether expressed or not. "Sense" is a genus for "meaning," just as "the signitive" is a genus for "the significative." However, there is a difference between the two pairs: in the *Investigations* Husserl distinguishes between two kinds of intentional acts, while in *Ideas I* he distinguishes between two forms of what is constituted by the acts.

§ 46. EXPRESSION AND THE INTUITION OF FACTS

THE SIGNITIVE INTENTIONS we come to by analyzing speech find fulfillment in the intuition of the objects they intend. Signitively intending the front of the house finds fulfillment in seeing the front of the house; the fulfillment is complex, involving the intuition, the empty intention as being filled, and the skewering act of identification.

Husserl insists that when we express what we perceive, while we are in a state of intuitive recognition, the "meaning-bestowing act" is not the intuition but the signitive act.[4] What gives meaning to our expression is not the intuition but the signitive intention fused with it. Words name and describe things not by a simple relationship between sounds and things, but through the mediation of signitive meaning, which is immediately expressed in the words. For example, if I see a squirrel and say, "A squirrel is running across the yard," my speech does not express the intuition but the meaning of the signitive act laminated on or fulfilled by the intuition (*LI*, VI, §§ 4–5). Someone who doesn't see the squirrel can have and express the meaning signitively, without intuition, and the meaning is exactly the same: "But an expression functioning symbolically [i.e. signitively] also means something, and means the same thing as an expression intuitively clarified. Meaning cannot first have been acquired through intuition" (I, § 21, p. 306). There is a difference between my act and that of the other person, but the difference lies over and above signitive and significant meaning: it lies in the dimension of fulfillment.

The meaning in my registration is the same meaning expressed in someone else's report. In my registration the "meaning-bestowing act" is not the intuition—if it were, the report could not have the same meaning as my registration—but the signitive act which is fulfilled by the intuition. This signitive act is also realized, without fulfillment, in the report. In the terms we have prescribed, the "meaning-bestowing act" in both registration and report is the act of framing a judgment; but this distinction is not clear in *Logical Investigations*.

It is not surprising that even within intuition, the signitive act is what gives meaning to expression, because the signitive act is what gives sense to the intuition as well. The intuition is what it is only as fulfillng an empty intention.

There is no way of linguistically expressing the fulfillment of an intention by means of a component part of the speech that expresses the meaning in the fulfilled intention. No part of a sentence can express that what the sentence expresses is fulfilled. At best I can say, "I see that the squirrel is running across the yard," but this is a registration about the fulfillment, a second-level intention, not a straightforward expression of the

4. *Bedeutungsverleihende Akte* are the theme of *LI*, I, ch. 2, §§ 17–23.

intention itself. This impossibility of expression is not the fault of weak resources in our inherited language; it arises because the meaning of an intention and the fulfillment of an intention are two different dimensions. The first can be expressed, the second can be registered or reported.

Of course the meaning$_r$ of a reflective intention can be expressed in a formula like "I see that p." This is talk about the fulfillment, and expresses the meaning$_r$ of the intention$_r$ that intends the fulfillment as such. The reflective act has its own empty intention$_r$ and fulfillment$_r$, and again what is expressed from the reflective act is its meaning$_r$. The meaning$_r$ in the reflective act cannot be equated, however, with the meaning in the act reflected on: "I see that the squirrel is running away" cannot be equated as an expression with "The squirrel is running away."

These impossibilities become evident only to someone who thinks not just about the object meant, not just about the meaning, not just about the fulfillment, but also about the further, reflective intention that allows the speaker to say "I see that p." Since this is someone who thinks even *about* the speaker's reflective intention and its own fulfillment, he is reflective on a still higher level than the speaker, and the necessities and impossibilities he sees may not be clear to the speakers and reflective minds below him. This someone, of course, will turn out to be the transcendental ego that does phenomenology. He is not mentioned in *Logical Investigations*, but he is at work there because the necessities and impossibilities evident only to him are being expressed.[5]

§ 47. Excursus into Some Puzzles and Some Possibilities in Expression

WE DISTINGUISH between (1) the expression of a meaning being fulfilled ("X is y!") and (2) the expression of the

5. E. Tugendhat, *Der Wahrheitsbegriff bei Husserl und Heidegger* (Berlin: de Gruyter, 1967), p. 200: "Transcendental reflection as epochē in a new radicality opens up just that dimension in which pretranscendental phenomenology did in fact move." Aron Gurwitsch, "Critical Study of Husserl's *Nachwort*," in *Studies in Phenomenology and Psychology* (Evanston, Ill.: Northwestern University Press, 1966), pp. 108–9: "As Husserl emphasizes in the *Nachwort*,

meaning in an act which, reflectively, intends the fulfillment ("I see that X is y"). In other words, it is an entirely different matter (1) to register a fact, and (2) to register a fulfillment, i.e., to register a registration. The second assimilates the first, and much of what is made explicit in (2) is latent in (1), but important philosophical differences exist between the two. Let us explore some of them, partly to anticipate issues we will treat more adequately later on, partly to show possible applications of themes we have developed, partly to raise some provocative questions.

We sometimes make statements whose effect is to bring about a new state of affairs. If the appropriate people, under appropriate circumstances, say things like, "I put you under arrest," "I sentence you to a week in jail," "I hereby accept membership in the club," they bring about someone's being under arrest, his being sentenced to jail, his being a member of the club. None of these facts prevailed before the words were spoken. When we announce that we do such things, we bring them about.

Such statements work as performatives, and they implicate the one who speaks them in two ways: (a) they make him conspicuously responsible for bringing the new fact about, and (b) they make him an ingredient in the whole new fact.[6] For the

---

everything rests on the comprehension of this change in attitude which was already now and then practiced in the *Logische Untersuchungen*—but which was not explicitly characterized as such prior to the *Ideen*."

6. J. L. Austin has introduced the term "performatives" into current philosophy. He contrasts performative linguistic acts with constative acts; see "Performative-Constative," in *Philosophy and Ordinary Language*, ed. C. Caton (Urbana, Ill.: University of Illinois Press, 1963), pp. 22–54; "Performative Utterances," in *Philosophical Papers*, ed. J. O. Urmson and G. J. Warnock, 2d ed. (London: Oxford University Press, 1970), pp. 233–52; *How to Do Things with Words* (Oxford: Clarendon Press, 1962), pp. 3–11. He gradually becomes dissatisfied with the distinction, primarily because constatives themselves seem to function as performatives. Some commentators have tried to salvage the distinction, others have said it should be abandoned. See the essays by Black and Forguson in *Symposium on J. L. Austin*, ed. K. T. Fann (London: Routledge and Kegan Paul, 1969), pp. 401–19.

Our discussion is not meant to lock horns with Austin, but there is a Husserlian distinction which might be of some use in the debate about his categories. We should distinguish two kinds of achieve-

man who was arrested was arrested by me; I am involved in the fact as the arresting policeman. Or I am made into a member of the club whose invitation I formally accept.

To register a registration involves mentioning myself as registrar: "*I* see that X is y." Such a statement also has a performative dimension. Moreover, (*a*) it makes me stand out as the one responsible for the claim that "X is y" is being verified, but (*b*) it does *not* make me ingredient in the fact whose registration I confirm. It just makes me a witness to the fact, not a member involved in it. Saying "I see that X is y" does not make me part of X's being y, but saying "I arrest you" does involve me in your arrest.

Bringing about a legal or institutional fact brings about a new part of the world, and implicates us in the world. Such achievements through language both reflect and bring about the speaker's being as part of the world. We are also part of the world through sensibility and through our implication in instrumentality. But registering ourselves as witnesses when we register a registration makes us stand out of the world—except insofar as our registration as a witness is also a public or legal fact and means, for example, that we will have to appear in court. Then our being a witness is treated mundanely and not transcendentally. Because Husserl stresses the scientific and contemplative aspect of being human, he underscores the

---

ments or performances. (1) One is the establishment of a new public, conventional, or legal fact, through the appropriate use of words: acquiring property, arresting someone, becoming a member. Such achievements can occur only when appropriate words are publicly expressed. (2) The second is the achievement (*Leistung*) of registration, or even the registration of registration. This does not need public expression, although it usually involves it and always can involve it. For example, suppose I have never seen a helicopter but have read descriptions of them. While I am sitting alone outside, one flies overhead. I can register it for what it is, even if I never tell anyone about it. From then on, I am someone who has seen a helicopter; I can be my own public for such acts. Furthermore I can meditate, alone, about myself as registering or having registered this object. I could say, "I see (have seen) this helicopter." But I could not acquire property or arrest someone without public expression.

Constatives are always performatives in sense (2), and may also be performances in sense (1) if we register ourselves publicly as witnesses. Furthermore, for Husserl even framing a judgment is an achievement or performance, generally a public one in sense (1), but also possibly restricted to sense (2).

detachability of mind from the world; treatment of instrumentality, sensibility, and legal or public performatives would emphasize the involvement of man in the world. However, these factors are specifically human only because of the detachability brought about in man's capacity to be truthful and to stand out of the world. What Husserl explores underlies them; his thought is not "more impoverished" than that of those thinkers who explore such themes.

But isn't the simple registration of a fact already a performative? Doesn't it make me stand out as a witness? Why is it necessary to utter the redundant "I see that X is y"? Why not just say "X is y"?

True, the registration is a performance, and that is why Husserl calls it fulfillment. But the statement "X is y" does not explicitly register the fulfillment. As it stands, it might serve merely to report the fact, or to repeat someone else's conviction. Only a statement like "I see that X is y" explicitly registers a registration, and makes it explicit that the registration is my own. It picks me out in a way the simple registration of fact does not.

Is the event of fulfillment a fact or episode in the world that can be registered or reported like any other, such as the fact that the tree has fallen or that the apples are in the basket? If framing a judgment and achieving fulfillment—components in being truthful—are somehow not just like ordinary mundane episodes, they cannot be registered and reported right along with the others in the concatenation of ordinary facts. So the assertion "that I see that p" does not just add another fact to the facts "that p," "that q," and "that r."

Actually, fulfillment *can* be taken as an ordinary fact—"the tree is falling and John sees it fall"—but then its distinctiveness as an element in being truthful is neglected. It is treated as a psychological or sociological or legal fact, and many paradoxes result if we try to show, within these parameters, what truthfulness is. This is the ambiguity of acts achieved by transcendental consciousness: they may be considered as mundane and psychological, but their true sense is revealed only when we take them as somehow not a part of the world. The epochē and transcendental reduction are supposed to help us do this systematically.

If the event of fulfillment—as well as the event of framing a judgment—is somehow not a part of the world, the registration of fulfillment is likewise not a part, and in the same way.

"I see that p" is registration of a fulfillment; corresponding reports of the same would be: "I saw that p," and "I will see that p." What is the status of "He sees that p"? It is different from a registration of my own fulfillment, but it is a registration nonetheless; someone else is being registered as a witness. However it does not make me stand out, the way "I see that p" does, for in uttering it I do not take responsibility for the truth of what he sees.

Just to play out the complications a bit more: I can say, "I see that he sees that p," and I do take responsibility for registering him as a witness, but the interesting problem here is the relationship I have to p. Must I also be willing to register or report p to make such a statement? It seems I must, if I truly take him to be engaged in a fulfillment. My thinking almost melts into his. But if I want to dissociate myself from him, I must say something like "I see he thinks-he-sees that p."

Registering a report is similar to registering a registration, but there are interesting differences. When I register a report by saying something like "I say that X is y," I pick myself out as the one responsible for the truth claim, but I do not constitute myself as a witness of the registration of the fact. I merely constitute myself as the authority who guarantees that "X is y" is true. I may make this claim on grounds other than my own fulfillments.

The fact I register myself as reporting is absent, and there are many attitudes which I, my interlocutor, and my audience can take toward it. This variety is reflected in the variety of ways I can register myself as reporter: I can say "I say that p," "I know that p," "I state that p," "I warn you that p," "I promise you that p," "I bet that p." When I choose one of these possibilities, I constitute myself as a guarantor of a special kind: as telling, as warning, as promising, as betting. And perhaps other cultures can register authority in ways that are not established in our conventions and language. I don't have such flexibility in registering a registration. Although some of these modulations may enter, the main point in registering a fulfillment is simply the verification "that X *is* y," and the assertion that I am the one who intuits it as such.

In skimming these questions and possibilities, let us move beyond (1) the expression of a meaning being fulfilled and (2) the expression of the meaning in an act reflectively registering fulfillment or report, and examine (3) the expression of

meanings in those intentions which are carried out in transcendental phenomenological reflection. These intentions can
focus on the reflective registration of fulfillments; they can also
focus on all the lower levels as well, on world-directed meanings,
intentions, and fulfillments.

A special problem arises with the expression of the meanings
in these intentions. Using a term coined by Thomas Prufer, let
us call the language used to express phenomenologists' meanings
"transcendentalese." Is transcendentalese continuous with the
ordinary language with which we register facts and register
fulfillments? There must be some continuity, because the judgments expressed in ordinary language have to be assimilated by
transcendentalese and described by it; somehow everything said
in ordinary language can be repeated or quoted in transcendentalese. And if registration of fulfillments can repeat and
quote ordinary registration of facts, why can't phenomenological
registration do the same? But then how does transcendentalese
distinguish itself from the vernacular, and how does it manifest
the discontinuity between the focus from which it speaks and
the focus of ordinary discourse?

Husserl certainly takes the intentions and registrations of
transcendentalese to be contemplative acts, but do they also
have performative dimensions? As such, how do they differ from
registrations of fulfillment? Does the phenomenologist or philosopher take responsibility for what he says in some new and
special way, different from the way we normally do when we
register fulfillments in the natural attitude? Who is the speaker
of transcendentalese and how can he have any interlocutors?
What is the nature of an empty intention and a verification in
transcendentalese? Is transcendentalese the last language, or
is there another beyond it, one that expresses meanings from
a still more reflective stance?

All these problems arise ineluctably once we start analyzing
the structure and meaning of fulfillment. They emerge out of the
questions asked in *Logical Investigations*, but they cannot be
handled within the parameters set by that book. We need the
tools and perspective provided by the transcendental reduction.
Without these tools and perspective, or others that might perform the same service, we cannot recognize transcendentalese
for what it is; we cannot recognize philosophical discourse for
what it is. We would keep confusing it with ordinary talk about
things and facts in the world.

§ 48. WHAT IS NOT EXPRESSED BY EXPRESSION?

EXPRESSIONS DO NOT EXPRESS acts or referents. They also do not express images that may be associated with their meanings (*LI*, I, §§ 17–18). Use of an expression may or may not indicate that the speaker has such an image or idea before him in his mind's eye, but this is not what the words express. This is easy to establish since we usually have expression without mental pictures, and the same picture can be associated with different meanings.

Expressions thus express meanings and not acts (which they indicate), nor objects (to which they are used to refer), nor images (which they may or may not indicate). But although expressions do not express acts or objects, they involve them as necessary supplements in the concrete. There can be no meaningful expression without acts or referents. A wider whole involves meanings, expressions, acts, and referents as nonindependent parts.

Husserl's definition of expression does not coincide entirely with ordinary usage. We do speak of gestures, signs, and even words "expressing" our moods, our acts, what we are "doing" internally, and Husserl would insist that these are cases of indication signs: "We at once see that ordinary speech permits us to call an experience which is intimated an experience which is expressed" (I, § 7, p. 277). Such signs of our experiences, strictly speaking, do not have a meaning. We might also say, in ordinary language, that a certain speech "expresses" its object well or badly, and this too would be forbidden in Husserl's philosophical use. His stipulations are made in order to bring out important differences that ordinary language obscures. He cuts off some of the ambiguity of ordinary usage in order to have philosophical univocity and precision (I, § 5).

In his later work Husserl admits the following sense of expression: something experienced prepredicatively, in simple sensuous perception, can be said to be "expressed" if it becomes articulated categorially and if the categorial articulations in turn find expression in speech. He says "the sciences aim at predications [in words] that express completely and with evident fitness what is beheld pre-predicatively" (*CM*, § 5, p. 13; see also § 4, pp. 10–11). According to this usage, an object prepredicatively experienced can be "expressed" more or less adequately in what we say about it. But this does not contradict the stipulations of *Logical Investigations*, for the categorial meaning is still the immediate exprimend, and the object of prepredicative experience finds expression only through the articulations.

§ 49. IMPRESSION

HUSSERL DOES NOT HAVE MUCH TO SAY about the perception of material things in *Logical Investigations*. What he does say is modeled on his understanding of expressions. An analogy is operative: as verbal sounds are to meaning, so sensuous presentations, "impressions," as we call them, are to things.[7] An intentional act animates the stuff of expressions to constitute them as meaningful, and thereby constitutes a meaning as well; likewise, a perceptual intention animates sensations to constitute them as impressions of a thing, and thereby constitutes the thing as well. The stuff of expressions is "interpreted as" expressing this or that, the stuff of sensations is "interpreted as" the presence of this or that thing. If operative verbal sounds are said to "express" a meaning, the interpreted sensations could be said to "impress" a thing in our awareness. An interpreted sensation is an impression; it is also the sensuous appearance of a material object.

Husserl adopts this "matter-form" schema—in which a datum is "apprehended" or "animated" or "interpreted" by an act so as to present something beyond itself, whether a meaning or a thing—from the general psychological and philosophical principles of his day.[8] One of the chief philosophical services it performs is to prevent us from taking the relationship between a thing and the presence it has in our sensibility as a causal relationship, as though the thing caused impressions in us and forced us to infer from them what it, the thing, must be like in itself. A thing and its impressions, in this latter view, would be related as something indicated is related to its indication signs. But a thing does not cause impressions, any more than

7. *LI*, V, § 14, pp. 566–67. See also his essay, "Psychologische Studien zur elementaren Logik," *Philosophische Monatshefte*, XXX (1894), 183–85.
8. See R. Sokolowski, *The Formation of Husserl's Concept of Constitution* (The Hague: Nijhoff, 1964), pp. 56–57.

meanings cause expressions; Husserl says, "We are not dealing with an external causal relation where the effect conceivably could be what it intrinsically is without the cause, or where the cause brings something forth that could have existed independently. Closer consideration shows it to be absurd in principle, here or in like cases, to treat an intentional as a causal relation" (*LI*, V, § 15a, pp. 571–72). The phenomenological relationships here are not causal but expressive and impressive; from the side of the subject, the awareness of meaning in expression and thing in impression is not inferential but interpretative.

There remain difficulties in Husserl's theory of sensation and perception, but its main value, not always acknowledged by critics, is to avoid the causal explanations that have dominated modern theories of perception, and to avoid the unreal problem of how we infer things from our sensations.

Implications of Husserl's position are brought out in his later lectures and manuscripts on the perception of things. In particular, to state how a thing is given in its impressions, Husserl uses the term *sich bekunden* in *Ideas I* (§ 52). A thing is really "manifest" or "presented" in its impressions, even though it is more than any one of them and transcends, as an identity, its whole continuum of impressions—just as a meaning is really given in expressions, even though it transcends all the expressions it may have. Unlike indication signs and pictures, which do not immediately present the objects meant through them, and unlike effects, which do not present their causes immediately, impressions do present the thing-identity which "announces itself" in them.

However, the analogy "meanings are to expressions as things are to impressions" is only an analogy. At least two important differences exist between expressions and impressions. First, the expressive verbal patterns are more thinglike than the impressive sensations. They are themselves material objects; it is always possible to focus on them as material masses. They are, Husserl says, constituted by an act appropriate to them and distinct from the act that constitutes meaning: "The acts in question are naturally perceptual or imaginative presentations: in these the expression (as physically meant) is constituted" (*LI*, V, § 19, p. 583; see also I, § 10). The full act of expression is a fused, double act, with the act of meaning founded on the act that fashions the expressive stuff. We characteristically live in the act of meaning; we do not focus on the expressive substrate except reflectively. But the material expression and its act are a distinct foundation for the act of meaning. Impressive sensations, on the other hand, are not constituted as material objects or masses; they are not correlated to distinct acts (V, § 15b, p. 573). We simply let the impressions happen; we do not fashion them the way we formulate words. In perception there is only the one act of perceiving, correlated to the object intended. Sensations function as a foundation in this but do not have the subsistence of expressive stuff. Sensations are present in consciousness, but not as correlates of special acts.

Second, because they are fashioned, expressions are conventional. What a certain word expresses is arbitrarily associated with this particular sound, and other sounds can and do express the same meaning. Moreover, an object meant signitively is only conventionally associated with the impressions of the sounds that work in such intending. A directly perceived object, on the other hand, makes impressions that it alone can make. The way it modifies our sensibility is the work of the object itself, not the result of choices and conventions established at one time in the past (VI, § 26, pp. 741–42). True, the style of emphasizing elements in sensibility may differ, depending on one's culture and one's own psychic history; but such differences in style presuppose impressions that are natural and not the result of choice.

So as regards content, an object and its impressions are intrinsically and naturally united, while a meaning and its expressions, or an object and its names, are extrinsically and conventionally bound.

§ 50. SENSATION

BOTH EXPRESSIVE MATERIALS and impressive sensa are subordinated to the intentionalities that they found: we live in the understanding of meaning, or in the perception of things. But they can always be thematized reflectively. We have already seen this with regard to expressions, but sensations too, Husserl claims, can be considered purely as states we endure, apart from their function of presenting an object, in abstraction from the apprehension that interprets and animates them.

Husserl calls an impressive sensation an "appearance" (*Erscheinung*), and he stresses the ambiguity of this term (V, § 2, p. 538). A "red patch" can be either the objective aspect being presented in the animated, interpreted impression, or it can be the lived-through sensation taken in abstraction from its objectification. One example Husserl uses is the sensation of pleasure, which is a poor example because it is dubious whether we should consider pleasure a distinct sensation: "A sensation of pleasure attaches to the idea, a sensation at once seen and located as an emotional excitement in the psycho-physical feeling-subject, and also as an objective property—the event seems as if bathed in a rosy gleam" (V, § 15b, p. 574). Another example is from hearing: " 'I hear' can mean in psychology 'I am having sensations': in ordinary speech it means 'I am perceiving'; I hear the adagio of the violin, the twittering of the birds etc." (V, § 14, p. 564). This problem, of course, is the problem of *Abschattungen* (see above, § 34).

Not only is it possible for us to think, abstractly, about sensations apart from their function of presenting objects; sometimes we actually experience sheer, nonintentional sensible states. "When the facts which provoke pleasure sink into the background, are no longer apperceived as emotionally coloured, and perhaps cease to be intentional objects at all, the pleasurable excitement may linger on for a while: it may itself be felt as agreeable. Instead of representing a pleasant property of the object, it is referred merely to the feeling-subject, or is itself presented and pleases" (V, § 15b, pp. 574–75).[9] Such pure sensation is analogous to the expressional debris left when meaning is taken away. Words bereft of meaning are a debris of sound, and impressions bereft of animating apprehension are a residual state of dumb sensibility.

It is interesting, and perhaps a symptom of the peculiarities of modern as opposed to ancient thinking, that Husserl compares the sensuous part of expression—the letters and syllables—to sensations in the perception of things. Aristotle has a similar comparison, except that he compares letters and syllables to the elements, either the "so-called elements" of earth, air, fire, and water, or the basic powers of hot-cold, fluid-solid, which seem to be the true physical elements in his philosophy (*Metaphysics* 7. 17. 1041b11–33). Both letters and material elements are called *stoicheia* in philosophical Greek. The Greek alphabet of the cosmos becomes, in Husserl, the alphabet of feelings and sensations within consciousness. True, they are

9. At this point Husserl is not sure whether sheer sensation can exist as a concrete state of consciousness, but later he seems to admit it can; see *PP*, § 29, p. 163; *Ideen II*, § 10, pp. 21–23.

sensations whose normal function is to present the qualities and profiles of objects; nevertheless, in Husserl there is an assimilation into consciousness of something philosophically elemental which dwells outside of consciousness in the Greek view of mind and cosmos.

In Husserl, the sensation is not held over against consciousness. Unlike words, the sensation is not constituted by a distinct intentional act. How then is the sensation—whether functioning impressionally as an appearance or not—present to consciousness?

Obviously not through the mediation of still other impressions or sensations, for it is not a thing, and such mediation would set us on an infinite regress. Rather, according to the doctrine of *Logical Investigations*, the sensation is simply the experiencing of the sensation; it is the continuous unity of living through this state of sensibility. Experiencing the sensation is not an awareness over against the sensation, as perceiving a thing is a process over against its object; experiencing the sensation is the sensation itself: "It is in this sense that what the ego or consciousness experiences, are its experience: there is no difference between the experience or conscious content and the experience itself. What is sensed is, e.g., no different from the sensation" (V, § 3, p. 540).

In undergoing sensations there is no "transcendence," no move beyond what is immediately and simply given, no awareness of an identity beyond what is immediately present, no residue of a sign-function of any sort. What is given is not interpreted or apprehended as presenting anything beyond itself. Consciousness just rests in what is there. Sensibility is the basement of consciousness in the *Logical Investigations,* and in experiencing its sensations consciousness does not differentiate itself from them. It takes no distance.

Conscious acts are also immediately experienced, without need for impressions as intermediaries between them and consciousness. But acts are not as fundamental as sensations, because all acts are founded on sensa, whereas sensibility can be there without the support of intentional acts.

§ 51. REMARKS IN RETROSPECT

IN THE *Investigations* there is a logical progression in Husserl's treatment of each of the following pairs: (1) indication signs and what they indicate, (2) expressions and meanings expressed, (3) impressions and things perceived, and (4) sensations and sensing. After the first, each is modeled on and contrasted to its predecessor. The relation between indications and indicated objects is the start and the easiest to manage because it deals with two independent objects or facts, related by the gentle force of association. Expression and meaning are less distinguishable, as the meaning is within the expression and the expression embodies the meaning. Still, one is only a sign for the other: an expressive whole is two and not one. Impressions and things are still less differentiated because impressions have no material subsistence, not even the evanescent kind enjoyed by words; moreover, impressions cannot be replaced by other impressions in a kind of "translation" of what is perceived, but are wedded naturally and not by convention to this particular thing. Finally, in the sheer sensing of sensation all otherness collapses and the feeling is identified with what is felt.

Each step moves toward greater condensation. Each removes some of the otherness and transcendence of the pair before it. In Husserl's philosophical analysis, once indication signs are established, each pair is first introduced as like its predecessor, then described for what it is in itself by being contrasted to its predecessor. We are led to register what each pair is by determining what it is not, after we have been shown what it is like.

Once we have philosophically discovered these levels, we can look back and see how mind works to transcend presences in different ways and so to constitute itself in different degrees. In pure sensibility there is no mind and no transcendence, only immediate awareness. In perception the immediacy of the impressional continuum is overcome and transcended by awareness of the thing that is there in the impressions, but not part of them. When expressions are interpreted mind moves away from the confinement of the real presence of things to the possession of meanings signitively, apart from things; here certain material masses or sounds serve as the expression of identities of meaning that are transcendent to them. Finally, in indication signs the mind can move from an object or fact to another entirely independent object or fact.

These four levels are treated in *Logical Investigations*. In Husserl's later writing still other transcendences are described, as the four levels give way to many more. Within sensibility there is the transcendence of retentional and protentional awareness in inner time; there is the transcendence of memory, of the forgotten past, of other minds, of the spatial world, of the idealized scientific world as against the lived world, of written as against spoken language, of eidos as against the individual, of imaginary objects as against particular images and acts of imagination. In each of these the mind is made to move from what is present toward what is absent, toward something absent which is not of the same order as what is present—the thing is not an impression, the meaning is not an expression, the eidos is not an individual. And the mind holds both the absent and the present together in a single but differentiated consciousness (*APS*, p. 337, n. 1).

Because the absent meant in such transcendence is of another order from what is present, the movement of transcendence breaks apart the homogeneous wholeness of what is present: meaning breaks the homogeneity and wholeness of pure sound, things break that of impressions. A whole is broken and a new whole is formed encompassing the transcendent and the transcended: the thing and its impressions, the meaning and its expression, the eidos and its individuals, the other mind and its body. This motion of mind, forming wholes and breaking them in order to move on to new wholes, reaches closure when it comes to the final whole beyond which, according to Husserl, further questioning is meaningless: the whole of transcendental subjectivity, the field that phenomenology cultivates.

Genetic phenomenology, a discipline which Husserl formally isolates only rather late in his career,[10] traces the necessary sequence of wholes in consciousness. "Another 'constitutive' phenomenology, the one concerned with genesis, follows the history, the necessary history of this objectification, and thereby the history of the object itself as object of possible knowledge" (*APS*, p. 345; see also pp. 338–39).

The work of mind is to carry out its transcendences and yet to remain identical with itself throughout them all.[11] Mind never turns into one of the objects it constitutes; it does not turn into

10. See I. Kern, *Husserl und Kant* (The Hague: Nijhoff, 1964), § 31.

11. Aron Gurwitsch, "A Non-egological Conception of Consciousness," in *Studies in Phenomenology and Psychology*, p. 298: "The ego is then a synthetic unity of these psychic objects, chiefly of the dispositions and the actions—that is to say, it turns out to be a transcendent unity of transcendent unities. All these objects have their support in the ego, and the latter performs their permanent

an ordinary part of the world. It remains transcendent to them all, when seen from a phenomenological point of view.

As it executes one or other of its transcendences, the mind actualizes itself out of its own potential. When it is not doing this, it relapses into a potential state, of which there are different kinds. A mind that has done mathematics is endowed with mathematical habitualities, so it is different from one that has never done mathematics, even when both minds are at rest (*CM*, § 32). A mind that has brought about eidetic intuitions is different from one that merely senses the pull toward eidos. A mind that has framed judgments is different from one that has only repeated diffused opinions.

Mind perceiving is different from mind somnolent; mind judging is different from both. Mind reflecting phenomenologically is actualized differently from mind actualizing any mundane transcendence, even natural science.

On this point Husserl might be compared with al-Farabi and his distinctions between (*a*) potential intellect; (*b*) intellect in actuality, brought about when the forms of existing things come to be in it; (*c*) acquired intellect, achieved "when the intellect in actuality thinks the intelligibles which are forms in it, insofar as they are intelligibles in actuality"—that is, achieved when the mind contemplates objects as phenomena;[12] and (*d*) agent intellect, the separate being that is the efficient cause making the potential intellect into an actual one, and making the potentially intelligible object become actually intellected. The hardest part in comparing Husserl and al-Farabi is to find what corresponds in Husserl to the agent intellect. Is there any need for something to correspond to it? If not, why not? Does the perpetually active form of inner time-consciousness have a place in this comparison? What is the place of language, and that of the desire for science?

The logic of parts and wholes, the contrast of presence and absence, and the persistence of identity within a manifold, all cooperate in the mind's work of transcendence.

In *Logical Investigations* the paradigm for the mind's transcendence is its ability to experience indication signs; in

synthesis. It is not, however, a support distinct from that which is supported. . . . Such a support would be more or less indifferent to what it supports."

12. al-Farabi, "The Letter concerning the Intellect," trans. A. Hyman, in *Philosophy in the Middle Ages*, ed. A. Hyman and J. Walsh (New York: Harper and Row, 1967), p. 217.

recognizing a sign we hold a presence and an absence together in one differentiated consciousness. But this starting point in the *Investigations* is not the absolute starting point, chronologically, in Husserl's career. His earlier work uses the logic of transcendence and presence and absence within the context of mathematical thinking, so to come to the beginning we would have to go back to the *Philosophie der Arithmetik*.

§ 52.   BEYOND SENSIBILITY

IT IS APPROPRIATE at this point to go a step further than *Logical Investigations*. As we have seen, four levels of consciousness are distinguished in the *Investigations*: indication and the indicated, expression and the expressed, impression and the thing impressed, and sheer sensation. In the last of these, sensing and sensum are identified. Through his reflections on inner time, Husserl came to see a distinction in sheer sensation between the sensum and the experiencing of it.

In Appendix XII of his *Lectures on the Phenomenology of Inner Time Consciousness,* in a passage written after 1911, he makes a critical remark about his earlier doctrine: "Sensation here is nothing other than the inner consciousness of the content of sensation. . . . Thus it is understood why in the *Logical Investigations* I could identify the sensing and the content of sensation. Since I moved inside the frame of inner consciousness, there, naturally, we did not find any sensing, only what is sensed" (pp. 176–77; Churchill translation modified).[13]

In this text Husserl distinguishes between sensing (*Empfinden*) and what is sensed (*Empfundenes*) or the content of sensation. He observes that in the *Investigations* he remained "inside the frame of inner consciousness," that is, he discussed only what was sensed, and did not reflect on the process of being aware of inner objects. He stayed within the frame, and

13. I have been helped very much by John Brough in getting clear on Husserl's doctrine of inner time-consciousness. See his doctoral dissertation at Georgetown University, "A Study of the Logic and Evolution of Edmund Husserl's Theory of the Constitution of Time-Consciousness" (1969), and his essay, "The Emergence of an Absolute Consciousness in Husserl's Early Writings on Time-Consciousness," *Man and World,* V (1972), 298–326. On the importance of app. XII, see p. 313 of that essay.

did not examine the frame itself. In the *Investigations* he did not succeed in prying loose the flow of inner consciousness—which will turn out to be the absolute flow of inner time-consciousness —from the contents or inner objects constituted within that flow. In the studies associated with his lectures on time, he succeeds in this differentiation, and distinguishes an absolute flow of inner consciousness from the series of sensations and acts, the inner objects, that appear within it. He differentiates sensing from what is sensed.

Husserl moves beneath what the *Investigations* consider the basement of consciousness, sensations and acts as immediate experiences. He finds a murky flow of temporal awareness beneath, which is responsible for them as experiences.

Perhaps it is possible to identify the passage in which Husserl becomes clearly aware of this distinction for the first time. In his edition of the lectures on time, Rudolf Boehm has included a number of manuscripts which had previously gone unpublished. We are interested in Number 50, which was written sometime between October 15, 1908, and the summer semester of 1909 (p. 324, n. 1). Throughout the text Husserl asks how a flowing consciousness can be a consciousness of succession. At any instant of my conscious life, how can I be aware of instants that have elapsed? How can the past be around in the present?

We need not trace all the aspects of this problem now. For our purposes, Husserl's conclusion is important: "Therefore sensation, if we understand this as consciousness (not the immanent, enduring red, sound, etc., i.e., the sensed), and also retention, remembering, perceiving, etc., is untemporal, viz. it is nothing in immanent time" (no. 50, pp. 333–34). The expression is rough, and some words are ambiguous. To paraphrase the point we wish to stress in this text: "Sensing (as opposed to the content sensed) is not an object in inner time."

The experiencing of inner objects (sensed qualities and acts) is not itself an inner object. It stands outside the flow of inner objects. These inner objects have a temporal station in my conscious life, and are thus temporal entities; but the experiencing of them is outside this flow of inner temporal objects. It is not a member of their series (see *PP*, app. XII, pp. 414–15).

The reason for this conclusion comes a few lines earlier in the text. Looking back on his own efforts Husserl says, "Wasn't it an absurdity to consider the time-flow as an objective motion? Yes! And yet, on the other hand, [primary] remembering is something that has its own Now, and the same Now as, e.g., a sound.

No. That's where the fundamental mistake was. The flow of the modes of consciousness is not a process, the Now-consciousness is not itself now" (no. 50, p. 333). In this passage, which is as dramatic as anything in Husserl will ever be, two points are made. (a) The inner time-flow, which is the experiencing of inner objects, is not itself inside the procession of inner objects. The flow of inner time-consciousness, the flow of experiencing, is not a motion that can be mingled with the sequence of inner sensa and acts; much less can it be mingled with processes in the objective, spatial world. It is the frame for inner objects and their sequence; hence it is not among them. (b) Since the inner time-flow does not mingle with the succession of inner objects, and since it is inner objects, like sounds, that are said to be "now" or "later" or "earlier," the parts of the time-flow cannot be said to be "now" or "later" or "earlier" in the same way. Parts and events in the time-flow do not share the temporal station of parts and events in the sequence of inner objects, sensa and acts. "The Now-consciousness," says Husserl, the inmost awareness which is aware of an inner object as now, "is not itself now." It would be a confusion to measure the parts and events in the inner time-flow by means of the measures used to identify parts and events in the procession of inner objects.

The passage is complicated because Husserl is also talking about how elapsed consciousness is still present in the actual instant of inner awareness. After having said that "the Now-consciousness is not itself now," he continues, "The being of retention, which is 'together' with the Now-consciousness, is not 'now,' it is not simultaneous with the Now; this would make no sense." Since the absolute flow of inner time-awareness is not itself in time, we don't have to ask whether retention is simultaneous with the now-consciousness. They don't have to be said to share the same time, because neither is in time at all. They are "together" but not "simultaneous," and their togetherness remains to be analyzed.[14]

The primitive elapsing of the now-consciousness into retention is an "event" outside time, not only beyond the worldly time of clock and calendar, but beyond the immanent sequence of sensa and intentional acts. This is the emergence in Husserl's thought of an absolute flow of inner time-consciousness, "more

14. A more settled expression of this temporal "togetherness" can be found in ZB, no. 54, p. 375. See also § 38 of the text of the lectures.

immanent" than the procession of inner objects, acts and sensations, which make up the basement of consciousness in *Logical
Investigations*.

It is not accidental that this absolute dimension comes to
light in connection with Husserl's doctrine of retention. For the
retentional and protentional consciousness is what provides the
manifold for constitution of the identities—acts and sensations
—that are constituted by the absolute flow. It is at this point in
the text, apparently, that Husserl uses the term "retention" in its
technical sense for the first time.[15]

Husserl closes with the words "These are highly important
things, perhaps the most important in all of phenomenology"
(p. 334).[16] He says this because these reflections open up the
domain of the "true and final absolute" for phenomenology
(*Ideas I*, § 85), the domain where the most primitive parts are
engendered, and where we find the manifolds and identities
that condition all others but are conditioned by none.

§ 53. CONSCIOUSNESS OF INNER TIME IS NOT MUNDANE

SINCE THE FLOW of inner time-consciousness is outside
the objective time of clock and calendar, and also beyond the
private time of inner temporal objects, the life that is led in this
domain is in no way a mundane life. The reflections of text
Number 50 are a temporal way of establishing the nonworldli-
ness of the transcendental ego.

Gadamer has observed that even in the *Crisis*, the most

15. The first use of "retention" appears to be in no. 50, p. 333, l.
23; see n. 2 on that page, and see p. 211, n. 1. Uses of the term before
this point are later interpolations, as Boehm remarks in the footnotes.

16. Boehm stresses the importance of this passage in his introduction, pp. xli–xlii; see also "Husserl und Nietzsche," in *Vom
Gesichtspunkt der Phänomenologie* (The Hague: Nijhoff, 1968), pp.
226–27. Earlier, Husserl expresses some suspicion that the flow of
inner experiencing is different, in an important way, from a regular
process, and that it must be distinguished from inner objects which
are experienced, but he does not get clear about it until no. 50. See
the anticipations in no. 26, p. 207, ll. 17–23; no. 45, p. 301, ll. 22–23;
and the remarks on p. 427. Brough ("Absolute Consciousness," pp.
307–10) shows that in no. 39 Husserl already distinguishes inner
objects from the experiencing of inner objects, but that he is not yet
clear on the distinctive nature of such experiencing.

persistent problem Husserl feels he must overcome is the tendency of all philosophers to take the ego as a part or member of the world: "The transcendental ego is not an ego in the world. To recognize this and hold it fast is the overwhelming difficulty." [17] The tendency to make the ego mundane is the "fundamental mistake" Husserl overcomes in text Number 50, where it appears as the tendency to take the inner time-flow of the ego as being itself in time; it is the constant problem of falsely objectifying the self.

What does it mean to say that a new dimension of absolute consciousness is differentiated from the sequence of inner objects, the sequence of sensa and acts? Let us put it in terms of language and expression. It means that while I am capable of making statements, intuitively, about an object in the world, or about facts in the world, it always remains possible for me to start talking about my sensations, which are ingredient in my perceptions, or to start talking about my perceiving objects or facts, or to start talking about my framing and expressing judgments or registering facts. I can articulate new truths, and frame new judgments, no longer about mundane objects and facts, but about these inner objects, my sensations and acts. Furthermore, my judgments can find fulfillment in registrations about my inner objects. These new judgments, the fruit of reflection, are not reducible to those that are made about mundane objects (houses and trees), nor are they verified by perception of mundane objects or facts (*Ideas I*, § 45).

The possibility of making such new kinds of judgments shows that I have been experiencing something besides trees, houses, and other mundane objects: I have been experiencing my own sensa and acts. This means that I do not just perceive the house, I also experience the perception of the house. There is therefore a distance between me and my perceptions, my judgings, my sensations. The place where this othering between me and my inner states of consciousness occurs is the domain of inner time-consciousness. The flow of inner time-consciousness allows an inner object to be constituted as a unity within a manifold of temporal phases. It also allows my self to be constituted as the one to whom these inner objects appear.

The first experiencing of my inner objects goes on non-thematically; it takes place while I am directly concerned with

17. "Die phänomenologische Bewegung," *Philosophische Rundschau*, XI (1963), 27.

objects in the world. I can always change my concern to a reflective awareness of inner objects. When I do this, the objects in the world become nonthematically, marginally present to me. In this reflective stance I can, claims Husserl, give an eidetic description of the structure of my sensations and acts. When done rigorously and exhaustively, this is descriptive phenomenology.

However, phenomenology also has a further task. It must reflect on my first reflection, and show how that first reflection is possible. This is done by showing how the flow of inner time-consciousness allows the first reflection to take place. In this second reflection we focus not on mundane objects, not on inner objects like sensations and acts, but on the temporal profiles through which inner objects are constituted and made available for reflection. The same phases of inner time-consciousness that allow inner objects to be constituted also allow reflection on these inner objects to take place. Our second reflection shows how all this happens. In the second reflection we do a "phenomenology of phenomenology," and show how descriptive phenomenology is possible (see *FTL*, § 107c, pp. 288–89 and n. 1; *EP II*, p. 276, n. 2; *CM*, § 63).

None of this is done in *Logical Investigations*, where sensations and acts are simply taken as ultimates. How they are experienced, and how we can talk about them, is not treated.

6 / The Inside of Time

Omnia, Lucili, aliena sunt, tempus
tantum nostrum est.
—Seneca, *Epistulae morales ad
Lucilium* 1. 1

κρύψαντες γὰρ ἔχουσι θεοὶ βίον
ἀνθρώποισιν.
—Hesiod, *Works and Days* 42.

WE HAVE MOVED from the consciousness of signs, through perception and sensibility, into absolute time-consciousness. We will keep the logic of this argument alive by exploring the part-whole structures, unities in manifolds, and transcendences that are at work within the domain of inner time.

§ 54. SOME DISTINCTIONS AND TERMS

1. ONCE HUSSERL'S THOUGHT on time had developed, he often distinguished three levels: (*a*) temporal objects in objective, worldly time, like melodies, races, local motions, or illnesses; (*b*) inner objects or immanent objects, which are sensations and acts and the combination of sensations animated by intentional acts; and (c) the absolute, time-constituting consciousness.[1]

1. For example, see ZB, no. 40, pp. 286–87; no. 52, p. 358; no. 54, p. 373; and in the main text of the lectures, § 34.

During the first years of his study of time, until about 1904, Husserl did not make much of the distinction between (*a*) and (*b*).[2] What he says about time-soaked objects applies indiscriminately to both; his description of perception of the temporal object holds both for the perception of an objective thing or process and for the "inner" perception of acts and sensations. Overlooking the distinction between (*a*) and (*b*) has bad effects; it makes it impossible for Husserl to realize that inner objects are not constituted in the same way that mundane objects are. This in turn makes it impossible for him to isolate (*c*), the absolute flow of inner time, because it is identifiable only as the domain of consciousness specifically underlying (*b*).

The distinction between (*a*) and (*b*) began to emerge with consistency and clarity in texts just prior to the lectures of 1904–5.[3] The distinction between (*b*) and (*c*), as we have seen, began to emerge with consistency and clarity only in 1908 (see above, § 52).

2. We must distinguish between the parts that arise in a temporal object and the parts that arise in the consciousness of a temporal object. (*i*) Parts of the temporal object are called the now-phase, the just-elapsed phase or phases, and the coming phases. Sometimes they are called the now, past, and future phases. These are all phases of the object. (*ii*) There are parts in the consciousness that enjoys a temporal object; these are called the now-perception, "primary" or "fresh" memory (as opposed to the "secondary" memory of full-blown remembering), and expectation. These names were used until 1908, when Husserl introduced the terminology that has since become classical in this matter of time, and spoke of primal or central impressions, retentions, and protentions.

It is important not to confuse (*i*) and (*ii*). In particular, a "now" or "now-phase" should not be ranged with retentions and protentions; the former belong to (*i*) and are phases of an

2. The manuscripts Boehm has collected in section I, pp. 137–86, dated about 1893–1901, mention differences between inner objects like acts, sensations, and "appearances," and objective things like melodies; but they do not speak of the two as radically different in their temporality. Husserl moves quite easily from one to the other. See no. 1, pp. 147–48; no. 2, p. 153; no. 5, pp. 156–57. The tone is generally used as the paradigm for a temporal object; see no. 12.

3. In no. 19, the first manuscript in section II, Husserl begins to distinguish systematically between "inner" and "outer" temporal objects, and focuses on the structure of inner objects.

inner temporal object, while the latter belong to (*ii*) and are phases of the consciousness of an inner temporal object.[4]

To return to our distinctions under (1), until Husserl distinguished between (*a*) and (*b*), (*i*) was used indiscriminately for both (*a*) and (*b*), and the status of the consciousness composed of (*ii*) was not clearly identified. After (*a*) was distinguished from (*b*), and after (*c*) was isolated in 1908, (*i*) began to be used primarily for (*b*) and (*ii*) was applied to (*c*).

Consider the whole made up of a now-perception, primary memory, and expectation—or, to use the later terminology, the whole made up of a primal impression, retention, and protention. This whole is called (*iii*) a momentary phase of consciousness, and is sometimes named a *Querschnitt*, a segment or slice of the flow of consciousness.[5] It is "thick" (ZB, no. 27, p. 210, l. 23). It encompasses the parts (*ii*) that are actually at work in consciousness. It is, as we shall see, a continuum because it contains these parts; and as one segment succeeds another, a continuum of continua is engendered.

In Husserl's later philosophy this segment, the part of one's conscious life that is alive and actual, comes to be called *lebendige Gegenwart*, the living present. In respect to the constitution of time it is more elemental than (*a*) a present actuality in the world, and even more elemental than (*b*) a present actuality in the stream of my sensations and acts. It is the present actuality of (*c*), the absolute consciousness.

3. The word "phases" has been used throughout this development. It is used analogously by Husserl. It can mean (*i*) parts of a temporal object: the now-phase, elapsed phase, and coming phases; (*ii*) parts within a segment of the flow of consciousness: the primal impression, retentional, and protentional

4. John Brough ("The Emergence of an Absolute Consciousness in Husserl's Early Writings on Time-Consciousness," *Man and World*, V [1972], 315), clearly brings out this distinction and criticizes commentators who have failed to see it: Seebohm, Diemer, and Sokolowski. Seebohm, incidentally, continues to overlook the distinction in *Zur Kritik der hermeneutischen Vernunft* (Bonn: Bouvier, 1972), pp. 61–63. The distinction is brought out neatly toward the end of no. 54 in the manuscripts Boehm has edited; on p. 372, ll. 21–26, Husserl asks whether we must distinguish between the "tone-now" and our central consciousness of it. He replies in the affirmative on p. 382, ll. 27–31.

5. E.g., ZB, no. 24, p. 199; nos. 32 and 33. See also APS, pp. 316–17.

phases; (*iii*) momentary segments of the flow of consciousness.[6] To try to reduce ambiguity, we will always use "phase" or "phases" in sense (*i*), to mean parts of temporal objects.[7] We will use appropriate words like "primary memory" or "retention" for (*ii*), and "segment" or "living present" for (*iii*).

§ 55. PRESENCE OF THE PAST IN INNER TIME-CONSCIOUSNESS

FOLLOWING THROUGH the argument of *Logical Investigations,* we have come to inner objects, sensations and acts, and have distinguished these objects from the absolute awareness we have of them. Each inner object is a unity; a sensed sound is a unity that is experienced durationally. If the sound continues unchanged in regard to pitch, timbre, and loudness, it still goes through a manifold of temporal phases. We can distinguish phase 1, phase 2, phase 3, phase 4, and so on. These phases are the manifold within which the sound is constituted as an identity.

While we are enjoying phase 6, the earlier phases are no longer immediately present the way phase 6 is. However, they are still at work in the constitution of the sensed sound; they are still functioning in the manifold that presents the sound as a unity. In what way are they still present?[8] They are present because each elapsed phase is presented through a successive series of profiles. The temporal object is a unity in a manifold of phases; but each phase is a unity in a manifold of its own.

Each phase is a phase of the temporal object. It is analogous to a "side" of a spatial object. Each side of a spatial object is

6. Husserl lists the term's various senses in no. 30. Correlative to the sense of "phase of consciousness" as a thick segment of the flow of consciousness, one can also speak of a thick "phase" of the temporal object given in that segment.

7. This is the sense it has most of the time in Husserl. See ZB, pp. 212, 215, 226, 239, 262–63, 275–86, etc. Some passages in which it is taken in sense (*ii*) are p. 333, ll. 26–34; app. VIII; and § 39 of the main text of the lectures. Note the ambiguity of "phase" in *APS*, pp. 323–25.

8. For the following see ZB, no. 39, esp. pp. 275–76, 282; no. 53, pp. 362–68 (this text uses spatial profiles as an analogy for temporal ones).

present to us in a series of aspects: the way it looks from this angle and from that, from this distance and from that.

Now consider the temporal phases in an inner object. While we are enjoying phase 2, phase 1 is still given *from the vantage point of phase* 2. Phase 1 is given in a certain perspective; a certain profile of it is being presented. What we are immediately given is not phase 1 pure and simple, but this profile of phase 1—the way it looks from the vantage point in which we enjoy phase 2 immediately. We are immediately presented with profile 2 (phase 1). If we have moved on to the direct enjoyment of phase 6, we still have phase 1 at work, but now under a new profile, from the vantage point in which phase 6 is directly present. We are immediately given profile 6 (phase 1).

Phase 1 is therefore the unity that is constituted in the series of profiles 1, 2, 3, 4, 5, 6 . . . (phase 1). Each of these profiles is different from the others.[9] Phase 2 and all the other temporal phases of the object are likewise constituted in a manifold of temporal profiles appropriate to each of them.

The only time a phase is not given through some profile or other is when it is being immediately enjoyed in its direct presence, as a now-phase. Once it elapses from immediate presence, the phase itself is never again absolutely immediately given; but its subsequent temporal profiles are immediately given along with subsequent actual now-phases.

While we are directly enjoying phase 6, we are also in the direct presence of profile 6 (phase 1), profile 6 (phase 2), profile 6 (phase 3), profile 6 (phase 4), profile 6 (phase 5). Phases 1 to 5 are "absent" and transcendent to consciousness at this point, but their appropriate profiles are just as immediately present as phase 6 is.

This is the absolute and adequate consciousness of the present experience: it enjoys not all the *phases* of the inner object, but the phase we are actually enjoying plus the appropriate *profiles* of the elapsed phases. This is the well-rounded whole of absolute consciousness, sheer presence with no absences or transcendences, nothing co-meant which is not immediately given.[10] To reach this absolute center, it is not enough to distinguish the various temporal phases of an inner object; the temporal profiles of each phase—each phase's "modes of

9. See *APS*, p. 322: Husserl speaks of "the tone-phase which fades away in the continuity of retentional modification." See also *APS*, app. XIII.

10. *EP II*, app. XXVIII, p. 466, ll. 1–4; p. 468, ll. 25–31; *CM*, § 9.

temporal orientation"—must be taken into account (*ZB*, no. 53, p. 364, n. 1).

In our natural, nonphenomenological experience, we never focus on the profiles in which elapsed phases appear. Non-phenomenologically we experience the immanent object, the sensed sound or experienced act, which endures and constitutes itself as an individual identity within the manifold of phases. We may perhaps refer to one or other of the phases of the immanent object, but we cannot focus on the profiles of these phases until we begin to reflect phenomenologically. That is, all nonphenomenological consciousness involves self-transcendence, even when it is limited to the experiencing of inner temporal objects; all nonphenomenological consciousness reaches beyond the immediately given to intend something that is absent and transcendent—in the case of inner experiencing, it intends the inner object, which is always partly absent, in its elapsed phases as well as in its present phase (no. 51, p. 350). Only phe-nomenological reflection focuses on what is absolutely present to inner consciousness: the now-phase and the accompanying profiles of elapsed phases. These profiles are essentially over-looked by the nonphenomenological consciousness, because a new kind of reflection is needed to bring them to light.

Only phenomenological reflection can be aware of what Husserl often calls the "wonders" and the "marvelous struc-ture" of the absolute, inner time-constituting consciousness (no. 39, pp. 276, 280, 283; see also *APS*, p. 310). It alone becomes aware of the manifold of profiles which are experienced but never thematized in nonphenomenological awareness, which considers the identity but overlooks the manifold.

§ 56. THE MANY KINDS OF REFLECTION AND INNER TIME

WE MUST BE MORE PRECISE about what kind of phe-nomenological reflection brings the structure of inner time to light. As we have seen, we can reflect on our judgments—on supposed facts as supposed—and also on objects as supposed. We can also reflect on our acts and sensa and generally on our stream of consciousness; we can do so in various ways.

1. In ordinary psychological reflection, we consider acts and sensa as objects or processes in the stream of consciousness. We

do not shut off our world-belief, so these objects or processes are not radically distinguished from things in the world. While reflecting in this way we can, Husserl claims, carry out an eidetic description of the elements and structures of psychic objects.

2. If we perform the epochē and transcendental reduction, we continue to reflect on our acts and sensa, and are able to carry out a descriptive phenomenology; but now we have an appreciation of the true nature of inner objects as they work in intentionality. Structurally this reflection is not different from that in (1); the difference between the two arises because the world-belief is suspended in one and not in the other.

In both kinds of reflection, we continue to overlook the profiles in inner time-consciousness. Even in (2) we focus on acts or on their phases, but not on the profiles of the phases. This kind of descriptive phenomenology is still naïve because it does not account for itself. It does not show how its own reflections are possible.

Reflections like (1) and (2) thematize an inner object, but they always look at it directly in its elapsed phases. Such reflection does not focus on the profiles of the elapsed phases: it overlooks them. Even when these reflections are iterated, when they reflect on other reflections—this feat is possible because reflections too are inner temporal objects—they overlook the profiles of the phases of the temporal objects they focus on. Such reflections iterated even to infinity cannot overcome this handicap.

3. There is need for a new kind of reflection which focuses on the profiles of phases in inner temporal experiencing. This reflection makes a new kind of phenomenology possible, a critical inquiry which overcomes the naïveté of the simple descriptive phenomenology brought about through (2). Husserl sometimes calls it a phenomenology of phenomenology, or a phenomenology of the transcendental reduction (see above, § 53, and below, § 60). It discloses the elements in inner time-consciousness. When it looks at what the other reflections overlook—the profiles of temporal phases of inner objects—it sees what makes the other reflections possible, which those reflections never manage to see. And by discovering this intimate structure of inner time, this critical phenomenological reflection is also able to see what makes its own self possible.

In summary, the structure of inner time explains how the following are possible: (a) the immediate experiencing of inner objects in the stream of consciousness, (b) ordinary reflection

on inner objects, (c) the reflection at work in descriptive transcendental phenomenology, and (d) the critical phenomenological reflection on the absolute flow of inner time-consciousness.
It also explains why we do not have to move another step, why
we reach philosophical closure in the domain of inner time-
consciousness.

§ 57. The Datum in Inner Temporal Consciousness

Profiles of elapsed phases are still around in consciousness with the presence of a now-phase. It is one thing to
say that profiles are copresent with a now-phase; it is another
thing to explain how this can happen.

1. Husserl's first attempt to explain this is not successful. To
explain how the various phases of a temporal object are present
to consciousness, he makes use of the "matter-form" schema of
constitution which he introduced in the *Investigations*.

In ordinary experience we are given a datum or sensuous
content, and can apprehend or interpret it as the impression of
a perceived object, or as the impression of a picture of an absent
object, or simply as the impression of a symbol by means of
which we intend something signitively. These differences are
brought about by differences in the animating act of apprehension, and not by differences in the datum, which is neutral as
regards how it is to be interpreted.

Husserl tries to apply this schema to our experiencing of
inner temporal objects, such as sensed sound. He claims that
even here we have a datum which is neutral, in this case
temporally neutral, since we are dealing with differences in
time. It is then apprehended or interpreted by different kinds of
consciousness, and is made to be either the impression of the
actual now-phase of the temporal object, or a representative, a
profile, of an elapsed now-phase.[11] Consciousness would interpret datum *A* as being the impression of an actual now-phase,
and datum *B* as the profile of a phase that has elapsed.

This explanation is laden with inconveniences, and was
subsequently rejected by Husserl. The major problem is this:

11. This doctrine of Husserl is directed against Brentano, who
tried to place the sense of pastness in the datum or content. Husserl
places it in the "ways of apprehending" the datum; ZB, nos. 14, 15.
See Brough, "Absolute Consciousness," pp. 304–6.

the datum cannot be temporally neutral; it *has* to be a present datum if it is to be around for apprehension and interpretation. Even if it is supposed to represent an elapsed phase of the inner object, it has to be present now to serve that function. And if the datum is present, where do we get any direct awareness of pastness, of the falling into absence which characterizes temporal objects? Consciousness is glutted with the present; the datum is temporally indigestible. We may interpret a datum as representing something just past, but the something just past is not, and cannot be, directly presented to us. We cannot break out to a direct awareness of the nonpresent.

Another difficulty is that the matter-form schema applied to the experiencing of inner objects is obviously an awkward complication and leads to an infinite regress. It forces us to put intermediaries between our inner objects, sensa and acts, and the consciousness that experiences them; the sensed sound would need a datum between itself and our sensing of it. But now this datum itself is sensed, and so needs another datum, and so on to infinity.

It should be obvious that one of the reasons Husserl tried this unsatisfactory approach was that he did not sufficiently distinguish between (a) temporal objects in the world and (b) inner temporal objects. He tried to handle (b) with tools that belong to (a).

So his explanation through the matter-form schema cannot be sustained, but what is to replace it? How is the experiencing of inner temporal objects to be correctly described? We must make a detour through Husserl's description of memory and imagination; certain themes that he develops there will be used for the correct analysis of immediate experience of temporal objects.

2. In perception we have an object present to us; in memory and imagination we re-present something. How does this re-presentation take place? We will discuss the problem chiefly in terms of remembering.

Spontaneously, we think remembering involves an internal image or picture, an idea of memory—we will call it the phantasm—which is taken to represent something that is no longer present to us, although it once was present. The phantasm is, somehow, a copy of the impressions or appearances of the thing. But the phantasm is a present datum; it is given here and now, and interpreted or recognized as an image. We take remembering to be a form of pictorial consciousness. Imagination is analogous, except that we do not take the phantasm as a picture of something once present as an impression.

Around the time of the *Logical Investigations*, in some of the early texts dealing with time, Husserl put forward just this kind of analysis of remembering. We find it in Numbers 7 to 10 and Number 15 of the supplementary texts in Boehm's edition of the *Lectures*. In mentioning this doctrine later, he refers to it as one he held "in the early years at Göttingen" (ZB, no. 41, p. 288).[12]

In Number 18 a new analysis is developed.[13] There are two important points in the new explanation: the first is what we might call the "two-track" structure of remembering, and the second is the removal of a present phantasm as an ingredient in memory.

(a) While we perform an intentional act, such as the act of perceiving a tree, we are also aware of the act and experience it. If E stands for the experiencing of the act and A_1 for the act, we have $E(A_1)$. When we remember the same tree, we relive the portion of our conscious life that was the original perceiving of the tree. We have a re-presentation of the act A_1. If re-presenting or remembering is symbolized by R, we have $R(A_1)$, and since the re-presenting or remembering itself is an act, we now have $E[R(A_1)]$. E is, of course, the present experiencing of the act of remembering (ZB, app. XII; see the early formulation of this, no. 45, p. 297, ll. 26–27).

In such re-presentational consciousness we have two tracks of temporality. We have the living experience E, but we also have, nested within the temporality of E, the re-presented flow of A_1. The flow of time-consciousness can transcend itself in such a way as to allow another flow to be present within itself (no. 45, p. 299; no. 54, p. 369).

To be more exact, and to suggest a refinement of Husserl's own formulas, the symbolic expression for remembering should be: $E_2\{R[E_1(A_1)]\}$. For when I reproduce a prior act in memory,

12. See no. 46, p. 311, ll. 3–6. In no. 15, p. 173, Husserl says, "My interpretation is the following: The usual remembering is a pictorial apperception, just like expectation." This is an Aristotelian position; see *De memoria et reminiscentia* 1. 450b11–451a17.

13. Boehm says this text may date from 1901. See p. 137, n. 1. Perhaps this is too early. No. 18 differs a lot from no. 15, which is dated December 20, 1901. No. 18 is the last in section I of the manuscripts edited by Boehm, and the first in section II is dated 1904. Could no. 18 have been written between 1901 and 1904?

I also reproduce my original experiencing of that act. I reproduce my living through the act. The same structure would hold if I remember myself as going through a state of sensation, as opposed to performing an act; letting S stand for a state of sensibility, we have: $E_2\{R[E_1(S_1)]\}$.

In his writing on the problem of other minds, Husserl will use the two-track structure of remembering as an analogy to describe how other minds can be present to my own. He will be able to claim that even a single consciousness transcends itself, since in its present station it can re-present a prior portion of its own life; analogously, and with the appropriate qualifications made, it is possible for a consciousness to entertain within itself the presence of another mind's life.

The re-presenting and reliving of a past act should not be confused with reflection on the act. In a reflection we thematize an act that we are still living through; remembering does not thematize a past act, but revivifies it and goes through it again— at a distance, with a sense of its otherness to the present process of remembering.

Obviously, reliving a past act in memory involves making the object of that act present again as remembered (app. XII). In re-presenting my perception of the tree by my window, I re-present the window tree as well, as it appeared at that time. Using Husserl's formulas, if V_1 stands for re-presenting an object which was once perceived in the act A_1, it is an essential law that $R(A_1) = V_1$.

(b) In this new explanation, remembering does not involve having a present phantasm which is interpreted as the picture of something past. The schema of matter and form, datum and apprehension, does not apply any longer to memory. Instead, "The earlier consciousness is reproduced completely" (no. 18, p. 181). Memory is not a pictorial consciousness, with a phantasm serving as the picture; instead, the pictorial consciousness and memory are now contrasted to one another. When we see a picture of a historical event,

> we have a pictorial representation, the perceptual presentation gives us an analogue, one we are aware of as a picture. In memory this is not the case. "The theater all lit up"—this is not a more or less analogical picture, we don't mean something similar to what appears now; we mean what appears itself; the appearing theater, that which appears with the character of being now. Isn't this representation through identity, and not through mere pictorial similarity? (no. 18, p. 184; for a later statement, see APS, p. 305).

In remembering, what is present now is a reliving of a former part of my own stream of consciousness, with the sensibility and the objects that were present to me then. The sensibility and the objects are "inside" the repeated track of conscious life; they are not in my present track as something that serves as a picture for the past (no. 41, pp. 289–93). All I experience immediately now, in my present track of consciousness, is the reproduction, the reliving of my former track of awareness. Memorial consciousness involves two tracks, two "nows" with one nested inside the other: "I do not just exist and just live, but a second ego and a second entire life of an ego is made known, is mirrored in my life, i.e. is represented in my present remembering" (*APS*, p. 309).

I remember an explosion by having myself perceiving the explosion. This is the only way I can have the same explosion-event again. I do not have a picture of the explosion, for a pictorial consciousness is single-tracked. When I perceive a picture, there is a present datum which is interpreted, by an act which is also present, as the image of something else; but the time-stream of what is imaged is not nested inside as a second track.

Memory essentially requires being aware of the otherness betweeen the reproduced track and my present act of reproducing; if I lose this awareness of difference and absence, I slip into hallucination: "This would no longer be remembering, but a (hallucinatory) perception of what is past, but not as past" (*ZB*, no. 18, p. 182).[14]

Imagination has to be explained in the same way. In imagination I do not have a sensible phantasm which is like a sensuous datum except that I interpret or apprehend it as an image or picture of something. Rather, in imagination I reproduce myself

14. There is a neat progression on the issue of phantasm and memory in no. 18. (*a*) On p. 179, l. 26, to p. 180, l. 12, Husserl starts to see problems with the phantasm in remembering; he has accepted it until now. (*b*) On p. 182 he still calls for a "picture" (l. 25), even though he is clear that memory is a two-track consciousness. (*c*) On p. 182, l. 35–36, he admits the picture here is not an ordinary one. (*d*) On pp. 183, ll. 31–36, 184, ll. 16–24, and 185, l. 31 to 186, l. 2, he clearly admits that remembering is not a type of pictorial consciousness; in memory we have the same datum we once perceived, not a picture of it. The process in Husserl's thought is a gradual recognition of the difference between remembering and the pictorial consciousness. They had been mistaken, philosophically, for one another.

as perceiving and acting. There are two tracks of consciousness again, one nested inside the other, and my phantasm is within the inside, reproduced track. It is not a present datum pure and simple (*EP II*, § 44, pp. 112–13).

While I am actually perceiving something, I have a sensuous datum or an impression which I apprehend or interpret as being the appearance of a tree or a house. The matter-form schema works in ordinary perception. But when I reproduce a prior track of my conscious life, is there a datum to be apprehended or interpreted? Is there a datum between my present act of remembering and the stretch of conscious life that I reproduce? To use the formula $E[R(A_1)]$, is there a datum between R and A_1? Obviously, there is not. Here we just have the sheer, immediate adhesion of one track of consciousness against the other. No mediating datum or impression is needed. The same is true in the case of imagination.

As long as we expect a phantasm as the datum and picture for memory and imagination, we do demand a sensuous impression which must be apprehended or interpreted, and we do try to use the matter-form schema. But a closer analysis of memory and imagination shows that this is not needed, and that it would lead to contradiction.

With his new description of memory, Husserl reaches a kind of constitution that does not need the schema of matter and form, content versus apprehension. The constitution of an object as remembered does not need the schema.

To summarize Husserl's new position: when I remember the Nymphenburg gardens I also remember myself walking in the gardens and perceiving them. I could not remember them in any other way; I must re-present myself when I re-present them. But this is not a pictorial consciousness. When I do enjoy a pictorial awareness—when I experience a tableau as a painting of Wellington—I do not copicture myself or re-present myself as a mediator necessary to making the picture appear as picture. The pictorial consciousness does not require two tracks. It takes place in the immediate present.

(*c*) Husserl's analyses may help resolve some dilemmas concerning dreams, memory, and imagination.

Dreaming is a two-track state of consciousness, even though the inner track is so dominant that the outer, encompassing track practically loses its self-possession. When we remember ourselves dreaming—and the concept of dreaming can be analyzed only within the context of remembering our dreams—we go into a three-track structure, and we (1) remember ourselves as (2) experiencing ourselves as (3) going through something at a distance.

This structural explanation of dreaming is based on the textures of inner time. The alternative is to try to find marks or criteria in the content of the dream that serve as symptoms that we are dreaming: for example, the incoherence and discontinuity of dreams as opposed to wakeful experience. But such criteria never explain how we can immediately recognize "that it was only a dream." A special kind of reflection is required for that.

If there are dreams that cannot be remembered, perhaps in them the outside track does fuse with the inside one. Then no reflection is possible, not even the subsequent reflection and self-control made possible by remembering; the self is the victim of its images. Such fusion may have effects in our subsequent conscious life, but they are effects of causes, not the consequences of motives that we can evaluate and manage to some extent. It is probably the case that most experiencing, including dreams, takes place on a continuum stretching away from this extremity of fusion. That we can remember a dream indicates that we had some distance from it when it took place, i.e., the dream was a two-track awareness.[15]

As regards memory and imagination, Husserl knows that he differs with the general trend of modern thought: "Reproduction is not, as Hume and the sensualistic psychology since Hume believe, something like a copy of a perception or a weaker echo of it, but a fundamentally new kind of consciousness" (*APS*, p. 325). If memory and imagination were the Hobbesian "decaying sense" (*Leviathan*, I, § 2) or faded impression, we would need some mark or criterion in the idea itself to distinguish it from perception; loss of force and vivacity is usually suggested. But this is a relative matter, depending sometimes on our dispositions or the situation in which we experience, and we are left unsure whether we are perceiving or only remembering or imagining things, let alone dreaming them. Husserl's structural explanation shows that memory and imagination are new kinds of conscious life and new forms of transcendence; they are not determined by attributes in the content of our experience.

Such differences in kinds of intending come to light when

15. Husserl may have a different interpretation; he seems to say we lose our distance when we dream. See *APS*, pp. 308–9, and also pp. 499–500.

we get used to reflecting on intentionality and on correlative modes of appearance. Trying to explain differences in appearance exclusively by appealing to differences in the content of what is experienced betrays a failure to change the natural, world-directed focus of mind.

3. Husserl's new analysis of remembering and imagining allowed him to resolve the vexing problem of how retentional consciousness works. But he did not immediately apply his new principles to the description of actual, nonrepresentational experiencing. There was a period of time in which he had established the two-track structure for memory, but still thought a kind of phantasm or present datum was needed for "primary memory" or retention to apprehend. For example, in Number 33, which Boehm says was used in 1905, and in Number 39, which comes from a course given in 1906–7, Husserl admits that only the immediate now-phase of a temporal object presents a sensum (*Empfindung*), but he also postulates a "phantasm" (no. 33, pp. 233–34) or a "reverberation" (*Nachklang,* no. 39, pp. 280–81) of the sensum as a datum representing elapsed phases.[16]

So he sees there is a difference between the datum for the current impression and the datum for its associated "primary memories," but he is unable to do philosophical justice to the difference—unable to give it its proper philosophical expression—because he still feels the need for a current datum for all intentions. Of course, to call the datum for primary memories a phantasm or reverberation instead of a sensum does not at all avoid the inconveniences which, we have seen, follow upon postulation of a temporally neutral datum: in either case, the datum is a present datum and does not account for the sense of pastness.

4. In Number 44 Husserl sees difficulties with this view (p. 296, ll. 4–11). At the beginning of Number 47 he again raises the problem of the status of a sensory content or datum in the consciousness that has elapsed from immediate perception to primary or fresh memory: "One speaks of the reverberating, the fading, etc., of the sensuous representants, when true perception goes over into fresh remembering. But according to these studies it is clear that the faded, reverberating contents are no

---

16. ZB, no. 39, p. 280, nn. 1 and 2; p. 283, nn. 2, 3, 4. Originally, Husserl spoke of "representation" here, but later changed it to "retention" or other words.

longer sensuous contents at all, and are not 'contents' in the original sense. It's hard to make sense here. What is the talk of 'contents' getting at?" (p. 311). A few lines later he starts working out his new and final position.

He now simply denies that there is any content or datum for elapsed phases of the temporal object. He had tried to say that as each phase of the object elapsed, a datum was still available —a kind of phantasm or reverberation or decaying sense— which was newly interpreted by the primary memory as a profile of what is just past. Now he denies the need for this problematic and indigestible datum. When a phase elapses, the impressional consciousness that enjoyed its direct presence also elapses: it turns into and is revivified as a primary memory or retention ("retention" appears as a term in no. 50; see above, § 52). Since the former impressional consciousness is kept alive as a primary memory, the phase correlative to it is also kept around in the present, but in a new profile, in a new mode of temporal orientation, as just past.

The elapsed phase of the object is kept alive "inside" the revivified impressional consciousness, inside the primary memory. There it is now intuited "as past," and consciousness breaks into the direct awareness of pastness. It was prevented from doing so as long as we insisted on the need for a present datum that would be interpreted as a profile of the past.

Husserl is able to conceive of primary memory this way because he had already taken secondary remembering in much the same fashion. Removal of the phantasm as a present picture in secondary remembering is a prelude to removal of a faded or decaying sense datum in primary memory. Textually, he appeals to the model of secondary remembering and imagination just before he registers his new theory of primary memory, and he compares the latter to the former (no. 47, pp. 312, 317–18; no. 54, p. 376).

§ 58. AN IMPLICATION OF HUSSERL'S NEW THEORY OF PRIMARY MEMORY

IF NO SENSUOUS DATUM has to intervene between awareness and the elapsed phases of an inner temporal object, none has to come between the present central awareness and the actual now-phase of the object. Any vestige of a datum or sensuous content between an inner temporal object and the awareness we have of it is washed away. There is an immediate adhesion between this awareness and inner objects. This awareness turns out, in a few pages, to be the "absolute" consciousness that differentiates itself from inner objects. There is then no mediating sensuous datum between absolute consciousness and the inner objects it experiences.

This is the second case of immediate adhesion between consciousness and object we have encountered; the first was that between the act of secondary remembering and the reproduced acts that are revivified within it. We now have two cases of constitution which do not require the distinction between apprehension and a datum or content of apprehension. However, the schema of datum versus apprehension is still valid, and will continue to be valid, in Husserl's descriptions of how we perceive spatial things in the world. Recall the distinction between (a) things in worldly time, (b) inner objects, sensa and acts, and (c) the absolute, time-constituting consciousness. There is immediate adhesion and no intermediate datum for interpretation between (b) and (c). But a datum for the perception of (a) is still needed, and is provided by the sensa in (b). These sensa continue to be animated by the intentional acts which are also objects in (b).

§ 59. Primary and Secondary Memory

Although primary memory, in its first conception, is modeled on secondary memory, especially in the matter of removing a present datum, the structures of the two modes of consciousness remain essentially different.

1. **Primary memory or retention** is a part within the absolute flow of consciousness, the level in which experiencing of acts and sensa goes on. Secondary memory is an act, a full-blown inner object, which is itself experienced. Retention is a part of (c), secondary memory a member of (b).

2. Primary memory is part of an ongoing experience. It remains continuous with the present, and is actually a part of the present segment of inner awareness. The phases given through primary memory have never dropped into forgetfulness or fallen out of mind. The same individual temporal object that was presented in them is still being presented in the actual now-phase; its phases form a continuum with the now-phase at its

edge. A remembered act or portion of the flow of consciousness, on the other hand, has fallen into forgetfulness and is discontinuous with the present. It is defined as that which is brought back, repeated, or represented, a second track of the temporal flow distinguished from the present flow of experience.

3. Since secondary remembering repeats a portion of conscious life, it can be achieved only because of the temporal flow in unrepeated experience. The structure of retention and protention permits this immediate flowing to happen, and so primary memory is a condition of the possibility of secondary remembering.

4. Retention is our first and most elementary intuition of the past. Since no central impression exists without its comet's tail of retentions, every ongoing experience is infected with a sense of pastness. All presences are experienced as slipping away; even in the living present, what we have is taking its temporal distance from us (*APS*, pp. 317, 325). Still, this intuition of pastness is different from the more radical past given in secondary remembering, where we are presented not with something slipping away, but with what has slipped. The object is given as more distinctly over and against us; it is more thoroughly objective.

Husserl attributes great importance to secondary memory in the constitution of objects. What is given in immediate experience, even with retention and protention, is "still not an 'object'" (p. 327). The consciousness without memory cannot appreciate what it perceives as something it can go back to, repeatedly, through remembering it; it cannot perceive "objects" as such (p. 326). Husserl agrees with Kant that reproduction and recognition are required for the sense of objectivity, and says these capacities are the work of remembering, not of direct perception (*APS*, p. 327; *ZB*, app. IX). Without remembering there can be no "life of the mind" (*Geistesleben*), no life involving recognition, evaluation, willing, and action (*APS*, p. 326).

Remembering also makes us notice the *presence* of what is perceived; it makes us aware of its temporal dimension. When I am busy with an object in the present, I am busy with the object, not with its temporal station. The temporal dimension is there, but is not noticed. When I remember the object, its pastness is thematically given and cannot be overlooked unless I fall into a hallucination. The power to remember brings the temporal dimension into focus and makes it possible for us, during the actual presence of an object, to thematize its presence: we are now capable of appreciating, because of the memories we have of other perceptions, that this object can and will be absent at some time, and available only in memory.

5. Within an actual segment of conscious life, all the parts that phenomenology distinguishes are moments. The central impression and its retentions and protentions are moments to each other, and so are the now-phase and its elapsed and coming phases. We can isolate a single central impression, or a single retention, only abstractly. They are not singly given. Furthermore, it makes no sense to ask how many retentions there are in a given segment, because they form a continuum, and distinguishing them is the same sort of process as breaking up any continuous manifold. But remembering is chopping the life of consciousness into pieces, for it isolates portions of the flow and presents them by themselves. They are experienced as independent wholes in memory. In this process, we come to orient ourselves in our conscious history. We register parts, relationships, motives, and set up patterns of self-understanding. We attempt a rational attitude toward ourselves. Further, self-possession through memory is both played off against and implicated with expectation and plans; we remember in order to perform. Our attempts at registration stretch into the future.

§ 60. SELF-AWARENESS AND REFLECTION

WHILE WE PERCEIVE THINGS, frame judgments, or perform other intentional acts, it is always possible to turn our attention reflectively on our acts and sensations. Reflection is made possible by the structure of inner time-consciousness. In perceiving (a) something in the world, I also experience (b) my act of perceiving and its ingredient sensations, which are constituted as inner objects; my act of perceiving can give away to an act of reflection which focuses on the act of perceiving or its sensations. The act of reflection is itself an inner object and, like all inner objects, is experienced and constituted by (c) the absolute flow of inner time-consciousness.

We can reflect on our own acts and sensations because of their endurance through time.[17] An act or sensation is not just

17. ZB, app. VIII: "Without this [viz., the elapsing of cental impressions into retentions] a content would not be thinkable as a lived experience [Erlebnis]; lived experience, in principle, would otherwise not be given to the subject as a unity—nor could it be

present in its emergent now-phase; elapsed phases are also there in profile. We can be passively solicited by them, and may respond actively by performing the reflective act of focusing on the inner object as it is still present in these elapsed but functioning phases. The inner object has never fallen out of mind into the absence of forgetfulness; from being actually experienced it can slip directly into being the object of reflection. As ordinary consciousness moves on, it is always incipiently reflective this way.[18]

But inner objects, although immanent in consciousness, still stand over against the domain of pure immanence, the domain of absolute consciousness. Even acts of reflection are not part of absolute consciousness. Reflection is an inner object in (*b*), one that focuses on other inner objects in (*b*); it is experienced by the flow in (*c*). Also the flow in (*c*) makes reflection possible by holding the elapsed phases of all the objects in (*b*).

Besides this kind of reflection, Husserl claims that still another self-awareness is possible within (*c*). The flow in (*c*) is so structured that besides allowing the units in (*b*) to be experienced, it also allows a manifestation of the flow to itself (ZB, § 39; no. 54, pp. 378–82). This peculiarity of the absolute consciousness cuts off any infinite regress of underlying flows that would otherwise be required to explain our awareness of each. The inner objects in (*b*) need the flow (*c*) to be experienced, but flow (*c*) is aware of its own self, so no further levels are necessary.

How does the absolute flow of consciousness appear to itself? The only parts within this flow are the central impression, retentions, and protentions. Each of these is correlated to a particular now-phase of the inner object in (*b*). Each retention is a revivified central impression, and by being revivified it keeps alive its corresponding now-phase in the appropriate profile.

The awareness in (*c*) is dual. There is experience of the inner object being presented through the continuum of phases, but there is also awareness of the retentions as they build up a continuum. This is analogous to remembering, in which we are aware of the remembered theater and also of our perceiving in the theater of that time. The difference is that in remembering

---

given—and so it would be nothing" (my translation). See also app. IX.

18. See Gerd Brand, *Welt, Ich und Zeit* (The Hague: Nijhoff, 1955), § 12, and K. Held, *Lebendige Gegenwart* (The Hague: Nijhoff, 1966), pp. 104–12. See *APS*, p. 320.

there are two tracks of consciousness, and the "now" of the theater is contrasted to the "now" of remembering. In the immediate awareness that goes on in (c), retentions are copresent with the central impression.

Shall we say that retentions are simultaneous with the central impression? This would not be correct; simultaneity is a concept applicable to units in (a) and (b). Two explosions can be simultaneous, and so can a sound and a color sensation. Retentions and the central impression they attach to are together, but not simultaneous (see above, § 52). Their togetherness is not in time because it is the condition for time. We naturally want to use terms like "simultaneous," "before," and "after" to describe this togetherness—and the separation which is also involved in it—but such terms are not really applicable; as Husserl observes, we do not have names for these wholes, parts, and relations (ZB, § 36; no. 54, p. 371). Even calling the process of inner time a "flow" is metaphorical.[19]

The turn of mind that focuses on absolute consciousness and distinguishes its parts is, of course, the critical phenomenological reflection which reaches the living present and, among other things, is able to carry out the phenomenology of the phenomenological reduction (see above, §§ 53, 56). It is different from ordinary reflection, which manages to focus on the inner objects in (b); it is also different from the reflections carried on in ordinary descriptive phenomenology, which also look at the inner objects in (b), but do not get into the parts and structure of (c), the absolute time-constituting consciousness. That is the exclusive preserve of the final phenomenological reduction.

§ 61. THE LIVING PRESENT

THE ACTUAL SEGMENT of conscious life, the *lebendige Gegenwart,* is an absolute concretum because everything happens within it: remembering, expecting, perceiving, judging, being passively affected, and even doing phenomenology—all are

19. ZB, no. 54, p. 371, l. 13. See Ms C 2 I, 1931, p. 5: "All these expressions, which involve the words temporalization [*Zeitigung*], time, world, and also object, when they are not mundanely used, have a sense that first comes out when the transcendental-reductive method is systematically exercised; and so their sense is completely foreign to the natural language."

nested inside the living present, while it is not nested inside anything else. We cannot get down to anything more basic because all further divisions—into central impressions and retentions, for instance—are abstractive. The living present is the theater in which the whole spectacle of conscious life is available for phenomenological viewing. Even the past and future are present only inside it; the living present is a present for my past and future.[20]

During some of his lectures in the early 1920s, Husserl introduced an "apodictic reduction" as a methodological device to get to the living present.[21] It means limiting our phenomenological attention to the segment of consciousness actually at work, and "shutting off" our intending the future and past that stretch beyond it. This manoeuver is like the transcendental reduction in *Ideas I,* in which we bracket the world and its objects, then find them all again as phenomena inside the residue left by reduction; in the case of time, we bracket everything temporally outside the living present, then find it all again inside the present, since even the future and past, as well as forgetfulness, take place there.

In the transcendental reduction the world is transformed into phenomena in my stream of consciousness; in the apodictic reduction the whole stream of consciousness is transformed into phenomena within the living, flowing present. This present is stretched, containing the central impression, retentions, and protention; presence, absence, and identity go on even in this elemental place.

There is a certain philosophical naïveté in intending the past and future, just as there is naïveté in intending objects in the natural attitude.[22] In both cases we entertain a transcendence

20. See *PP,* app. XXIII, and Ms C 2 I, 1931, p. 1: "The primal phenomenon of flowing is the phenomenon of all phenomena. [Das 'Urphänomen' des Strömens ist das Phänomen aller Phänomene.]"

21. *EP II,* § 38, p. 80: "I now distinguish this transcendental reduction or phenomenological reduction from the apodictic reduction, which is bound up with it. The latter indicates a task first made possible through the phenomenological reduction. Before I exercise apodictic criticism, I must have a field for the criticism, here a domain of experience, and I first have this one—that of transcendental self-experience—thanks to the method of phenomenological reduction." See also § 46, p. 126, ll. 25–28; § 52, p. 164, ll. 20–30; § 53a, pp. 169–72. The apodictic reduction is more promised than achieved in the main text of *Erste Philosophie.* See also app. XXVIII, p. 467, ll. 24–36.

22. *EP II,* § 53a, pp. 170–72; *FTL,* § 102, p. 270; § 107c, pp. 288–89.

without accounting for it. Each reduction is an attempt not to deny the transcendence, but to understand it and describe its components of empty and filled intentions and their synthesis.

By performing the apodictic reduction we get to the living present, and are able to perform a criticism of descriptive phenomenology, the science that was made possible by the transcendental reduction. We enter into the phenomenology of phenomenology, or the phenomenology of the transcendental reduction. To put things in a schematic way, we might say that the concrete whole for the natural attitude is the world; the concrete whole for descriptive phenomenology is the stream of transcendental subjectivity; and the concrete whole for the phenomenology of phenomenology is the living present.[23]

The living, flowing present is the subject of many studies in Husserl's C manuscripts, which were written in 1927–33, and in other essays from this period.[24] It is hard to describe because to make it static is to destroy what it is, so words must be found to describe it as a continual flow; it can only be intuited in passing.[25] Some way must be found to describe how the central impression lapses into retention, and thus becomes other than the present and yet is recapitulated with the new central impression. This

23. On the living present as the final concretum, see Ms C 7 I, 1932, p. 5: "I am actual and concrete as the enduring present, that is my concrete being. [Wirklich und konkret bin ich als ständige Gegenwart, das ist mein konkretes Sein.]" Also C 13 III, 1934, pp. 6 and 11; C 17 I, 1931, p. 42: "The present is the 'absolute reality,' it is the most authentic reality as primitive temporality. [Die Gegenwart ist die 'absolute Wirklichkeit,' ist eigentlichste als urzeitigende.]" See EP II, app. XXVIII, pp. 466–67, where Husserl talks about making a reduction to this concrete presence.

24. Held's book, Lebendige Gegenwart, gives an excellent introduction to some problems in the C manuscripts, and provides many excerpts. Brand's Welt, Ich und Zeit is another important source. Thomas Seebohm has written two books dealing extensively with time-consciousness: Die Bedingungen der Möglichkeit der Transzendental-Philosophie (Bonn: Bouvier, 1962), and Zur Kritik der hermeneutischen Vernunft, but they do not deal specifically with the C manuscripts.

25. See Ms C 13 II, 1934, p. 9, where Husserl calls primitive temporality "a 'pre'-time [Vor-Zeit], which is not yet a form of objects for the ego which lives in this stream of consciousness. . . . As 'pre'-being it is unexperienceable and unutterable, and as soon as the unutterable and unexperienceable is shown—i.e., experienced and made theme of a statement after all—it is made ontic [ontifiziert]." See also Ms C 17 IV, 1932, pp. 7–8.

passing is more basic than even a single impression/retention—more basic than a single "part" in the conscious flow—because the impression/retention is a synthetic identity made possible by the othering and gathering at work in the passage. This original separation and reconciliation is the primitive event that underlies all objects. Consciousness on this level is not a thing or a substance; it is a happening. The deepest ingredient of consciousness is not a substance but an event; Husserl calls it *Urgeschehen* and *Ursein* (Ms C 2 I, 1931, p. 8).

Describing this is hard not only because sheer event escapes words, but also because it is the place where parts are engendered for the first time. The parts at work here are not supported by any more basic differences or parts. In the central impression "lies the source of all manifolds" (Ms C 4, 1930, p. 13). In dealing with higher-level phenomena, like things or other minds, we can always take the notion of difference for granted because these structures are built on more basic identities in difference. We can, for instance, identify one aspect against another by appealing to the different places and times from which we have perceived them; we can identify higher temporal objects by reference to different times in which we perceive and remember them. But in inner time and the living present we do not have any props. We reach difference and otherness in its most primitive form, and sameness in its most primitive form as well. Nothing can be taken for granted here because there is no level more basic to grant us anything. Here the same and other, identity and difference have to be caught in their most primitive separation from one another; and since language and names assume prior recognition of identity within difference, we seem to be left without words to describe the primitive othering of the same.

We always have the formal terms of presence, absence, and identity, and in fact we have used these to talk about inner time. But we need terms to show specifically how these formalities are realized in inner time and how they differ there from other realizations.

It should be remembered that the living present is complex not only in having a continuum of central impression, retentions, and protention; it also involves the phases of an inner object, phases which are correlated to the impression, retentions, and protention. The inner flow of consciousness is always accompanied by something it is an awareness of. We never have the naked form of time; inner time-consciousness is inner experiencing.[26] So as regards inner experience, Hume is correct: whenever we try to find a self, we always run into some inner object, a sensation or an act; the self on this level is the experiencing of these inner objects.[27]

The self is not a prepackaged whole; it is constituted as an identity within differences. For example, when I remember myself doing something, the remembering and remembered self are recognized as the same, and the self on this level is the identity in these two ways of being present and absent. The self as agent of judging is different from the self as agent of perceiving, but both are ways of being for the same self. This self is also identified with the unity that comes to be in the living present, but the feeble self on this level is just able to enjoy sensations and is not even capable of appreciating their difference from him, since remembering is required for that. Still, it is my self.

The process of temporality in the living present is prior to the developed personal self. Husserl sometimes calls it anonymous, prepersonal, and automatic.[28] As identities within the life of consciousness, we owe our selves to it.

There are great problems here.[29] Are these structures truly intuited and registered, as Husserl claims, or are they constructs? How are identities constituted here? How do we resolve the paradox of a present that is both permanent and flowing? Is univocal discourse possible here without paradox? Or must we appeal to philosophical metaphor? Husserl is convinced that this domain can be explored with the univocal concepts of his rigorously scientific philosophy. He does not make idle claims, but only the publication of his manuscripts on time will allow us to see and judge what he has accomplished.

26. *APS*, § 27, p. 128, ll. 5–32; *ZB*, app. VI, pp. 153–54 in Churchill's translation.

27. *A Treatise of Human Nature*, bk. I, pt. II, § VI, ¶ 3. Of course, even though there never is an ego without inner experiences, this does not mean that the ego is just the sum of inner experiences. The self crystallizes and actualizes itself against the psychic stream of consciousness. But on the level of the living present, the self is just the form of inner time-consciousness.

28. Held, *Lebendige Gegenwart*, pp. 97–104, 118–22.

29. Part II of Held's book examines several of the "enigmas" (*Rätsel*) of inner time-consciousness.

§ 62. SPATIAL VERSUS TEMPORAL WHOLES

SPATIAL WHOLES, whether things or phantoms, must be distinguished from temporal wholes. Each has profiles appropriate to itself. The profiles of spatial wholes are disjunctive and exclusive, the profiles of temporal wholes are assimilative. A profile of a spatial object is the impression made by the object from a certain point of view. It does not contain in itself the other views the object provides to other viewpoints. Rather, it points toward these other looks of the thing; they can be acquired only outside the present point of view. Each look is exclusive of the others. When one is present the others are absent. There are no alternative points of view for an inner temporal object. There is only the present. All looks are available here, and only here. Elapsed looks are assimilated and still at work in the present; there is no other way we can have them.

This property of temporal wholes can be expressed formally. Suppose we are at the point of enjoying phase 4 of a temporal object. Profile 4 (phase 1), profile 4 (phase 2), and profile 4 (phase 3), along with anticipated phases, are copresent with the now-phase. This whole is a continuum. It is a concretum, and comprises what is given to the actual segment of conscious life. Call it continuum$_4$.

When we come to enjoy phase 5, we include profile 5 (phase 4), and also profile 5 (phase 3), profile 5 (phase 2), profile 5 (phase 1), and anticipated phases. This is a new continuum, a new whole and concretum. Call it continuum$_5$.

As each now-phase succeeds another, we engender a continuum of continua$_{1,2,3,4,5}$ . . . .[30] What had been a whole becomes assimilated as a part of the new whole. What had been a concretum becomes assimilated as an abstractum in the new totality. Continuum$_4$ is not available anywhere except as assimilated into continuum$_5$, and subsequently into further wholes as they arise. Each profile in continuum$_4$ is also only available in this way. In this respect temporal profiles differ from spatial ones, which do not assimilate one another.

For example, when we are at now-phase 5, phase 3 is only available under profile 5 (phase 3). But phase 3 had originally

30. See ZB, no. 32, p. 231, ll. 28–31; no. 33, p. 233, ll. 3–4; no. 53, p. 365, l. 6 to p. 366, l. 20.

been assimilated into the concretum surrounding phase 4; inside continuum$_4$ it was present as profile 4 (phase 3). When we move on to phase 5, the concrete continuum$_4$ becomes assimilated into continuum$_5$, so profile 5 (phase 3) is an assimilation and new perspective on profile 4 (phase 3) as well. That is, profile 5 (phase 3) presents phase 3 as having gone through profile 4 (phase 3). It does not present phase 3 immediately, but as having traversed the continuum of profiles it must go through to get to its present one. Phase 3 is thus profiled in its recession from the actual present; the change in a temporal object must be presented in its presence.

There are boxes inside boxes in temporal constitution, and they melt into one another. Husserl says each whole continuum$_x$ becomes profiled in the motion of temporal consciousness: "The whole continuity of earlier profiles undergoes profiles once again" (ZB, no. 39, p. 276).

We have developed the formal structure according to which an inner temporal object, like a sensation or act, is experienced. But the experiencing of such an object is itself temporally extended, and so its parts are assimilated into one another in the same way. The parts of the experiencing are the central impression, retentions, and protention.

The segment$_3$ of conscious life involving the central impression$_3$ and its retentions and protention is a whole and a concretum; when we move on to the next segment$_4$, the whole becomes assimilated as a part and an abstractum in the new concrete whole. Both the inner temporal object and the experiencing of an inner temporal object are thus assimilative wholes, not disjunctive and exclusive as spatial objects are.

Because a spatial object is experienced as having other profiles besides those given in perception, it has a kind of transcendence to experience which is not found in the immediate experience of temporal objects, where everything is assimilated into what is now present. The transcendence of spatial objects motivates and justifies the epoché and transcendental reduction in *Ideas I*; the assimilative character of temporal experience lets the life of consciousness escape the epoché and remain as a residuum for the transcendental reduction. It is still available as a field on which we can frame judgments.

§ 63. PRESENCE AND THE PRESENCED IN INNER TIME-CONSCIOUSNESS

AN INNER OBJECT, a sensum or act, appears as an identity in a manifold of temporal phases. Each phase appears first in a central impression as a now-phase, then is retained and continues to appear through a series of profiles: profiles 1, 2, 3, 4, 5, 6 (phase 1).

Question: You once said, "The only time a phase is not given through some profile or other is when it is being immediately enjoyed in its direct presence, as a now-phase" (above, p. 142). I ask, why is its actuality as a now-phase not just another profile among many? Why is it not one among the temporal profiles within which the phase appears as an identity? You seem to violate your own rules about identities in manifolds, for here you take the identity—the phase—as something which is first given "nakedly" and subsequently presented clothed in profiles. You make the identity one of the members of the manifold through which it appears. Didn't you say this cannot be done?

Response: What you describe as an exception to the normal rules of identities within manifolds is indeed the case in inner time-consciousness. If an inner temporal object were infected with spatiality, if its "now-phase" were a "side" or "aspect" that might be intuitively present many times over again, in different profiles each time, your objection would hold. We would have to distinguish the phase from the profile of its present actuality, because we could have the phase again later in another actuality; we could go back and look at the same phase (side or aspect) again.

But the peculiarity of inner time is precisely the removal of this sort of difference between the actual phase and its actual presence. We can't have the phase in another actuality. Its actuality is unique. The profiles that are subsequently engendered in retention occur because that unique actuality gets repeated or retained continuously, and there can be many repetitions or retentions, so a difference arises between one profile and another, and between the phase and its profiles. Some transcendence is already at work in retention. But repetition or retention can never make the present actuality alive again, and so no such difference or transcendence intervenes between a now-phase and its actuality. **An instant never holds center** stage twice.

Let us amplify this with images. There are two pictures one might have in the mind's eye when thinking about inner time-consciousness. The first probably captivates those who approach the subject by reading Husserl, the second those who come through Heidegger.

1. In the first picture: there are inner objects, sensa and acts. Each inner object appears through a manifold of temporal phases. Over against the temporal phases is the flow of absolute inner time-consciousness, the sequence of central impression, retentions, and protention. The absolute flow (*c*) is pictured as a regular stream of consciousness; it resembles our ordinary stream of moods, feelings, and acts in (*b*), except that it is more elemental.

It is easy to see why this picture predominates among Husserlians: Husserl pried level (*c*) loose from level (*b*) with great difficulty, and the former always kept the flavor of the latter.

In this picture we imagine a now-phase, and over against it a central impression "looking" at it.

2. But we might also picture this as: the now-phase—shining; and: the elapsed phase shining—shining again.

What difference is there between the now-phase and its shining? What difference is there between the presenced and its presencing? What difference is there between the now-phase and its actuality? Not a difference like any other.

But doesn't the now-phase shine for someone who sees it? To say that would be to project a built-up self into the conditions that found the self. This shining is more elemental than full perception. This is the anonymous, prepersonal presencing which must come to pass as a condition for feeling, perceiving, remembering, judging, as presenced to the self.

This sheer passive shining is being truthful in the most elemental way. Ontology: being truthful.

In this picture we replace "central impression" by "shining," and we replace the retention of an elapsed phase by a "new shining" of the original shining.

In the Husserlian picture we may wish to think abstractly and detach the form of inner time-consciousness from its content. This would yield the form of primal impression plus retentions and protention; and we must keep in mind that this form always has to have a content presenced in it. In the Heideggerian picture the analogous abstractive detachment is to isolate the shining, plus the shining again of elapsed shines, plus the awakening of the shining to come. This is the form of inner time-presencing; it is perpetually energetic, and separates and gathers itself. Of course, in this form, something shines; we must keep in mind that the form of shining is an abstractum and needs a content which shines in it.

As the shining continues to take place, what shines gradually differentiates itself from the life of shining, and the self which enjoys what shines consolidates itself too.[31] But the event of shining never stops, no matter how forgotten and overlooked it becomes when the self acquires bigger things to play with.

§ 64. HERMENEUTICS

BY ELIMINATING THE PHANTASM and allowing consciousness a direct presence of the past, in retention as well as in remembering, Husserl opens the door to the conception of man as existent in history. Heidegger and Gadamer advance Husserl's insight through their exploration of hermeneutic experience.

Husserl's move shows that the past is not something to be reconstructed out of materials which are atomically present. Such an inconvenience would follow if we had access to the past only through present data. Past and present would be disjunct pieces and human being, caught up in only one of those pieces, the present, would have to try to manufacture the other out of materials quite unlike it. No sense of pastness could directly appear.

In fact we live constantly in the atmosphere of the past. The Dead Sea scrolls, the fields and bridge at Sharpsburg, temple ruins in the Yucatan, and Euclid's *Elements* are not things that we interpret as indication signs of the past. They are perceived as old and venerable realities, present as historical and ancient, their pastness not inferred but intuited. And even new things arise either as continuations of or as innovations against what has gone before. The present is not separated, piecelike, from the past, but emerges "momentarily" continuous with it.

31. *Being and Time*, trans. J. Macquarrie and E. Robinson (New York: Harper and Row, 1962), § 72, p. 427. §§ 65–66 show that *Zeitigung* is beyond clock and calendar time, and develop what Husserl discovered as the absolute sphere of inner time-consciousness in 1908–9.

Although the past is always around, it remains to be appropriated (*Being and Time*, § 74, ⊄ 9; § 75, ⊄ 6; § 76, ⊄ 6). Until its possibilities are actualized and framed, it is just vaguely there; in that inauthentic state it is not truthfully effective as past, nor actually present as itself. The inclination to separate past and present arises in such inauthentic existence. When appropriation of the past fails to take place, the vapid present seems detached from what has gone on before, and one tries to "free" the modern and the new from the "lifeless" grip of history (§ 75, ⊄ 8). Present, past, and future fall apart, and the self with them. For what is rootlessly achieved in this way is not worth reappropriating later, and has neither future nor persistence.

Although the languidly available past makes human being inert, it is necessary as a condition for authentic appropriation; for the vague and heteronomous state of a tradition is the setting within which its truthfulness can be actualized again by those who are capable of doing so (§ 68a, ⊄ 7). In bringing this about they act not as solitary **geniuses**, but in service of the charged and structured process which gives them their potential. Ultimately, they act in response to the goodness which this process reflects.

Hermeneutic experience occurs in the fine arts, science and mathematics, farming, in the use of tools, in skills, in clubs and organizations, families, religion, politics, warfare, styles of clothing, medicine, in liking to live in a certain town, and in other ways of being in the natural attitude. It also occurs in philosophy, and we will be able to examine how it does so after we have shown the characteristics of philosophical judgment.

7 / Raising Questions about Appearances

THERE ARE FOUR SECTIONS IN *Ideas I*. The first deals with the problem of essence, the second tries to move from a nonphilosophical attitude to the consciousness appropriate to phenomenology, the third discusses phenomenological method and presents some basic structures of consciousness, and the fourth examines the theme of evidence. Section 2, with its transition into philosophical consciousness, operates with the triad of the world, the material thing, and the cogito. These three elements provide the context, motive, and object of the move into the philosophical attitude.

§ 65. THE WORLD

WHAT IS "THE WORLD"? Ordinary experience presents the world as extended indefinitely in time and space; I do not and cannot encounter spatial or temporal borders to the world I experience. The world includes many objects and many different kinds of objects: inorganic things, plants, animals, men, and other sorts of things as well, some hard to classify. It includes things directly present to me, but also things marginally present or totally absent. It even includes things that will always be absent, in fact, from me and from all men. Within the world it is possible for me to move my focus from certain things which are present to others which are only marginal or are totally absent; when this happens the things originally present become marginal or absent. This world also includes values, goods, instruments of use, friends and enemies, ugly and beautiful things (*Ideas I*, § 27; *PP*, § 6).

These varieties in kinds of beings, modes of givenness, and values are all present to me when I do what comes naturally. But another kind of world arises in response to a peculiar activity I can carry out, the work of doing arithmetic. This work produces a world of numbers which is different from the original world, in that the number world is there only as long as I do arithmetic. I do not have to do anything so special or artificial to make the natural world come around for me, nor does the natural world emerge out of the background of a still more aboriginal world. The arithmetical world does not destroy the natural world; it is nested within the ordinary world and leaves it undisturbed, though out of focus, for the time we do arithmetic (*Ideas I*, § 28).

The world includes other men who have their own viewpoint on the world, without causing it to become a different world. The world can tolerate a diversity of views without ceasing to keep its identity. The world can also tolerate errors, illusions, and hallucinations without ceasing to be one and the same world (§ 29).

Correlated to the one world is a fundamental belief in that world, a *Weltdoxa*, the fundamental conviction of the thereness of the world (§ 30). This is not a particular act of consciousness —there is no identifiable moment at which it was acquired—but an underlying state of belief, a permanent conviction which remains intact even when errors are found. Errors and corrections, in fact, make sense only within this conviction of the world. It is the most basic conviction of consciousness—what could be more fundamental?—and all other particular convictions rest on it. It does not rest on anything else. It is a conviction peculiar to the world, different from a doxa correlated to particular things. It is not an expanded version of the belief I have in my desk or chair; the world is not a large thing, for it contains in a way things cannot, and is related to things in a way different from the way things are related to one another. And correlated to this one world, there is the one world-belief.

Other philosophers have asserted that there is one world. Aristotle says that even though the form of the world could be repeated elsewhere, there is only one world because all the matter is used up by this world: the elements move to their natural places, and so all the earth is here at the center, surrounded by the water, air, and fire (*De caelo* 1. 8–9).[1] This is one world without any relation to consciousness; it is one by elemental necessity. Aquinas says there is one world because it is made and governed by one God; it is subject to one plan and finality (*Summa theologiae* 1. 47. 3). This is a single world correlated to a single divine mind. Kant asserts there is one phenomenal world because of the exigencies of human consciousness. The forms of sensibility order everything into one space and time, and the idea of the world closes the chains of hypothetical syllogisms, encompassing all conditioned things in the unity of the unconditioned world (*Critique of Pure Reason* A. 405–20). Kant's world is single because of the order achieved by the forms and ideas of consciousness, which forms and ideas are not intuited but philosophically inferred as conditions of possibility for the exercise of science.

Husserl's one world is correlative to the single conviction of one world. It is characteristic of his differences with Kant that he appeals to something that can be given intuitively, the *Weltdoxa,* and not to elements of consciousness that must be postulated or constructed (*Ideas I,* § 30; *Crisis,* § 30; *PP,* § 11).

In the case of all these thinkers, the question about one or many worlds is decided not by an empirical investigation of how many we can find, but by determining how one is to talk, philosophically, about the widest context of what can be present to experience. For Husserl the widest context, the most encompassing whole for natural, nonphilosophical experience is the world, and the most fundamental component in natural experience is world-belief.[2] This world-belief does not, of course, fabricate the world, but is correlative to it.

Husserl claims there is no formal contradiction in asserting another world in addition to the one we have, but that it is "really" incoherent to speak of another; it would be like talking about two births for the same man. No rules of syncategorematic form or formal consistency are broken, but the content does not

1. Aristotle also gives an argument based on the claim that there can be only one moving principle for the cosmos. See *Metaphysics* 12. 8. 1074a31–38.

2. *PP,* § 7, pp. 67–68, and § 19; *EJ,* § 29, pp. 137–40. See also Husserl's remarks in an essay, "Grundlegende Untersuchungen zum phänomenologischen Ursprung der Räumlichkeit der Natur," in *Philosophical Essays in Memory of Edmund Husserl,* ed. M. Farber (New York: Greenwood, 1968), pp. 318, 324. The essay was written in 1934 and brings out intersubjective dimensions which are not as clear in the earlier works.

allow us to speak this way. The philosophical term "world" does not blend with "two, three, or many," but only with "one." "The world . . . does not exist as *an* entity, as an object, but exists with such uniqueness that the plural makes no sense when applied to it" (*Crisis*, § 37, p. 143; see also *Ideas I*, § 48). "This is the world; another world would have no meaning at all for us" (*Crisis*, § 71, p. 255). Any second world would also, qua world, be the encompassing horizon for experience, and as such it would merge with the one we have. And if this new world were claimed to be the world of certain other minds, then it would obviously be an experienceable world and as such would fit, in principle, into ours.

In asserting the impossibility of more than one world, Husserl is talking about the real world, but as correlated to consciousness—not as an individual thing but as the encompassing whole within which all things and modes of presence and absence take place. The world is intuitively given as the final and total background for things.

§ 66. WORLD-BELIEF AND EPOCHĒ

BY CONSIDERING THE WORLD as correlated to the underlying world-belief, we have taken a first step in mastering this belief, and the world, philosophically.

Husserl proposes that we imitate Descartes. We are not to doubt the world—for that changes the modality of our belief, and we are not free to do that unless reasons are given, and none are—but we *attempt* to doubt our conviction of the world.[3] We are free to attempt to doubt, even if we have no reasons for it. We can always arbitrarily adopt this much distance from any doxa. The outcome may be that we find that no reasons for doubting exist, but the ability to try is always there: "The universal attempt to doubt belongs to the realm of our perfect freedom" (*Ideas I*, § 31, p. 107). The attempt at doubting sets up a neutral attitude toward the conviction in question. It does not change the modality of the conviction, but suspends it for the time being and brackets the object of belief.

3. *Ideas I*, § 31; *Crisis*, § 69, p. 237; *PP*, § 37, p. 188. Husserl does not accuse Descartes of truly attempting to deny everything, but he says what Descartes does practically amounts to that. See *Ideas I*, § 31, p. 109: "One can say that his universal attempt at doubt is really an attempt at universal negation."

Husserl proposes that terms like "putting out of action" are best applied to neutralization of acts of consciousness, while "bracketing" is applied to neutralization of the object of the conviction. We put our acts out of action and we bracket the things, facts, attributes, and ultimately the world, which are the objectives of our acts (p. 110). He also introduces the term "epochē" as a name for neutralization (p. 109).

Neutralization is a peculiar move in regard to modality. After it is executed, we keep a neutralized certainty, a neutralized probability, a neutralized falsehood, a neutralized negation. The original modality of the conviction is not turned into a different modality by this step. The convictions are kept, but changed in a unique way; they become "transvalued."[4] Consciousness has the capacity to make this move and often does so in the quite ordinary step of attempting to doubt. But neutralization is not entirely the same as the attempt to doubt.

The move to neutrality is the nugget Husserl wants to pick from the attempt to doubt. He concedes the epochē could be reached in other ways: the attempt to doubt is employed "only as a device of method, to highlight certain points" which can be brought out through it (p. 107). He says, "We extract only the phenomenon of 'bracketing' or 'disconnecting,' which is obviously not limited to that of the attempt to doubt, although it can be detached from it with special ease, but can appear in other contexts also, and with no less ease independently" (p. 109).[5]

How does the epochē differ from the attempt to doubt?

The attempt to doubt is naturally performed in order to change the modality of our belief in a certain object or to

---

4. Husserl speaks of the "transvaluation" of the objects and the world (*Umwertung*); *Ideas I*, § 31, p. 109. Boehm mentions this in comparing Husserl and Nietzsche; see *Vom Gesichstpunkt der Phänomenologie* (The Hague: Nijhoff, 1968), pp. xv–xvi.

5. Husserl has strong words about the way some misunderstand his epochē. Some critics think it leaves us with "world-images" which we must try to compare against a "real" world. See *EP II*, app. XXX, pp. 481–82: "Those who make such objections do not know how naïvely they speak and think, they do not know how much they overlook or . . . push aside the concrete problematic on which all true philosophy depends. . . . It would be totally useless, it would be an empty argumentation in reply, if one wished to enter into such empty arguments, which are so far from the real issue. The only possible answer here is to build up phenomenology itself, according to its method, problematic, and concretely executed work."

reconfirm, with new reasons, what we already believe. The epochē is not performed to adjust our normal convictions this way; it is supposed to make us able to think about our natural beliefs as natural beliefs. The attempt to doubt is always performed in the service of our mundane convictions (*EP II*, § 42, p. 98). Neutralization as such can be an end in itself.

The disconnection from a convinced life effected in the attempt to doubt is carried out in order to return to the same life with better conviction; the epochē is supposed to initiate a new kind of cognitive life: "Through the abstention which inhibits this whole hitherto unbroken way of life a complete transformation of all of life is attained, a thoroughly new way of life" (*Crisis*, § 40, p. 150). "So when I cease to take myself as a child of the world [*Weltkind*], as a natural man—I then have ready an endlessly open field of a new kind of experience" (*EP II*, § 52, p. 166). The new life may also serve the ordinary life, but its value is not exhausted in this service. It is worth living for its own sake.

Epochē can be applied to particular convictions or, Husserl claims, to the underlying world-belief. When the latter is done we apply it in one stroke to all convictions nested within the world-belief, including those of mathematics. In *Ideas I* and *Cartesian Meditations* Husserl tries to begin philosophy by neutralizing world-belief; in other works he tries to do it piecemeal, applying the epochē gradually to individual convictions until the whole is covered (*EP II*, § 46). Sometimes he criticizes the approach of *Ideas I* (*Crisis*, § 43). But the invariant in all this, and the part that cannot be rejected, is the neutralization of natural belief. We have to step outside natural convictions and, without rejecting them, think about them as natural convictions if we are to do philosophy.

Philosophy defines itself as the question of what natural experience is, and so defines itself against natural experience. If man is the part of the world that lives with other men and has a world given in ordinary experience and opinion and science, philosophy is also the study of man as the subject and agent of ordinary life and science. Since the world is the encompassing whole given to man in doxa and in natural science, philosophy is, in the words of Francis Slade, also scrutiny of "the world in its human involvement." [6]

6. Slade mentions this in a short unpublished note called, "Socrates: The Nature of Philosophical Inquiry." This text has helped me very much in formulating the issues of the present chapter.

The intersection of man and the world is the process of natural experience/appearance, through which both man and world are constituted, and this process is the immediate subject for philosophy (*Crisis*, § 52; *PP*, § 41, pp. 207–8).

Because the philosophical attitude contemplates world-belief and ordinary opinion, as well as the sciences founded on them, it escapes from their domination. Phenomenology is not subject to any mundane convictions, not even the *Weltdoxa*. It cannot use any of them, not even those of the sciences, as premises in its argument (*EP II*, § 53a, p. 170; *Ideas I*, § 32). It has to generate its own argument as a self-enclosed whole. True, it "depends" on ordinary experience and convictions because it thinks about them, and what it says must cohere with them; but they persist in phenomenology as neutralized, without the power to dictate, in their terms, what should be said next. They are not honored by philosophy as its "axioms" or premises.

At the same time, phenomenology does not interfere with natural experience. The convictions of ordinary life and science are adjusted only by evidences proper to those convictions; beliefs in biology change with biological experience, beliefs in history change with historical experience, beliefs about one's job change with experience in it. Philosophy does not substitute for such evidences, nor for the effort required to bring them about. It does not give views of "how things really are" as a short cut to avoid the labor of evidence. The natural sciences and opinions retain their methodological independence over against philosophy: "Phenomenological explication does nothing but explicate the sense this world has for us all, prior to any philosophizing, and [which it] obviously gets solely from our experience—a sense which philosophy can uncover but never alter" (*CM*, § 62, p. 151; see also *PP*, § 37, pp. 191–92).

In the classical Greek understanding, man is constituted as living with other men in a political community; prepolitical or suprapolitical existence is not humane. Man has a world made present to him in the opinions of his society. Philosophy is thinking about these opinions, the experience that generates them, and the world, city, and man constituted thereby. Because it contemplates these things, philosophy is to some extent distinguished from them, but it does not cease to be humane, because it preserves political and ordinary things. However, it appreciates them in a way not available to someone who lives his life with others, in political society, without reflection. As Socrates was clearly aware, examining ordinary life carries a certain threat, not because such scrutiny is evil, but because it can be turned from true scrutiny to partisan attack. Instead of being philosophical inquiry it becomes an attempt to acquire political power; it then represents one part of the body politic, and not disinterested thought about it.

Husserl is not far from this conception of philosophy. He appreciates the world as given through doxa, and man as constituted by living in the element of belief and ordinary experience with other men. But there is one shift of emphasis. The society he sees as constitutive of men, and the subject of philosophical scrutiny, is the community of scientists, not a political community. Even when his phenomenology is expressed as a kind of hermeneutic, it is the tradition of science he examines, not the traditions of a political society (*FTL*, Introduction, pp. 1–10). When he addresses himself to a crisis in public life, it is the crisis of the community engendered by Western science (*Crisis*, § 6). Even the *Lebenswelt* is defined precisely as something different from science.

The equivalent of degenerate, "partisan" philosophy in Husserl is the tendency to let one mundane science or opinion take over the role of philosophy, which should be disinterested and transcendent to the whole of ordinary experience and science. It may be psychologism, mechanism, or a mathematization of nature and man, but in each case the science of a part is allowed to rule over the whole. The epoché is a device contrived by Husserl to prevent this from happening. It is also supposed to make us aware of the philosophical enterprise as a possibility available to us. By following his argument, and especially by grasping the sense of neutralization, we are supposed to secure the philosophical attitude and keep it uncontaminated.

Husserl admits we will have great difficulty in doing this: we tend to slip back into the natural attitude and delude ourselves into thinking we are still doing philosophy. It is hard to sustain the philosophical attitude, he says, because our natural tendency of mind is toward the mundane, and it takes effort and practice to counter this: "for the eye is habituated only to the objective" (*PP*, § 38, p. 194). The pull toward the natural attitude is like the pull toward partisan argument which is always a possibility for disinterested philosophical discourse.

However, Husserl claims, it is always within our freedom to neutralize our beliefs and thus initiate philosophy, just as it is always in our freedom to attempt to doubt anything.

This is a bold claim. Does everyone have it in his power to

neutralize and study his convictions philosophically? Are there conditions that must be met? Obviously Husserl presumes we must have learned to frame and verify judgments, and that we have come to recognize the difference between opinion and registration, before we do philosophy. He also presumes we have learned to verify "professionally," that is, that we have become habituated to science.

If we have become scientific, and if we follow the argument leading to the epochē, he presumes we can all achieve the disinterested philosophical attitude, provided we have the "will" to live an intellectual life of radical autonomy and responsibility (*EP II*, § 28, pp. 6–7). Husserl stresses the importance of this will. It expresses itself in a decision to live a life of complete intellectual self-justification. Every philosopher must make such a decision at some time; he is constituted as philosopher by it. It is, Husserl claims, a "self-creation," and no one can enter into philosophy without it (§ 30, p. 19). The decision rules the whole future of one's life (§ 28, pp. 6–8; § 48, pp. 143–44; § 50, pp. 155–56).

The decision and the will behind it are evoked by the ideal of an absolutely responsible and autonomous life (§ 28, p. 8; § 30, p. 25). This value can never become fully actualized; it remains a Kantian ideal, for individuals and for the community, but it gives sense to the progress that men make toward it in the history of thought, once they are put on the right road of philosophy by phenomenology's "fundamental meditations" (pp. 196–97, an essay on individual and corporate life lived in radical responsibility).

The structure of temporality, claims Husserl, allows a total decision, governing the rest of one's life, to be made; for the whole of life is latent in the living present. We are able to survey and master the whole of life, philosophically, because of its assimilation into the present. The decision to begin philosophy, with its similarity to a radical and total ethical decision, is related to the structure of inner time (§ 50).

Certain individuals make this decision and are enabled to enter the life of responsible thinking once phenomenology has cleared away several misconceptions which aborted earlier attempts at it. These individuals work as the "functionaries" of scientific humanity (*Crisis*, § 15, p. 71; *EP II*, p. 197). But their treasure and enjoyment are not private. Husserl says that once I become philosophical, I come to know that "what is best for me is the best for every man, and the demand [*Forderung*] for such a life must be made, by me, on each person, and by each person on himself; also, that I must try to prompt [*bestimmen*] each person to it and make him responsible for choosing such a life and living accordingly" (*EP II*, pp. 198–99). The ideal is that the human community should become a community of philosophers, since autonomous and responsible life, authenticity, is available, he claims, only through philosophy.

Philosophy's universality extends even to matters of ethics and value, since values and goods can be objectified and examined as true or not (*EP II*, p. 197). Only when this happens are they responsibly asserted and assumed, and since such objectification is the work of intelligence, phenomenology is able to provide a critical examination of the evidence appropriate to them.

Everyone who thinks at all exercises transcendental functions, and so can become philosophical (*Crisis*, § 58, p. 205). Hindrances to becoming philosophical are intellectual confusion, which Husserl hopes to have removed in principle, and a certain weakness of will. Husserl's expectation of philosophy for everybody is bred in the rationalist and Enlightenment tradition within which he thinks (*Crisis*, § 56, p. 197). It is very different from the Greek notion that nature does not make everyone philosophical. Indeed the fact that some men do think philosophically and others do not may not be something that philosophy has the power to explain. But nature has its own way with Husserl after all, because the argument by which he hopes to make philosophy generally secure and available, the argument for epochē and reduction, is of all his thoughts the one most commonly found intolerable. Husserl himself complains about the lack of response to his new approach, and attributes it to the pernicious aftereffect of philosophical confusion, or to the inveterate pull of the natural attitude, or to the bad will of superficial readers: "One is powerless against the misrepresentations of hurried readers and listeners who in the end hear only what they want to hear; but in any case they are part of the indifferent mass audience of the philosopher. The few, for whom one [really] speaks, will know how to restrain such a suspicion" (*Crisis*, § 35, pp. 136–37; see also § 48 n., and § 65).

Toward the end of his life Husserl felt more and more solitary as a philosopher. At one point in his correspondence with Ingarden he complained, "I have become a philosophical hermit." [7] Although he had once said Ingarden was a "complete" phenomenologist, and not one-quarter phenomenologist like Geiger, he later asserted that even Ingarden, his "dear friend," was not a companion on his own philosophical way. The point of difference is the epochē and reduction. "Speaking plainly, you just don't know what issues would arise for you if the real understanding of constitutive phenomenology were opened to you. You are still worlds away from it" "The hardest thing of all in philosophy is the phenomenological reduction, to penetrate and use it with understanding" (*Briefe,* pp. 23, 63–64, 73–74).

Perhaps the real reason for Husserl's distress is not, as he thinks, the inability of others to understand the reduction, but his expectation that an argument like that leading to the reduction can be a sure way to bring philosophers about. Hopes for a thing like that are bound to be shattered.

It is strange that Husserl should stress the importance of the will to autonomy and responsibility, and the life-changing decision, as the beginning of philosophy. It is such a puritanical way to start the philosophical life. Is it not true that one begins philosophy because one wants to and can't help it (Plato, *Crito* 46B)? And because one begins, vaguely, to appreciate certain things which, it appears, are good to know? All the decisions in the world are no substitute for that. And one acquires intellectual autonomy because one has become philosophical; one does not choose philosophy for the sake of autonomy. Husserl takes the beginning of philosophy as he does because he conceives the will as the imperative faculty, instead of accepting it as rational desire.

Of course, philosophy is not a hobby like collecting stamps or doing crossword puzzles. And one of its functions is to understand what good is achieved through the philosophical life, both for the individual who leads it and for the community within which he lives. Thinking about this good prevents philosophy from decaying into its sophistical imitations and thus corrupting other goods, whose actuality may either require the presence of philosophy or be threatened by unchallenged sophistry. As a contribution toward such thought about the

7. *Briefe an Roman Ingarden,* ed. R. Ingarden (The Hague: Nijhoff, 1968), p. 79. Husserl says he is thankful that at least he is able to possess phenomenological philosophy; he is confident that future generations will discover him. On Heidegger see pp. 40–43.

nature and good of philosophy, Husserl's remarks on epochē and reduction are valuable, but they will not make a philosopher out of someone who does not already remember what it is to lead the philosophical life.

Does this imply that not everyone can lead the good human life? No, it implies that the good and responsible human life need not be simply equated with the philosophical life. The philosopher does not need to say, as Husserl makes him say, that "what is best for me is the best for every man," nor is he obliged to "try to prompt each person to it and make him responsible for choosing such a life and living accordingly."

§ 67. NEUTRALIZED CONVICTION

WHEN THE EPOCHĒ is performed on our convictions, they persist in our philosophical consciousness. As we enter into the philosophical attitude and begin thinking and experiencing phenomenologically, our mundane acts are put out of action and their objects and the world are bracketed; any judgments constituted by such acts are suspended. All these things become transvalued.

How do these acts, judgments, and objects persist within the philosophical attitude? We cannot understand what philosophy is unless we understand how they are still available in the detached consciousness of philosophy, which preserves—and even justifies—these things while somehow dissociating itself from them.

Husserl gives us one analogy in the attempt to doubt, which is carried on in the natural attitude. A second analogy is given in his description of the psychological way to reduction in the *Crisis* (§ 69, pp. 236–37). A psychologist contemplates the acts, judgments, and objects of another person. He does not share that person's doxa, so he contemplates it in a detached way. However, his own world-belief is still at work, and he asserts the real existence of the person he examines, so these neutralized acts, judgments, and objects are subsumed into the psychologist's own natural attitude. He has to do to his own doxa what he did to that of his subject, and this move is qualitatively different from the first, since we are not the same to ourselves as others are. But at least we have another hint as to what neutralization is like.

A third analogy is that of indirect discourse or quotation.[8] If I say, "Joseph says the tire may go flat," and if I neither agree nor disagree but only report what he said, I entertain a judgment, and even an act and an object, as neutralized. But here again, this is done with the support of my own world-belief.

Consciousness can transcend itself in this peculiar way, by holding neutralized acts, judgments, or objects within an underlying world-belief, in the natural attitude. How does it make the further step of detaching itself from its own world-belief and all its own natural acts, judgments, and objects? What sort of autonomy and freedom are achieved by this?

How can Socrates be a loyal Athenian and yet distinguish his philosophical life from being Athenian?

Everything is preserved and won in the epochē, nothing is lost (*Ideas I*, § 50; *EP II*, §§ 40–41; § 43, pp. 110–11; § 52, pp. 167–69). Even the self as bearer of the natural doxa persists, and the philosophical self appreciates this self as identical with its own self. Socrates the Athenian is the same as Socrates the philosopher. The philosophical self appreciates himself as the same within a new set of differences, which are not appreciated by the self as agent of the natural attitude; therefore there arises a self-identity which is not appreciated by the agent of the natural attitude. Transcendental philosophy is left with the permanent burden of appearing incomprehensible to those who do not examine natural conviction (*Crisis*, § 57, pp. 201–2).

The persistence of the self and of ordinary doxa inside phenomenology will be discussed later. It is enough now to stress the peculiarity of this presence and its importance for determining the nature of philosophical thinking and discourse.

§ 68. The Material Thing

LET US RETURN to the argument in *Ideas I*. Once we have shut off the world-belief that underlies all mundane assertions, does anything remain to be said? Is any ground still available for judgments, or are we struck dumb by the epochē? Husserl claims we can still make judgments about consciousness,

8. Thomas Prufer has developed this approach to the reduction in his essay "Welt, Ich und Zeit in der Sprache," *Philosophische Rundschau*, forthcoming.

but to show that this is possible he must display the difference betweeen consciousness and things (§ 33, p. 112).

Husserl analyzes the perception of things so often in his writings as an example of phenomenological method that it becomes tedious. But its frequency is not due to lack of imagination; material things are especially important because other mundane objects and levels in the sense of objects—values, persons, animals, aesthetic objects, mathematical objects, tools —are founded on things, but things in turn are not founded on any more basic reality. They are the fundamental kind of object.

Husserl elaborates this by showing that in the awareness of any higher-level object or sense, like value, beauty, or person, we must distinguish between the full object of awareness and the part of the full object that is "seized" (erfasst) (§ 37). The full objective correlate of an act of valuation is the valued object, but only the object is directly seized; the value is there, but it would require a new act which reflects on the value itself to seize the value and make it thematic. Husserl mentions in passing that seizing an object involves making it possible to say something about it; that is, it means setting up the object as a subject for attribution (§ 37; see also EP II, pp. 193–94). We can, for instance, only talk about values when we change our concern from valued things to the values themselves, even though we can use value terms before this, while we are appreciating the valued objects.

This kind of split between full object and seized objects does not exist in our perception of things, and this is the only mundane intentional consciousness in which it does not exist. In the perception of simple material things, like wood, granite, or iron, the object and the object seized are the same. There is no level of object more basic than things to make the split possible. All other intentional awareness is broken into a level of thematic seizure and a level that is meant but not meant thematically; the presence of material things underlies all other experiential presences.

Since all mundane objects either are things or involve things as ingredients, the way things are experienced is the basic way of experience at work in the world. Husserl says sensible experience is the "primary experience" (Urerfahrung) and that it provides the "final source from which the general thesis of the world, which I perform in the natural attitude, feeds itself, that makes it possible for me consciously to find an existent world of things facing me" (*Ideas I*, § 39, p. 126).[9] Perception of things is the matrix for world-belief.

Husserl's strategy is to show that this fundamental experience of things is such that he not only can suspend the world-belief that "feeds" on it, but that he must look elsewhere than the world if he is to find a basis for final and apodictic philosophical science. The point of analyzing the perception of things is to show the detachability from the world of the consciousness that enjoys things and, on the basis of that enjoyment, has a world.

In presenting his own position, Husserl opposes what we can call the "double-thing" theory, the philosophical position that the thing we directly experience is not the real thing, that the real one is a second thing behind the one that appears. This second may be the thing of primary qualities, the mathematical thing, as opposed to the secondary qualities we can sense, or it may be the thing of atomic particles. In any case it is not the manifest thing. The one we experience is taken either as an image of the real one, or as an indication sign of the real thing, which in turn is the hidden cause of our sensations or images. According to this theory, finding the truth about things means determining which modifications in my sensibility can be coordinated with certain changes in the real thing, so that I can infer changes in the object from changes in my sensations (*Ideas I*, §§ 40, 43, 52). Access to the thing is by reasoning and inference, not by direct perception. We are left with a nonintentional consciousness. Mind directly knows only itself, and must figure out what things are really like. It has no presence of other things; they are meant only absently through inference. In principle they can never be given. When expanded to include all objects, this theory of a hidden real thing gives rise to the notion of another world besides the one we experience (*Crisis*, § 34d).

The Husserlian notion of intentionality fights its chief opponent in this matter of the perception of things. For Husserl

9. Because of the place of thing-perception in Husserl's philosophy, it is easy to appreciate the importance of the course he gave on the experience of things in 1907 (the so-called *Dingvorlesung*), at a time when his position on the reduction, perception, world, and inner time was finding its proper formulation. The introducton to that course has been published as *Die Idee der Phänomenologie*, ed. W. Biemel (The Hague: Nijhoff, 1958). See the editor's remarks, pp. x–xi.

argues that there are not two things but only one: the thing we perceive is the real thing and there is no other. He argues that the relationship between indication sign and thing indicated, and the relationship between image and thing pictured, are not appropriate models for the perception of things. Each of them is a special kind of consciousness in its own right and neither fits the kind operative in perception. Sometimes we do intend things through signs or through images—the signitive or pictorial consciousness of *Logical Investigations*—but that is different from perceiving the object. Only a confused use of such terms would equate them with thing-perception: when brought to distinctness, such judgments are "nonsensical" (*Ideas I*, § 43, p. 136).

What do we have in the perception of things? In perceiving a thing, my flow of perceptions and sensations is constantly changing; as I move around the object, for instance, many impressions are made and a steadily changing flow of perceiving goes on. But in all this the same object is constantly present. And on another level even the "secondary qualities" of the object turn out to be constants over against a flow of changing perceptions; the gray of this desk makes different impressions in different kinds of light and from different angles, but it is the same gray color. Even secondary qualities, as well as primary qualities and the thing itself, are transcendent to the stream of perceptions; all must be considered "objective" to consciousness.

The perception of a thing is this flowing mixture of presences and absences of the thing's profiles. Perception of an objective quality, like color, brightness, loudness, or smoothness, is also a blend of presence and absence of profiles of such qualities. Some thinkers have felt that because not all of the thing is given at once, the thing is not really given at all. In their opinion, we have only appearances of the thing; an infinite mind might enjoy a view of the thing in itself without the deficiencies of our perception, but such consciousness is not humanly available. We must make do with images and signs. Against this theory Husserl insists that a material thing is not perceivable in any way except through the profiling, impressional presence we enjoy. It is, again, nonsensical to speak of a view of the thing at once from all sides and profiles. Things are not presentable that way, not because of a fault in our finite minds, but simply because a thing is that kind of being. Husserl refuses to measure an actual perception against a constructed ideal; his description simply analyzes the essence of perception as it is intuitively presented to reflection.

Things are perceived in a blend of presence and absence because they are spatially extended. Extension is the state of having "parts outside of parts," to use the medieval dictum; one part can be present while others are absent. No thing can be compressed into a partless state if it is to remain a thing, and so the perception of a thing is bound to involve both empty and filled consciousness.

The profiles of things are disjunctive and exclusive. This infection of spatial absence carries a host of implications for mundane evidences. It does not only mean that we have to walk around things to see all sides or that we can slice a thing *ad infinitum* and keep getting new views of it. It also means we have to go places, make experiments, ask questions about other points of view, read documents (with the spatial character this involves, a text never being read without moving one's eyes), measure things and reactions, excavate, shoot rockets and turn telescopes, mix things, operate cyclotrons and cloud chambers, and carry out many other actions in order to "find out" what is the case. The spatiality of material being, and the peculiar absence it involves, is the cause of the labor required in mundane evidences. It even conditions the distinction between our power to make hypotheses and the need to verify them.

Because of the spatiality of things, the evidence is never all in, something more can always be found out, and no judgment based on such experience is free from conceivable correction or negation. Husserl claims that even world-belief is corrigible in principle, because it feeds on the perception of things. Our experience of the world is such that it is not inconceivable that it may be corrected or negated: "The world is not doubtful in the sense that there are rational grounds which might be pitted against the tremendous force of ever-confirming experiences [*einstimmiger Erfahrungen*], but in the sense that a doubt is thinkable" (*Ideas I*, § 46, p. 145).

§ 69. SELF-CONSCIOUSNESS

WE HAVE DESCRIBED how we perceive things. Do we intuit consciousness in the same way? Is consciousness a thing to itself?

The consciousness Husserl examines is that whose fundamental work is to enjoy the presence of things. It flickers on the margins of material things, and in feeding on them becomes able to feed on itself too. Its identity is constituted as the identity of that which has a world, based on the matrix of thing-perception; as its own identity and the identity of its acts and states are constituted, it is aware of these internal identities, as well as of the mundane identities of the things that are its primary focus.

How can consciousness be aware of itself? Is that not like fire living off fire?

Husserl claims there is such a thing as immanent perception: not just a marginal self-awareness, but a full, reflective act which has other parts of consciousness, sensations or other acts, as its objects (*Ideas I*, § 38). The inner object is made into an object of reference, and judgments about it can be framed. Objects and parts in consciousness can be registered. It should be remembered, incidentally, that reflection on acts and sensations is not the same as reflection on judgments.

We will discuss four ways in which inner perception differs from the perception of things.

1. Units within consciousness—sensations and acts—do not have the spatiality of things, so they do not involve the kind of absence that infects perceived things. At any moment of self-experience or reflection, there is no viewpoint of the object other than what is given. What is given is all there is, whereas in a spatial object what is given is only what is available from this side; the thing is appreciated as also being what is absent. An inner object of consciousness does not transcend what is present (§§ 42, 44). Inner objects do have another kind of contamination of presence by absence, which comes from their being temporal objects. But this is essentially different from spatial absence (§ 44).

2. Inner objects do not need the mediation of further impressions to be made present to consciousness. Sensations and acts are experienced or reflectively perceived without intervening data. Self-consciousness and reflection adhere immediately to their objects. Husserl says the impressional sense contents, "which are a real ingredient in the experience of thing-perception, do indeed function as profiles for something, but are not themselves in turn given through profiles" (§ 44, p. 140). This is another way of saying what was asserted in (1), for the impressional and profiled presence of things implies that they are

not given at once; the transcendence of the thing is its being other than any one profile or impression.

3. In principle, a thing can never show up as an immanent object, and an inner object of mine can never be presented to me as a thing. The two kinds of being and ways of appearance do not mix. Consciousness and the world based on things form two distinct domains.

> Consciousness, considered in its "purity," must be reckoned as a self-contained system of being, as a system of absolute being, into which nothing can penetrate and from which nothing can escape; which has no spatio-temporal exterior, and can be inside no spatio-temporal system; which cannot experience causality from anything nor exert causality upon anything, it being presupposed that causality bears the normal sense of natural causality as a relation of dependence upon realities (§ 49, p. 153).

A "veritable abyss" yawns between the two regions of being.

Therefore, in reflection both act and object are the same kind of being, while in transcendent perception act and object are two different kinds of being. Further, in reflection act and object are both ingredients of numerically the same stream of consciousness; consciousness does feed on itself in reflection, and is defined as the kind of being that can do so.

4. When we reflect on an inner object that is still at work in consciousness, the reflection and its object make up a whole such that the reflection is a nonindependent moment. An act of reflection has its own foundation as its intentional object. All this takes place within the living present. An elapsing inner object, before it escapes into forgetfulness, becomes the object of an explicit act of reflection which also emerges within the same living present.

The reflection could not come to be without the elapsing act, so the reflection has its own necessary condition as its intentional correlate. It is like a tree bending back to assimilate its roots, or a house turning in on its foundation. These analogies have a pronounced limp, because trees and houses are not conscious beings, and the trick we wish to describe in reflection is something only self-consciousness is capable of doing. But the analogies help to illuminate the fact that reflection focuses on its own foundation.

The act of reflection could not exist without the earlier temporal parts of the living present within which it is executed, and these elapsed phases comprise the object that the reflection thematizes. In an immanently directed act, Husserl says, "we have a nexus of two intentional experiences, of which at least the superimposed one is dependent, and, moreover, not merely grounded in the deeper-lying, but at the same time intentionally directed towards it" (§ 38, p. 124).

This has an important implication: "Every immanent perception necessarily guarantees the existence of its object. . . . The insight that it [the immanent object] does not exist is, in principle, impossible" (§ 46, p. 143). Since the object of the immanent perception founds the perception, the perception could not have come to be without its object. Hence the existence of the immanent perception guarantees the existence of its object. A house could not come to be without its foundation, so the existence of the house guarantees the existence of its foundation. In the same way, the existence of a reflection guarantees the existence of its object.

It is inconceivable that a reflection should come about without an object for it to reflect on; but it is not inconceivable that a perception of a material thing might take place, only to be followed by further perceptions which show that there was no perception in the first place after all, because there was no material thing. Husserl sees this radical difference between "immanent" perception and "transcendent" perception.

From what reflective stance do we make this claim about reflections and their objects? We are not just reflecting on inner objects when we make it; we are reflecting on inner objects and on reflection, and also on the living present within which they both take place. We are carrying out a reduction to the living present, and examining the kind of reflective experiencing that goes on in descriptive phenomenology. We are carrying on an apodictic critique of phenomenology itself, and giving a theory of the reduction. All this is not fully brought out in *Ideas I*.

Thus items (1), (2), and (4) give us two reasons for the unquestionability, the absolute and apodictic presence of consciousness to itself in reflection: (a) the object of reflection is also the condition for reflection, and (b) the object of reflection is given without spatial profiles, so we only assent to what is actually present.

With the help of reflection, experience entwines with experience and builds up its own totality, that of the stream of consciousness, into which no "thing" can enter as an ingredient part. The whole constituted in this way will be of "great significance" for Husserl, for it will be the residue left by the epochē and reduction.[10]

§ 70. PHILOSOPHICAL DETACHMENT OF CONSCIOUSNESS FROM THINGS

REFLECTION IS A NONINDEPENDENT MOMENT in the whole made by the act of reflection and its object. Reflection has its own foundation as its object.

No other consciousness is like reflection. In thing-perception and in remembering, for example, we can separate the act from its object. The act is a piece, not a moment, of the whole formed by act and object. What the act has as object is not its own foundation, and the act does assert an identity of which the immediate presence is only one profile.

(X) How can a thing-perception be detachable, an independent part, from the whole it makes with its object? Since acts are intentional, doesn't the act require an object as its supplement? Isn't the act a moment to its object, and isn't it founded on its object?

(Y) The step by which we detach a perception from its thing and make it present by itself alone, as an independent whole, is reflection. In a full-blown reflection we disconnect our focus on the thing and make the act our theme. The original act has been shut off and its object bracketed.

(X) But don't we still include the thing as meant? Don't we still have the thing-noema when we reflect philosophically on the act? Doesn't Husserl say that the transcendent object is kept as constituted by the act?

(Y) Yes, but this way of keeping the object transforms it radically. It means we have filtered out every shred of our natural adherence to it. Our consciousness is no longer split— as it is when we reflect within the natural attitude—into a doxa adhering to a thing and a reflection adhering to an act which, in

10. *Ideas I*, § 38, p. 125. On the stream of consciousness as an enclosed totality, see *Crisis*, § 63, p. 220: "Is it not the lesson of a deeper and not naturalistically blinded reflection that everything subjective is part of an indivisible totality?" In § 72, p. 263, he speaks of "being in possession of the totality of the subjective sphere" and takes it in an intersubjective sense.

our split consciousness, we see as "dependent" on the object and founded on it. Because we cancel the first part of this split consciousness, we have only the second remaining. The second, the pure reflective awareness, encompasses things only as correlates to mind, not as foundations for its acts. And since things no longer "found" acts, acts are not be considered as moments to things. They are detached as independent pieces.

The thing is left as that which is merely relative to consciousness. In this new perspective, the thing is a moment to consciousness. The thing is now appreciated as an unfinished identity within manifolds of appearance. We now pay attention, systematically, to how the thing appears. We think about its perceivability and intelligibility, and attend to the thing in its human involvement. We see that when considered in this way, the thing must be founded on consciousness as a nonindependent part, even though it can never show up as a real ingredient inside the stream of consciousness. It always remains transcendent to consciousness.

(X) Is it all a matter of attitudes, then? Suppose I concede that we can look at things in this peculiar way. We can look at things in lots of ways; how do I know this way reveals anything real? It seems like a trick played with mirrors, or perhaps with words, which are mirrors of being. Words like "whole" and "part," "moments," "pieces," and "foundation" are being used ingeniously to make us think something real is happening.

(Y) You are asking much the same questions that Husserl proposes at a strategic point of *Ideas I,* where he says, "We have learned to understand the sense of the phenomenological epochē, but not yet the possibility of executing it" (§ 33, p. 112). Let us suppose, as you seem ready to concede, that what is described as reflection is not nonsense, but a way of looking at something. Your objection, in saying it is only one attitude among many, amounts to the objection that it is only one abstractive way, among many others, of looking at things. That is, it isolates one part of reality—mind and its acts and states—and sees everything, even things and the world, in relation to this part.[11] It is

---

11. *Crisis,* § 41, p. 152: "This is not a 'view,' an 'interpretation' bestowed upon the world. Every view, . . . every opinion about 'the' world, has its ground in the pregiven world. It is from this very ground that I have freed myself through the epochē; I stand above the world, which has now become for me, in a quite peculiar sense, a phenomenon." See also § 66, p. 229.

not much different, really, from considering everything in relation to trees, or to insects, or to music, or to food.

(X) That seems a fair paraphrase, but I warn you that the
concession you demand lets you skirt an important issue. Not
everyone would concede that reflection presents inner objects
in the simple way you seem ready to accept, as though inward
looks look this way and see this, while outward looks look that
way and see that.

(Y) Correct; that is a major question. But the position
Husserl takes is not so naïve. We do, after all, make judgments
about judging, feeling, seeing, and remembering. Something is
judged about, even if it is just a performance. And Husserl is
quite clear that the "immanent perceptions" which are the basis
for such judgments are different from the acts that support
judgments about things. The whole treatment of spatial objects
and purely temporal objects is supposed to bring that out. It
sounds like a naïve position if you don't pay attention to the
details of his argument.

Back to our main question. Yes, we do have to adopt a special
attitude. But this attitude is not abstractive. It is not one among
many viewpoints on being. What it reaches is a whole, a concretum. The whole is the entire stream of the life of consciousness; to be more precise—this step is not very much developed
in *Ideas I*—it is the living present, within which the past and
future are assimilated and kept.[12] Because of the way consciousness can entwine with itself as it flows along, and because no
thing can ever show up as one of the ingredient parts of the
stream of consciousness, this is a pure totality.

(X) I don't mind that part. The part I don't like is that
things and the world are supposed to be swallowed up into
consciousness.[13] How can that be?

(Y) Your discomfort comes from a reluctance to let go of
the natural doxa. You keep taking consciousness as one thing
that is going to engulf other things (*CM*, § 41; *Crisis*, §§ 18, 53).

(X) Well why shouldn't I be reluctant to give up my doxa?

12. Some mention is made of the living present in *Ideas I*, but
not much. See § 46, p. 143, for example; the well-known passage in
§ 81, p. 236; and § 78, p. 221.

13. *Crisis*, § 53, p. 180: "The subjective part of the world swal-
lows up, so to speak, the whole world and thus itself too. What an
absurdity! Or is this a paradox which can be sensibly resolved, even
a necessary one. . . ?"

You said yourself that having a world and enjoying things is what makes up the human estate. What strange, uncouth monster do you want to make of me?

(Y) If you don't neutralize doxa you can never appreciate it for what it is. You remain caught by it. I'm not saying you should negate your convictions or doubt them. These are options within the natural attitude, and someone who can't get outside the natural attitude can't seem to help mistaking philosophy for denial or doubt (*EP II*, § 34, pp. 54–55). But philosophy sustains ordinary experience in a special, detached way; in fact, it's the only defense the ordinary has against sophistic assault.

Consider philosophy in its political context. If an Athenian were urged to consider his world as merely the world held by the Athenians, wouldn't he be reluctant to do so? If he thought as a good Athenian thinks, he would fear that by considering the Athenian world as just one among many worlds, he would lose the humanity he achieved by being an Athenian. And he would be right: he would become like a sophist, without loyalties to any city, unless he were capable of understanding the Athenian world as the Athenian world in a philosophical way, either through the gifts nature gave him, or with the help of someone like Socrates.[14] Socrates was both loyal and detached.

But in order to do this, he must begin to think systematically about things and the world as they disclose themselves to man, about man as that to whom things and the world are disclosed, and about the process of ordinary experience and science as the disclosure of being to man. He is bound to go awry in thinking about these things if he does not neutralize his doxa. He cannot think consistently about appearing as long as a shred of ordinary conviction remains unexamined and operative in his "philosophical" speculations, for this shred will twist his mind from thought about appearing to thought about things.

We don't abandon things when we do philosophy; we get to the heart of things, but the heart of things is not a thing, and shreds of the natural attitude entice us, in devious and hidden ways, to make the heart of things into a thing. This is why

14. See Plato, *Timaeus* 19E: "I am aware that the Sophists have plenty of brave words and fair conceits, but I am afraid that being only wanderers from one city to another, and having never had habitations of their own, they may fail in their conception of philosophers and statesmen, and may not know what they do and say in time of war, when they are fighting or holding parley with their enemies" (Jowett trans.).

Husserl is so madly insistent on the epoché and reduction. We have to renounce things in a mundane way in order to discover them philosophically.[15]

(X) But if philosophy just thinks about being as it appears to man, can it ever get to being in itself?

(Y) Being in itself does appear to man. That is shown by Husserl's rebuttal of the "double-thing" or "double-world" theory. What appears to man in both ordinary and scientific experience is real being.

(X) But that is only being as it appears to man. There must be a better way of grasping it. Can't philosophy give us being as it is purely in itself?

(Y) You are asking philosophy to be a new experience of being, with special access to being that the ordinary and the scientific do not have.

(X) It should do something like that if it is worth its salt, and if it is going to tell us anything. Every other particular kind of experience has its proper access to being. And how can philosophy correct ordinary experience if it doesn't see things as they really are?

(Y) Philosophy doesn't correct ordinary experience. Better ordinary experience does that. Better biology corrects false biology, better carpenters correct poor carpenters, temperate men correct the dissolute, good poets correct bad ones.

(X) I thought philosophy could do all that too, because it knows how things really are.

(Y) Philosophy can correct people when they try to talk about being, man, experience, appearance, truth, and the like, and also when they try to talk about virtue. For then they try to do philosophy and that road can get very foggy and confusing; it is easy to mistake one thing for another.

There is a sense in which philosophy does get to real being beyond what is available in human involvement. If a philosopher appreciates the Athenian world as only one profile of the world in itself, he realizes that the world is an identity transcending this one profile. It can have other profiles as well, but our philosopher does not have to enjoy these other profiles. Nor

---

15. *Crisis*, § 53, p. 180: "From the beginning the phenomenologist lives in the paradox of having to look upon the obvious as questionable, as enigmatic, and of henceforth being unable to have any other scientific theme than that of transforming the universal obviousness of the being of the world—for him the greatest of all enigmas—into something intelligible."

does he enjoy a vision of the world without any profiles; that would be nonsense.

An absolute Athenian thinks the Athenian world is totally identified with the world. He is right, in a way, for the Athenian world is truly a manifestation of the world in itself; but his inability to appreciate the Athenian world as an appearance of something different from what appears means that he falsely absolutizes the Athenian world. He accepts the Athenian world the way Husserl says we must accept inner objects given to immanent perception: as not available under other profiles. The firm Athenian thinks this way because he cannot think systematically about appearances.

The sophist knows that the Spartan and Persian world-profiles are different from the Athenian, so he likes to tweak the Athenian's gullibility and play off one opinion about the world against another. He claims he can liberate the Athenian from false conviction. But the sophist just sees disjointed world-views. They are all pieces to him. He does not appreciate them as profiles of an identical world. He lives and traffics in appearances alone, without being or world. So he cannot appreciate either the real world or the humanity constituted in ordinary experience; he treats them as mere opinion. Opinion, and the honors of men—which are based on opinion—are the ultimate reality for him. You can see why only philosophy can counteract his arguments and his way of acting and protect political life against him. Philosophy can make us judge truly about appearances.

(X) Isn't it a good thing to make people, especially the young, question the customs and prejudices of their country? Much of higher education is directed to making students into critics of the established social order.

(Y) People should be helped to think about appearances when they are of a proper age, but it makes all the difference in the world whether they are helped to think philosophically or driven into sophistic opinion about the world in which they live (Aristotle, *Nicomachean Ethics* 1. 3; Plato, *Republic* 7. 537E–539E).

(X) This excursion into Athenian politics is interesting, but would you please show me how it ties in with Husserl? He says very little about cities and nations.

(Y) Husserl is trying to do what Socrates did, but with a difference. He is not thinking about Athenian or German or American or Chinese world-profiles, but about the profile of

being that is given in science and to the perceptions and categorial actions that underly Western science. He does not do
philosophy in a political context, so the sophistry he must counter
is not political sophistry.

You know that Husserl makes a bizarre claim in § 49 of
Ideas I.[16] He says the world as we have constituted it on the
matrix of thing-perception could, conceivably, be annihilated,
and consciousness can be conceived as still existent despite this
calamity.

(X) I am familiar with that passage, and find it ridiculous.
It's a piece of nonsense. It's enough to discredit everything else
Husserl wrote. I know he qualifies it by saying we have no
reason to expect this to happen or to plan for it—presumably to
have such an expectation would be to take his statements in
the "natural attitude," and they are not meant that way. Nevertheless, even as a conceivability, it shows Husserl is just playing
with words. What sense could such a thing have?

(Y) Let's be patient. Don't talk like a stubborn Athenian.
Husserl claims that the world we have constituted on the matrix
of things is one profile of being. Being and what we have
experienced as the world and in the world are not simply
identical. Being and things are not simply identical.

(X) If they are not, what is being like?

(Y) For one, it can also appear as consciousness. And
please don't think I deny that material things are being. They
are being too, but they don't exhaust being.

(X) To say being also appears as consciousness is not to
say anything more than you've said before, because consciousness is one of the realities that appear in the world. Still, I accept that as being different from things. So now we have being
appearing as material things and as consciousness. It has two
profiles at least. Are there any more?

(Y) We must keep in mind that the term "profile" has a
special sense when we talk about being. Its original use was
concerned with the profiles of a material thing, the different
impressions it makes from various spatial viewpoints. Then we
used it in reference to various cultural views of the world,
which is the identity in all the views. In each of these cases, it
makes sense to speak of potentially infinite profiles. But it
would be Spinozistic of me to claim there are infinite modes of
being, and that we have access to only two of them, matter and

16. Husserl does it again elsewhere: See *EP II*, § 37, pp. 72–73.

mind. I don't have to say that. All I wish to assert is that being as such is different from things and consciousness, even though it appears in them. And of course, even as a philosopher, I cannot tell you what pure being is like, apart from its human involvement.

(X) On this point you are too modest. Think of the claim that being is one with itself, that it is not what is different from it, that it is not a nonentity, that it is accessible to mind, that it can be itself over again within differences, and that it is better for it to be than not to be. These and other claims like them are true of being in itself, apart from its human involvement. Some of them are true of being apart from its involvement with any sort of mind. Don't you say such things about being when you do metaphysics?

(Y) True, but even as philosophers we appreciate these characteristics of being through its presence in human involvement. No one of us, none of the "mortals," as the ancients used to say, can read them off pure being. And please remember that the characteristics you mention presume distinct differentiation within being. Someday we must give some thought to what precedes and supports the differences in being.

(X) You seem to have ontologized many things I always thought Husserl projected into consciousness. For example, when he carries out that so-called world-annihilation in *Ideas I*, he seems to be left with a self-thinking mind, a purely solipsistic stream of consciousness. Isn't this like fire feeding on fire? And how can you still talk of being here—except perhaps the being of consciousness?

(Y) Husserl is not left with a self-thinking mind. When he tries to conceive what is left when permanent material things are thought away, he says, "It might happen, moreover, that, to a certain extent still, rough unitary formations might be constituted, fleeting concentration-centers for intuitions which were the mere analogues of thing-intuitions, being wholly incapable of constituting self-preserving 'realities'" (§ 49, p. 151). And in *Cartesian Meditations* he proposes the things we experience in our dreams as an alternative to real material things (§ 7).

He has to keep some kind of transcendent identity for intentional consciousness to be aware of. Consciousness would feed on these identities and so be able to become an appropriate identity itself. It would turn out very much different from the kind of self we have become—feeding as we do on the spatial and unclosed identification of material objects—but the stream of experience would still constitute a self (*Ideas I*, § 49, pp. 151–52).

In this respect Husserl's stream of consciousness differs from Aristotle's self-thinking mind, which does indeed know only itself—it would be degraded by knowing anything else. And besides being deprived of intentionality, Aristotle's separate mind is also deprived of temporality. Husserl's pure consciousness remains a temporal stream.

(X) Husserl calls the pure stream of consciousness "absolute" being, in that it can be conceived to exist without the existence of material things (*Ideas I*, § 49, p. 152).

(Y) We should not let a word like "absolute" overwhelm us. Once we realize that being is not exhausted by material things, of course, consciousness turns out to be more durable than material things; since it can appreciate being as such, and not just material being, consciousness is an invariant in the difference between material being and being. When you take the world constituted on the matrix of things as only one profile of being, you must absolutize consciousness vis-à-vis the world, for consciousness becomes registered as invariant through the difference between being and the world.

But to say consciousness is absolute being is not to say consciousness is all that being is. Quite the contrary; for absolute being is only one disclosure of being, and is defined against another kind: the dependent and relative being constituted for consciousness. Being as such can be both absolute and relative, so it is beyond these differences. Consciousness need not have this constituted world as its other, but it must have some other transcendent to itself because it is intentional. So consciousness does not exhaust being.

In this respect Aristotle's separate mind could not call itself "absolute" consciousness, for it would not realize itself as absolute in contrast to anything relative, nor would it realize that being is not identified with its own thinking. In contrast, Husserl's transcendental consciousness is aware that being is not equated with itself. It knows that it is "only" absolute being. It appreciates that being is other than itself. And this appreciation is reflected in the temporality of transcendental consciousness, which is another kind of otherness, one inside the life of consciousness, even inside its living present.

(X) Now that's a breathless outburst, and it's left me staggering. I don't particularly like to talk about these things, and you've dragged me much farther afield than I want to go.

I don't have any idea what Aristotle's self-thinking thought says to itself. And I suspect this kind of talk brings back ghosts and spirits we can well do without.

(Y) You may not know what the separate mind says to itself, but you do know what Aristotle says about it, which is our issue here.

The consciousness Husserl discusses is not a Gnostic or Neo-Platonic mind that is outside the world in a thinglike way. Such conceptions, in fact, may be taken as unsuccessful attempts to think about mind. The stream of consciousness is outside the world the way a judgment, a verification, the framing of a judgment, remembering, and reflection are not in the world, and many philosophers you would consider quite sober have noticed peculiarities in the way such things exist.[17] The stream of consciousness is a deeper invariant actuality that underlies these actualities and sustains them even when they fall into a latent state.

(X) Well then you're talking about psychological things. There is no need to get metaphysical after all. This is what psychologists talk about all the time.[18]

(Y) They do talk about them, but not in a way that does full justice to them. Psychologists consider these things as objects or parts of the world, with causal connections to other objects or parts of the world. So do neurophysiologists. They try to discover regular patterns of dependence among changes in psychological objects, and between changes in psychological objects and changes in things outside consciousness.

(X) That seems fair to me. Consciousness, judgment, judging, reflection, and sensation are parts of the world in some sense, are they not? And this approach avoids the metaphysics which you are not able to escape.

(Y) What we have here is a struggle between two wholes. In a psychological view, one does not suspend one's underlying world-belief. The world is kept as the whole. It is the total horizon for being, events, and change. Mental objects and events take their place along with all the rest, and each man's self is a part of this world. In a phenomenological view, the world-belief is suspended. The whole we turn to is the whole of subjectivity, which had been taken as a part in the world-whole.

17. See above, Chapter 2, n. 22.
18. On how psychology misunderstands what it talks about, see *Crisis*, § 57, pp. 202–3.

Now the world and its things are considered as a part constituted by consciousness.

(X) That is a neat formulation of the problem, for anyone who likes global thinking. Now of the two choices, isn't it more sensible to take the world as the whole? Obviously you and I are only entities within the world.

(Y) You may remember that our discussion about being and the world began as we were comparing Husserl to Socrates. Socrates understands the world as not exhausted by the Athenian world. He would admit that Glaucon is an Athenian citizen, an Athenian "entity" if you will, but he also tries to make Glaucon see the Athenian world as one that might not-be, and to appreciate that he, Glaucon, would still be despite this calamity. His being as a man is not exhausted by his being Athenian, even though he would not have become a man had he not been Athenian, or Spartan, or a citizen of some city.

Now Husserl claims that the world constituted on the matrix of thing-perception, and explored and confirmed by the sciences and crafts, does not exhaust being. We are entities in the world, but the world could, conceivably, not-be as we have constituted it, and we could still be. The being of consciousness or mind is not exhausted by being the perceiver and registrar of material things.

(X) I don't admit the analogy. Obviously there can be a plurality of cities and cultural worlds. Sociology, political science, anthropology, and history show that. But that being could be different from what we have come to know has not been and cannot be shown by anyone. There is a world, and the various critical sciences tell us what is real in it; physics and chemistry tell us what is real in matter, biology tells us about living things, and psychology tells us about the mental life of men.

(Y) And which science tells us what is real about truth, appearances, verification, world-belief, meaning, and things like that?

(X) Psychology, since they are mental acts or parts of mental acts. Perhaps a sociology of knowledge would do it for groups of men. Linguistics might help in questions about language. For example, biology tells us what is real in living things, while psychology tells us what appearances, whether false or true, living things engender in our minds. Living things are real, but appearances are mental, so psychology studies them (*PP*, §§ 26, 27).

(Y) Psychology cannot distinguish between the true and false appearances of living things, can it?

(X) No, biology does that. You have to know the real thing to be able to distinguish between true and false appearances (*Crisis*, § 69, pp. 236–37).

(Y) But you just said biology examines things, not appearances. Appearances, being mental, are left to psychology.

(X) Well, there is a part of psychology that specializes in those particular experiences. It is the psychology associated with the experience of living things.

(Y) But biology still picks out which appearances are true and which are false?

(X) Yes, but let's not be narrow-minded about what the science of biology is. It's reasonable to call preprofessional but intelligent and critical judgments parts of the science. Biology in a legitimately wide sense includes all serious and rational judgment about living things.

(Y) I'm happy to concede that. Now biology, in the wide sense you have defined, must be able to talk about experiences and appearances of living things as well as about living things, because it has to pick out which are true and which are false. So it has to move over into what you have been calling psychology, at least to that special branch of psychology which treats the experience of living things.

(X) Nothing wrong with that, is there? These days everyone says that interdisciplinary cooperation is a good thing. Besides, the biologist and the psychologist can be the same man. In fact a biologist has to be a psychologist in the specialized sense we have determined, the expert in experiences and appearances of living things. And I suppose a chemist would have to be a psychologist in respect to experiences and appearances of material substances.

(Y) Then that part of psychology that deals with experiencing living things is really a part of biology, and not an independent science.

(X) All right, suppose I concede that.

(Y) And the part of psychology that deals with experiencing matter is really a part of physics and chemistry, and all the other parts of psychology are really parts of other sciences, like history, astronomy, political science, and economics. Then there is no psychology as a science in itself. The psychologist has been dissolved into all the other scientists.

(X) Wait a minute. I'll distinguish between other men as

scientists, and as ordinary, nonscientific persons. I concede what you say in part; psychology is largely swallowed up by other sciences. But there are many nonscientific actions in mental life, and psychology can still have them as its own preserve.

(Y) I'm afraid you closed that door when you said that biology is not to be taken just as a professional science, but that it extends to all reasonable judgments about living things. Presumably you would extend all sciences that way. This means that all of man's intelligent activity is used up in the various sciences and arts, so psychology has nothing left as its own special field for study.

(X) But there are things left over. There are things like emotional patterns, reactions to stimuli, and adaptation to environment. I know what you are going to say: you will claim that none of these involve man's critical thinking about things and the world. They do not involve truth, appearances, good or bad judgment, meaning, and verification.

(Y) Your anticipation is correct. To put it succinctly: these things do not involve man as being truthful.

(X) I'll concede that, and say psychology examines man's mental life in all other respects.

(Y) You mean it examines man in all respects except the one that makes him human.

(X) All right; but these other respects are part of man, aren't they?

(Y) They certainly are, and I am happy to leave them to your science, as long as you admit that man is studied in his humanness by some other way of thought.

(X) Agreed. And now the ball is in your court. What is this other way of thought? So far we have agreed that biology thinks about living things, and also about the true and false appearances of living things. Physics and chemistry do the same for matter. Is the sum total of the sciences and arts the way of thought that studies man in his ability to think? This would be a strange conclusion. Man would not be one thing, but dozens of things put together.

(Y) Sometimes a man can be dozens of pieces put together until he begins to think in such a way that the parts become registered as moments of a whole. No one of the sciences can provide this way of thought, because each provides one of the pieces; and psychology doesn't do it either.

(X) Don't tell me, let me guess. Philosophy can do it!

(Y) Let's avoid slogans. Let's just say there is a way of thinking that sets out to think about the whole instead of the parts. It has never achieved a full registration of the whole—perhaps the notion of such achievement has something self-contradicting about it—but it has come to realize that thinking about the whole has to be very much different from thinking about the parts. It can show, in detail, that an attempt to think about the whole in terms of the parts falls into incoherence and inconsistency; even the parts are not integrally preserved in such an attempt. The attempt to register the whole on the basis of world-belief is bound to avoid coming to terms with man in his humanness, as our discussion about psychology revealed.

(X) I'm afraid I let psychology get a black eye in that argument.

(Y) There's nothing wrong with psychology, and the same kind of argument could have been carried on about sociology or linguistics or any other science of man. They all run into difficulties when they present themselves as the science of truthfulness—which they sometimes do by claiming to show that there is no such thing as truth.

Actually, you may have conceded too much a moment ago. There is a sense in which psychology—to stay with that as the paradigm—does study specifically human things like language, verification, meaning, human perception and learning, and even truth, as mental parts and performances in men. But, in a subtle way, it does fail to account for the humanness of these things, and precisely because it keeps its own truth-interest or world-belief alive.

Look at it this way. Biology, history, other sciences, as well as the nonspecialized perceptions and judgments in ordinary life, are exercises in being truthful. Psychology, because it keeps its own world-belief alive, is also an exercise in being truthful. If psychology examines these other exercises, it does not share in their truth-interest; it turns them into objects, and makes them serve its own concerns. It is like a Spartan who comes to Athens and investigates the beliefs of the Athenians with a foreigner's curiosity.[19] At the other extreme, if psychology does subordinate itself to the truth-interest of other sciences, it becomes an appendage to them and loses its own autonomy. It is like a Spartan

19. *Crisis*, § 69, p. 240: "But the psychologist as such in his inquiry must, we repeat, take and have no position: he must neither concur nor refuse, nor remain in problematic suspense, as if he had some say in the validities of the persons who are his subjects."

who becomes an Athenian citizen and lives exactly as the Athenians do.

The secret of Socratic detachment is to avoid each of these extremes. It is to preserve the integrity of the truthfulness we are examining, to treat it with sympathy, to recover it herme- neutically, but also to remain distinct from and unsubordinated to it. Socrates remains in control.[20] In Socratic detachment, one thinks about being truthful, and to do this one cannot be a partisan or competitor in one of the regular exercises in being truthful.

Husserl tries to bring this attitude about through his epochē. In comparing his enterprise with psychology, he claims that a descriptive psychology is changed into a part of phenomenology simply by this suspension of its own world-belief. The small change makes all the difference. If you don't suspend mundane conviction, you may exercise truthfulness but you do not think appropriately about being truthful, and you run the risk of ruining its humanness because you are likely to mistake some- thing else for it.

(X) That seems to leave psychology more dignity than your previous remarks did. But it seems that psychology and all the sciences of man, including linguistics, do not do justice to man unless they become philosophical.

(Y) True. That is what it means for them to become philo- sophical: to do justice to what they study (*Crisis*, § 72, pp. 257–60).

(X) So philosophy is a kind of anthropology.

(Y) No, and perhaps some interpretation of Husserl is called for at this point. In disclosing what being truthful is, philosophy must also appreciate being as that which supports truthfulness (Plato, *Republic* 6. 509B).

(X) But I thought you had to shut off the concern with the world and with things.

(Y) Even though we may have to suspend our world-belief as a condition for thinking about man, we do not have to suspend something more basic, which we might call being-belief. After all, the epochē does not leave us with nothing at all. Even in Husserl's description in *Ideas I*, when we suspend world-belief we still scour around for another basis for judgment (§ 33). Something is still at work. This being-belief settles on pure consciousness as still available for judgment, and finally we

20. *Crisis*, app. XXIV, *Husserliana* ed., p. 486, ll. 13–22.

find that pure consciousness includes mundane being as its correlate. Through these steps, there is never an epochē of being-belief. If there were, nothing more would happen. The world and world-belief are nested, respectively, within being and being-belief, and man is the being that has a world because being appears to him. The concern with being defines man more fundamentally than the more limited claim that man is the being that has a world.

It would not surprise me if Husserl's argument would have been much less arduous if he had made this context of being, as well as the context of political life, more explicit. They are operative in his thinking, since they are parameters for all authentic philosophy, but he does not articulate them.

(X) Sure, but then you're off into metaphysics again.

(Y) It's only when you get into this way of thinking that you can make appropriate statements about truth, appearance, verification, and meaning.

(X) If that's what has to be done, I may as well leave those statements to someone else. My common sense will suffice for my problems. I've been an honest man all my life, I've managed to hold fairly decent opinions, I have verified a number of claims and have done a good job of it, and have dispelled some illusions, those of others as well as my own.

(Y) Everybody exercises truth, and honest men do it as a matter of habit. But to talk about it systematically is another thing.

(X) All right, I'll leave that to the experts then.

(Y) You take a great risk if you do.

Prospero: Abhorred slave,
Which any print of goodness wilt
  not take,
Being capable of all ill! I pitied
  thee,
Took pains to make thee speak,
  taught thee each hour
One thing or other: when thou
  didst not, savage,
Know thine own meaning, but
  wouldst gabble like
A thing most brutish, I endow'd
  thy purposes
With words that made them
  known. But thy vile race,
Though thou didst learn, had that
  in't which good natures
Could not abide to be with; there-
  fore wast thou
Deservedly confined into this rock,
Who hadst deserved more than a
  prison.

Caliban: You taught me language;
  and my profit on't
Is, I know how to curse. The red
  plague rid you
For learning me your language!
                      —*The Tempest,* I. ii

BEING TRUTHFUL involves taking a position by making judgments. What is a judgment, and what parts can phenomenology register in it?

§ 71. JUDGING VERSUS PERCEIVING

SENSIBLY PERCEPTUAL CONSCIOUSNESS is a foundation for judgmental consciousness; the former can exist without the

[205]

latter, and the latter emerges out of the former. In judgmental consciousness there is an explicit awareness of parts as parts; the subject is distinguished from its predicates, one member of a relation is distinguished from the other, a member of a group is distinguished from the others and from the group as a whole. In sensibly perceptual consciousness a manifold is lived through as we perceive the simple object in the continuum of its appearances, but the continuum is not distinguished into parts.

Judgmental consciousness is generally taken as that which predicates an attribute of an object, but Husserl expands the sense of judgment to cover categorial articulations of all kinds: predicating, relating, collecting, universalizing, and the like (FTL, § 39). He admits that predication has a primacy over the others, for some of them arise as special kinds of predication and all can be turned into predicative forms, but they do not thereby become reduced to predications. It is necessary to have a concept that covers all such articulations and respects their differences. The concept of judgment, in the breadth Husserl gives it, does this.[1]

Husserl's wide sense of judgment gives his reflections a scope beyond European languages. To the extent that a language, when spoken, articulates parts in what is given in perception—as opposed to serving as a sign of recognition or a sign of feeling—it enters into the judgmental domain whose characteristics Husserl describes. It is conceivable that the genius of one language family may arrange parts into wholes in a way that is quite different from what is achieved in another language group; but in all cases the formal structure of parts and wholes is operative.

Judging is called a spontaneous activity by Husserl. The contrariety of active and passive is used in many ways in his philosophy, depending on the level of consciousness we are concerned with; even a simple perception has active and passive moments. But judging is active in contrast to the passivity of perception, in the sense that it brings about a new kind of object, the categorial object. Perception does not bring about a new object on the base of an old object; the perceived stone is not a modification of a stone or other thing given in some more elementary way; it is simply the unmodified presence of stone. But

1. See also EJ, §§ 1–2, on the primacy of predication; § 13, pp. 60–62, on prepredicative judging; §§ 53–54, on relation and predication.

the stone as a component of a state of affairs or of some other categorial object involves something more than the perceived stone, and the new factor arises in response to the activity of judging. The stone is being actively intellected, and the spontaneous activity of thinking is needed for this to happen.

Besides its ability to constitute and register categorial objects, judging is active in another respect. It introduces a third factor between the state of affairs and the act of judging: the judgment or the fact as supposed. Perceptual consciousness does not build up a third entity. There is the act of perceiving, and there is its object; sometimes consciousness can intend the object in an empty way, but this does not constitute a third object between act and thing. But the activity of categorial consciousness, besides articulating parts in the object it considers, also establishes a new domain that can be distinguished from and even critically compared to the domain of registered facts, the domain of meanings.

Emergence of the domain of meanings allows communication to take place, since what one speaker can take over from another—with or without assent—is precisely this articulated judgment. Two speakers cannot perform numerically the same act of judging, but they can possess numerically the same judgment, for a judgment is an ideal entity, identically the same no matter when, where, or by whom it is expressed. It is even misleading to talk of "numerically" the same judgment, just as it would be to speak of numerically the same Pythagorean theorem; such objects cannot be counted.

But can't I take over the meaning of someone else's perception? Doesn't sheer perception, apart from the articulation of judging, establish an ideal sense that can be communicated? Can't this ideal sense be distinguished as a third entity between the act of perception and the thing perceived? Perception alone, apart from its capacity to become ingredient in judgmental consciousness, does not establish a communicable and expressible meaning. To claim that it does would be to fall prey to the mistaken belief that we learn to speak by being taught lots of proper names. Speaking is not putting labels on things; it is articulating and, simultaneously, expressing categorial wholes. If your interlocutor cannot judge at least vaguely, you cannot communicate with him; perception itself does not make it possible. Perception is meaningful, but only by virtue of its potential to work in the registration and verification of categorial wholes.[2] True, we sometimes use a simple name as a sign of perceptual recognition and are understood by others. But this is a limit case which is possible because normally there is more to be said, and usually such simple naming is only a preparation for subsequent judgment.

Without the possibility of categorial framing, the only "communication" possible is the kind one can have with an animal one knows well. One can "understand" what the animal feels or wants, but one cannot quote the beast.

Since judging generates something expressible and communicable, the man who judges in an original way is established as someone with a distinct position among his fellows. This is a third respect in which judgmental consciousness is active in contrast to perception; perception as such makes no public claims and does not make the perceiver distinctively responsible for what he sees.

Within the judgmental or categorial domain, as opposed to the perceptual, we must therefore distinguish (a) the act of judging, (b) the judgment, (c) the registered or reported facts, states of affairs, relations, or other categorial objectivities correlative to the judgment. Failure to distinguish the act of judging from the judgment results in psychologizing logical structures; it turns a logical identity into a psychological process. Failure to distinguish the judgment from the registered fact makes it impossible to distinguish mathematics from formal logic, and either renders the problem of the truth of judgments insoluble—by depriving judgments of the registered facts to which they conform when they are true—or naïvely projects logical structures into the world of things.

§ 72. EXPRESSION VERSUS JUDGMENT

A JUDGMENT AS MEANING is what is expressed in an uttered sentence. It is possible to turn our attention from the judgment to the sentence as an acoustical and expressive phe-

---

2. See *EJ*, § 63, p. 252, where Husserl says that if we break off perception at any time, we have still perceived the object; but if we break off judging before we finish the judgment, the judgment is not there. Judging is a production of a new whole in a way that perception is not; the judgment is not there until the whole is finished.

nomenon.[3] If we generalize a certain sentence—consider it as a type and not as a token—we can subject it to grammatical analysis, and its words to phonemic analysis; by expanding our study to other words and other possible sentences, we can describe the language it belongs to. This would be an analysis of something prejudgmental, because it studies the expression of judgment, not the judgment itself, which could be expressed in many other ways and in other languages. But although prejudgmental, the level of expression is a condition for the existence of the judgment, for unless the grammatical and phonemic parts of the sentences are distinctly articulated—distinctness being the sufficient differentiation of appropriate parts from one another—the judgment itself cannot come into being.

Because judgment and expression are moments to each other, there can be pressure exerted by one on the other. Patterns in expression may give shape to patterns in judgment; the character of a given language may pressure its speakers into judging along certain lines and not along others. But judgment and expression are two and not one, so the pressures can be resisted. The ingenuity of a speaker enables him to break conventional patterns and bring about judgments that most of his associates in the language consider exotic.

Because judgment and expression are moments to each other, one can develop while the other lags behind. It is possible to know what you want to say, and be unable to say it yet. But the only way to finally show what you mean is to find its proper expression.

Two ways an expression can fail are by being acoustically confused or grammatically incoherent. Grammatical incoherence will be treated later because it is involved with the distinct appearance of the judgment itself. Acoustic confusion exists when we realize that someone is talking, and hence pretending to express judgment, but we cannot distinguish the parts of the expression, not because we are unsuitably positioned to perceive them, but because the pronunciation is bad: "Even the sensuousness of the verbal sounds and of their articulation can be vague" (*FTL*, § 16a, p. 59). Someone mumbling this way may be led by the sensuous association of words, and may not be making judgments. If the mumbling becomes emotionally charged it

---

3. *PP*, app. IX, which the editor entitles "The Structure of Language and the Possibility It Permits of Study along Two Different Lines."

may be just an indication sign of the man's feelings, and not an expression at all.[4]

It is also possible to think and to frame judgments while writing, although real or imaginary speaking is usually entwined with this process. In its original sense alphabetic writing is made up of indication signs of units of acoustic expressions, but someone who knows how to write well enough can frame his judgments with the expressive support of written words, without the intermediary of silent or voiced speaking. In writing, the analogue to acoustic confusion is scribbling. The scribbler, as opposed to someone with bad handwriting—and sometimes the reader may have a hard time making the distinction—does not think when he pretends to write.

§ 73. VAGUE AND DISTINCT JUDGING

ANOTHER LEVEL OF ANALYSIS is the judgment itself, that which is expressed in expressions. The judgment is a whole on another level than the expressive whole, and its parts and combinations are different, even though conditioned by the expression.

It is possible for a judgment to be only confusedly or vaguely executed (*FTL*, § 16a; *Crisis*, app. VI, pp. 361–64). This can occur, obviously, when the expression is confused or vague, but

---

4. An expression can also fail by not bringing about the desired response in those who hear the judgment. The speaker has pronounced his expression adequately and coherently, but it was the wrong choice of expression for the audience at hand. (On another level, the speaker may have chosen the wrong argument, i.e., the wrong judgments.) This is a failure in what Aristotle would call the rhetorical aspect of speech (*Rhetoric* 1. 2. 1355b26–27) and in what Austin calls the perlocutionary act (*How to Do Things with Words* [Oxford: Clarendon Press, 1962], pp. 101–31). Success in the rhetoric of a speech assumes that the change in the auditors is brought about on the condition of their appreciating the judgments which the speaker expresses; so they must clearly hear his expression and articulate the judgments in turn, at least as judgments held by him.

Still another way for expression to fail is through unsuspected ambiguity. The speaker thinks the expression can harbor only one judgment, but in fact others could be found in it, and the auditor may take one of these others. Disastrous examples of this occur in ambiguous military commands.

it can also occur when the expression is distinct but the judgment only passively assimilated. Passive reading or listening, or verbal formulations that we let ourselves make without thinking, are examples; we let the expression come about, and it may be perfectly distinct phonemically and correct grammatically, but we do not frame the judgment. We do not put its parts together explicitly.

This state is possible because of the public and institutionalized character of expressions, which are subject to their own kind of inertia; certain words, phrases, and sentences suggest others that are often associated with them. It is also possible because judgments themselves, not just their expressions, can settle into a passive state where they work like sensible objects. They are there publicly or as part of our private store, and exercise an associative pull on our attention (*PP*, § 41, p. 210). Being led this way is associative dreaming, not thought, although it presents itself as thought because it uses expression. What is at work here is a kind of sensuous passivity peculiar to language, not the kind operative in daydreaming or undirected perception. The associative pull is not exercised by attractive images and things but by settled formulations of meaning. The capacity to think is also the capacity to think in this degenerate way, both the excellence and the weakness being peculiar to man.

The opposite of confused judging is distinct judging, the sufficient articulation of the parts of the judgment. The difference is a matter of activity. When we frame a judgment we explicitly perform the act of judging. The judgment is now there for us as a whole meaning, and its parts are present as parts. Distinct judging is only the intuition of the *judgment*, not yet intuitive registration of the facts judged, nor intuition of the things judged about.

Vague versus distinct judging is only one way in which a judgment can be absent and then present. When I simply name a judgment or refer to it, I also intend it emptily—for example, when I refer to "what you said in reply to his question," or to "the judgment most people would make about this." There need be no vagueness when we refer to judgments this way. The corresponding intuitive presence of the judgment is achieved, of course, when the judgment is framed.

Husserl's analysis reflects the way we come to make judgments. When learning a foreign language we first just exercise the expressional wholes we are given as models; when we can articulate these properly, we gradually become capable of framing a judgment and taking a position in our new language. Until we are confident of the expression we do not trust ourselves to make a judgment. Before we master the language we anticipate authentic judgments, but only emptily, for we cannot make them yet. What goes on when we learn our first language is not the same, however, for when we learn a foreign language we have already framed judgments in our native tongue, so we can explicitly intend what we are after. A child's anticipation of judgments cannot be like this.

Framing a judgment does not just bring about the existence of a judgment; it also constitutes the one who framed it as a speaker.[5] He has defined himself as the spokesman for such-and-such a position. The performance is essentially public because of the expression ingredient in judgment, and because the judgment expressed can be assumed by others. The judgment becomes the responsibility of the one who performed it, and others can call him to task for it, ask for reasons and explanations, expect him to defend it, thank him if it is true and helpful, blame him if it is not. One's self as a public speaker—which is different from one's character as a source of action—is constituted by the sum of judgments one has framed. Although judgments are detachable from individual speakers and sometimes become everyone's property, a speaker is never detachable from the judgments he has framed. Even if he abandons them, they once were his.[6]

Much of our thinking and speaking is the passive repetition of what "they" say.[7] Perhaps some people never frame a judg-

5. APS, § 14; EJ, § 66, pp. 272–74; Ideen II, § 22, pp. 99–100, and § 23, p. 103. The mind slips into inactuality when one does not think.

6. A self with his convictions is called a "monad" by Husserl; CM, § 33.

7. Heidegger has developed the notion of inauthentic judging by his analysis of das Man. In Being and Time, trans. J. Macquarrie and E. Robinson (New York: Harper and Row, 1962), § 34 n., he relates this theme to the problem of the vague consciousness in Husserl, referring to Ideas I, §§ 123 ff. Heidegger situates Husserlian themes within the wider context of the question of being, but he does not sufficiently consider the context of political philosophy. And even the question of being appears different if the political context is taken into account.

Heidegger advances beyond Husserl by explicitly raising the question of being in ways Husserl did not, and by raising the issue of publicness in a more appropriate way than Husserl, with his stress on the discourse of science, was able to do. But Heidegger's concep-

ment beyond reports about their feelings and the sensible attributes they see, touch, feel, hear, and taste in things; many frame judgments only in certain areas of competence and interest. Some frame judgments at the drop of a hat, without evidence, and are soon discovered to be irresponsible in speech; only the unwary take them seriously. At the other extreme someone may avoid the risk and conspicuousness of judging by remaining the mouthpiece of general opinion or the positions of others, but then he is a blank in public conversation.

§ 74. JUDGING WITH CLARITY

AN ENTIRELY DIFFERENT DIMENSION of judgment, which must be distinguished but not separated from those we have analyzed, is what Husserl calls its clarity. Clarity is the aptitude of judgment to conform to registered facts (*FTL*, § 16b; *Ideen III*, § 20).

A distinct judgment is intuitively present as a judgment or as a meaning. But the presence of the judgment is not the same as the presence of the things judged about. When I frame the judgment in a report—I say "The front door is open" while I am behind the house—the judgment is there but the door and its being open are emptily intended. Even when I frame the judgment in a registration of its fact, I may turn my attention from the fact as registered and focus on the judgment—the fact as supposed—and make the judgment, not the registered fact, present intuitively to my mind. This happens when I reflect.

Framing a judgment makes the judgment, not necessarily its registered fact, intuitively present. But the judgment can also be brought to the presence of what is intended through it. Two degrees are possible in this. First, the judgment can be brought directly to the registered fact it is correlated with. The fact can be actually registered, and its identity with the judgment recognized. The judgment is matched to the facts. This is the clarity of actual possession (*FTL*, § 16c).

Second, we can have a "clarity of anticipation," a

---

tion of the public is not adequate for political life; in terms of the kinds of human association distinguished by Aristotle in *Politics* 1. 2—family, village, city—Heidegger's thoughts are most appropriate for the village, not the city. A village is not based on any kind of constitution or "social contract."

"prefigurative clarity," an "intuitive but merely prefigurative consciousness" (*FTL*, § 16c; § 59; app. II, § 2a, p. 314; *APS*, § 19, p. 79). Here the sense *can* be brought to the presence of facts and matched against them, but it is not actually so consummated. The judgment is capable of matching facts, and is considered under the rubric of this capacity, even though the capacity is not yet actualized. We appreciate the judgment as capable of being fulfilled if we can imagine how we would saturate it (*CM*, § 25).

If a judgment has clarity of anticipation it is verifiable or falsifiable; if it has clarity of possession it is verified or falsified. A judgment can exercise its clarity of anticipation in a report; it exercises its clarity of possession only in registration.

A judgment executed with clarity is one that can enter into the process of adequation to registered facts; clarity is the dimension concerned with verification and falsification. The dimension of distinctness does not raise these issues; its concern is merely the presence of the judgment as such, not the judgment's adaptation beyond itself to facts. Different issues arise in each dimension, and different rules for forming wholes out of parts operate in each. The state of distinctness is governed by rules for formal consistency, while the state of clarity is governed by rules for coherence of the "contents" of judgmental meanings. A clear judgment is one whose partial meanings work together in the same language game, so that it makes sense to try to verify the whole judgment against facts.

We have already said that judgment is the identity within two states: (*a*) the absence constituted by vagueness and (*b*) the presence achieved in distinctness. We now fill this out: the judgment also requires (*c*) the state of clarity, of being actually or potentially laminated against facts (*FTL*, § 21). Judgment is the identity in all three states, because even a distinct judgment is made with the teleology of heading for facts as they are. Its sense is to be verified or falsified. Still, distinctness and clarity are two different dimensions, even though the full sense of judgment requires both as moments.

§ 75. FORMALIZING AND GENERALIZING

WE HAVE DISTINGUISHED a prejudgmental level, that of expression, and three states of judgment: vague, distinct, and clear. We must discuss three levels of formal structure which cross over the three states. But before doing that we must explain the notion of form.

Husserl distinguishes two kinds of abstractive processes, generalization and formalization (*Ideas I*, § 13). Generalization consists in moving from a certain content to a wider content which includes the first, like the move from dog to animal to living thing; it is possible to generalize in a step-by-step progression. The reverse of generalization is specialization, when our content is moved from a wider to a narrower one contained within it, from animal to dog to terrier. All such moves and subordinations are a matter of the contents of the meanings and objects involved.

Formalization takes place in one stroke, not step by step. It involves rendering the content of the meanings or objects indeterminate or indifferent, as "anything at all." The judgment or fact is not taken as empty of content, but as indeterminate in regard to content. What is left when the contents are rendered completely indeterminate is the formal structure that can be united with "anything whatever" and the various derivations that "anything" can undergo. A form like "S is p," claims Husserl, is an example of what is left after such variation.

Since no determinate content is left we cannot have generalization or specialization, but we can still subordinate one form to another: "Sp is q" is subordinate to "S is p." Subordination in formal structures is brought about by a further operation performed on the prior form, not by narrowing the breadth of the content in the meaning, object, or fact (*FTL*, §§ 13b, c). And obviously, deformalization—reinsertion of specific content into form—is different from specialization, narrowing a content to one of its subordinate parts.

Both generalization and formalization can be performed either on objects and facts or on meanings. When we generalize objects we get various levels of essences that are hierarchically arranged; when we generalize meanings we get concepts of wider or narrower scope. When we formalize objects and facts we get the system of formal ontology; when we formalize meanings—judgments—we get the various structures studied in formal apophantic logic.

Formalization is an abstractive process and yields moments, not independent pieces. Form and content, or "stuff" as Husserl sometimes calls it, are supplements to each other in the concrete judgment. We do not impose ready-made forms on pre-existent contents. The two moments exist in tandem (*FTL*, app. I, §§ 3, 7).

In the domain of meaning, the stuff-moments differ from form-moments because every part of the content involves a reference to objects intended through the judgments, while the formal parts do not. In a judgment like "The tree is green," the contents "tree" and "green" both have a referential dimension to realities beyond the judgment, in addition to having an affinity to one another as parts of a complex whole; while the formal moment "The —— is . . ." serves not to refer but to combine material parts of the judgment. The formal moment provides linkage, not reference.

The formula "The S is *p*" expresses a whole judgment but leaves the material cores indeterminate. The formula "The —— is . . ." expresses just the formal moment of the judgmental whole, while "tree-green" expresses the material moment. These formal and material parts are moments and not pieces. They exist concretely only together with one another. Husserl calls the concrete combination of form and stuff the "syntagma" (*FTL*, app. I, § 8).

§ 76. Morphology of Judgment Forms

THERE ARE THREE STRATA of formal structures in the judgment: the morphology of judgment forms, the rules for formal consistency, and the rules of truth logic. These are three levels of formal logic. They crisscross with the three judgmental states of vague, distinct, and clear.

The morphology of judgment forms simply collects the various formal moments that are possible in categorial articulation, not only for the judgment of predication, but for all kinds of judgment (*FTL*, § 13). In addition it classes judgmental forms according to their dependence or subordination to one another. "*Sp* is *q*" is derivative on "*S* is *p*," "*aRb.bRc* implies *aRc*" is derivative on *aRb*. As always, formal subordinations are the result of further operations performed on more basic judgmental forms.

Even confused and vague judgments have to conform to the rules of judgmental morphology. A combination of terms that is not well formed, like "king but or and"—or to avoid the confusion with grammatical malformation, a string like $R \ v \ / \ S$—is no judgment or judgmental form at all, not even a vague one. It is a heap of terms, not succeeding in combining to form a single whole; it is a debris of pieces of meaning, not a single complex meaning. If such a malformed string is combined even confusedly, there is no judgment, not even a confused one, that could later be identified with what is brought to distinctness. Nothing is being expressed. But if the string is well formed, even though vague, it is possible to identify it as the same as what is later articulated distinctly.

It is important to distinguish between the morphology of judgment forms and the morphology of the forms of expression, the grammar of a given language. A sentence may be grammatically malformed and still serve to express a well-formed judgment; "She's not much good for pretty but pretty much good for strong" is not elegant English but it does have an identifiable judgmental sense that can be properly paraphrased.[8] True, grammatical malformation can slide into judgmental malformation, and the borders may be hard to determine in certain cases, but the fact that they can be distinguished in some instances shows that there are two levels of rule-governed formations of wholes, judgmental and grammatical or expressive.

Jokes and plays on words often exploit the difference between the two levels. The expressive whole can be taken to express two different meanings which stand in a certain tension to one another because they cohabit the same expression; and yet we know which of the two is the point that caps the story, because it is the more surprising or embarrassing.

In poetry or in the lyrics of songs a still more primitive level begins to assert itself more strongly than in ordinary speech, the sensuous character of the expressions. To exploit the sensuous rhythms and color of a language, its grammatical form may be forced to suffer distortions, and the judgmental form may be so distended that we would be hard put to it to paraphrase or

8. Often translations provide good examples; here is one describing instruments of amusement in a catalogue: "ROOP-THE-ROOP. Two rockets, accommodated each 4 persons, equipped at the edge of arm, circle vertically, having quick revolution, so that visitors have much thrill by the turning somersault. DAMBOO. Four different animals go round, having the movement of up and down. This equipment is a favourable amusement facility for children. OCTPUS. Carriage, accommodated from 2 to 3 persons equipped at each top of 8 legs of octpus shaped device. All of legs are revolved and make a movement of up and down, so that visitors have a fun to be tossed by octpus legs" (*New Yorker*, October 9, 1971, p. 96).

even mark out sections, judgmental units, in what is being expressed.[9] And yet, unless the exercise falls into sheer word-music, there must be a vestige of grammatical form and judgmental composition, whose very distortions may be part of the structure of the poem or lyrics. One has to be skilled in a language to understand its poetry, partly because only then can one appreciate the significance of rule violations in it. Different poets may exploit different levels in their work—the judgmental, the expressive and grammatical, the rhythmic—but a great poet will master them all.

When an expression is ambiguous, it is possible to appeal to the intention of the speaker to determine the proper sense. But, unless he is to turn from meanings to things, the speaker will have to paraphrase the meaning in other words in order to identify it. He can never present the meaning pure and simple, apart from one of its expressive possibilities. If we deal with a written or recorded expression and cannot ask the speaker any questions, we must appeal to other things the same man has uttered to infer which of the possible meanings is the one he had in mind. In any case, even when direct questions are possible, the meaning is available only as played off against the level of expression.

§ 77. CONSISTENCY OF JUDGMENTAL FORMS: THE VOICE OF THE JUDGER

THE SECOND STRATUM of judgmental form is the level of consistency. Once various judgmental forms have been articulated, the possibility arises of combining two or more of them into a larger whole. In some cases this can be done, in other cases it is prohibited. The only rubric that prohibits combination of one form with another is the rule against inconsistency. "All S are p and some S are not p" is not a possible whole because the second half contradicts the first, and it does so "analytically," by virtue of the formal moment of the whole judgment. It does not violate morphological rules.

So long as the judgment remains in its vague state such in-

9. See J. Edie, "Can Grammar Be Taught?" *Patterns of the Life-World*, ed. J. Edie, F. Parker, and C. Schrag (Evanston, Ill.: Northwestern University Press, 1970), p. 333.

consistency may be tolerated. Even when vague the judgment must be morphologically well formed to be a judgment at all, but good morphology does not rule out inconsistency. The passivity of a confused judgment allows its owner to be held by one position and by its formal contradictory, because he has made neither position explicitly his own. He can say now this and now that because he is only the mouthpiece for general opinion which is awash with contradiction, since all its floating positions and maxims move from this place and time to that, and combine with one another in all sorts of ways. There is no identifiable speaker of public opinion, it is only what "they" say. And so we cannot look for consistency, for saying the same thing, from it; even a particular speech, a single complex judgment that lets its parts combine by associative inertia, can tolerate inconsistency because of this lack of an identifiable speaker. So if an individual lets himself be carried by what "they" say, formal inconsistencies will arise and be quite acceptable, both in particular speeches and in the sum of speeches he makes during his life.

The distinct state of judgment differs from the confused state in that the speaker actively articulates the parts of the judgment himself. It becomes his judgment and his position. He differentiates himself as a speaker from the anonymous, confused voice of public opinion, and his judgment differentiates itself from what "they" say. He and his position become conspicuous, identifiable, and responsible. When this happens no particular speech of his, no complex judgment, can afford to be formally inconsistent. If the speaker is talking literally—the cases of paradox and metaphor call for special analysis—he cannot, as an individual, hold two contradictory positions, because each destroys the other, simply by virtue of their form or linkage. The two judgmental articulations cannot be made together.

When a judgment is brought from its vague to its distinct state, the speaker may find that it is consistent in both states and that he has no need to abandon what he held vaguely. But the movement from one state to the other may reveal that the vague judgment falls apart into two or more inconsistent positions when made distinct. The speaker realizes that he did not hold a single tenable position at all—it turns out to have been several incompatible positions masked as one—so now he must distinguish and partially accept, partially reject his prior pretended judgment (see Plato, *Sophist* 230B–E, 252C).

The formal discipline that is matched to distinct judgments

is the logic of consistency, or consequence logic (*FTL*, §§ 14, 17). Husserl calls it apophantic analytics: "analytics" because it gives rules for consistency based entirely on formal moments in judgmental wholes, and therefore prescribes the structures for analytic validity; "apophantic" because it focuses on judgment as opposed to objects and facts, for there can also be an analytics, formal ontology, focused on objects and states of affairs instead of meanings.

In developing the sense of distinctness and consistency, we have stressed the role of the speaker of the distinct judgment and his emergence as an identifiable voice. Husserl does not emphasize this as much as we have, largely because he is concerned with scientific judgments. The speaker of science, as a network of judgments, is the scientific community; its voice is choral and not individual. It is already differentiated from the cacophony of common opinion and has submitted itself to the rules of consistency. It can be taken for granted that there is an identifiable speaker, or chorus of speakers, and the only problem left is to determine whether a given judgmental combination is or is not consistent. All the concern of analysis is with the complex judgment form.

We have expanded the scope of our inquiry beyond the voice of science to the constitution of any voice at all. This forces us to mention explicitly what Husserl does not state in *Formal and Transcendental Logic*, the requirement that the complex judgment we are scrutinizing for consistency be the judgment of one speaker. If there are two speakers, "All S are p" can be stated by one and "Some S are not p" by the other; only when the two judgments are combined into a whole to be asserted by one speaker do they become inconsistent. When we say the combination of these two judgments cannot be asserted as a whole, we implicitly mean that it cannot be asserted as a whole by one speaker, even though the individuality of the speaker is left unidentified; he is formalized as a voice, but he is not separated from the complex judgment, nor it from him. The formal moment of a definite speaker is a necessary supplement to a distinct judgment, but it is not a necessary supplement to a vague judgment, since the mouthpiece of what "they" say can support the latter.

Certain conditions must be fulfilled even for a mouthpiece of public opinion: one must learn the appropriate language, the governing part of growing into a way of life. This allows one to form the expressive wholes that are the necessary support for possession of any meaning, even that which is passively and inauthentically assimilated. One becomes the agent of grammatical form and judgmental morphology. But merely knowing the language does not constitute one as a definite speaker; one must frame judgments to achieve that distinction.

The distinct discourse of science, which is the horizon within which Husserl carries on his investigations, is only one case of distinct speech and identifiable speaker, even though in modern times it has come to be accepted by many as the only one. By expanding the horizon to include the constitution of voices and speeches of all sorts, it becomes possible to locate science and even "philosophy as a rigorous science" within the wider context of human affairs. In this perspective some dilemmas of Husserl's phenomenology—the problem of the discourse leading into phenomenology, the apparently arbitrary obsession with apodicticity, the epochē, the status of the transcendental ego—can be resolved and the contribution Husserl's thought can make to human affairs can be better appreciated.

§ 78. Truth Logic and Coherence

THE THIRD LEVEL of formal logic is truth logic, and it corresponds to judgments performed with clarity. Truth logic expresses the formal laws governing the process of bringing a judgment to adequation with registered facts (*FTL*, § 15).

Husserl claims that traditional logic does not distinguish sufficiently between laws in consequence logic, or analytics, and laws in truth logic. It confusedly takes, for instance, the laws of noncontradiction, of excluded middle, of identity, and of *modus ponens* and *modus tollens* now as rules for consistency, now as rules for truth; but when the two logics are distinguished the laws have to be formulated appropriately for each. The law of noncontradiction in consequence logic would state that if one judgment is valid as a meaning, its contradictory in form cannot be held as a meaning; two contradictory judgments cannot be distinctly given as copossible. The law of excluded middle would claim that of two contradictory judgments, one or the other must be capable of distinct "mathematical" existence (*FTL*, § 20).

Now if we put these laws into truth logic, the law of non-contradiction states that of two contradictory judgments we can expect only one, and not both, to be verified or matched to the facts (*FTL*, §§ 20, 77). Only one can be found to be correct, and if one is matched to the facts then a priori its contradictory cannot be. The law of excluded middle states that every judgment can indeed be brought to the facts and either verified or falsified; i.e., there is no judgment that is not decidable against an appropriate state of affairs. Further, the law of excluded middle implies that once a judgment is decided as true or false, it is so once and for all; evidence at one time is a permanent evidence that lasts through time. Husserl claims that the principle of identity can be interpreted this way in truth logic, as a statement of the permanence through time of a judgment's truth status. He adds that it also refers to the intersubjective truthfulness of a judgment.

All these formal rules, and others besides, deal with the judgment in its adequation to registered fact (*FTL*, § 78). They are principles of truth logic. In the logic of consistency their analogues would deal with the existence of the judgment as such, and the possibility of its coexistence with other judgments.

The two domains have traditionally been confused because the judgment is teleologically oriented toward matching facts and thus the logic of consistency is a condition for bringing about truth. But the two domains must be kept distinct because the sense of each of the formal disciplines is different. However, we can appreciate the difference only if we climb out of the formal disciplines and examine the intentionality that works through consistency into truth. This phenomenological examination is not possible as long as we are carrying out one of the formal enterprises themselves.

Formal principles in truth logic, such as those we have examined and others like the presuppositions of truth and falsity, the identifiability of judgments, and the decidability of judgments, are "idealizing presuppositions" in our exercise of verification (*FTL*, pt. II, ch. 3, p. 184). That is, they are not based on empirical generalizations of what has been experienced, but express various ideal components of the sense of truth. Many judgments have never and will never be matched to facts, but the sense that they are made to be matched is still in them.

We have examined some formal rules governing the truth of judgments. Another set of formal rules determines that the parts of a judgment may themselves be syntactic formations. In "*S* is *p*," for instance, *S* may be a state of affairs, "*T* is *q*," or a relation, *aRb*. However, if we keep unpacking syntactic formations, we finally come to parts which have no syntax within them. Ultimately, says Husserl, we come to unmodified judgments about individuals (*FTL*, § 82). These judgments are the basis for all higher-level ones.

When we examine the truth of such individual judgments, when we discuss how they can match appropriate facts, we find that the material cores, the stuff-moments which we have not mentioned in our formal treatment of truth logic, now become relevant. If a given judgment is to be matched to registered facts, the material cores of its parts have to be coherent (*FTL*, § 87). They must belong to the same language game or "object" game. Material moments like "tree-large," "man-tired," or "lamp-bright," do form coherent wholes when united as parts; others like "sleep-orange," "vice-swift," or "stone-witty," if taken literally and univocally, do not. That is why it makes no sense to try to verify or falsify a judgment like "His sleep is yellow," or "My vices are fast."

A judgment with incoherent contents cannot enjoy clarity, not even the clarity of anticipation. If inconsistency in judgmental form disqualifies a judgment from being brought to distinctness, incoherence of content disqualifies it from being brought to clarity. And now a mutual implication comes to light: consistency is required as a condition for bringing a judgment to truth, and so distinctness is a condition for clarity; but coherence of the material cores is necessary as a condition for bringing a judgment to distinctness, so clarity is a condition for distinctness. An incoherent judgment like "All sleep is orange," Husserl claims, is beyond contradiction and consistency because it does not constitute a whole of meaning (*FTL*, §§ 88–89). It fails to do so not because of morphological deficiency or formal contradiction, but because the partial elements in its material core do not make a coherent whole sense. The stuff-moment "sleep-orange" is not an "ideal possibility" and the judgment of which it is a moment—we must always remember that material wholes are only abstracta that need judgmental form to exist concretely—also is not a real possibility as a distinct judgment.

§ 79. THE RETURN OF JUDGMENT TO PERCEPTION

INCOHERENT MATERIAL WHOLES are impossible as meanings because it is impossible to experience the parts of such wholes in the unity of a single perceptual intuition. I am able to verify a judgment with the material core "tree-green" because in the perception of a tree I can encounter green as a latent part of what is experienced. But in the experience of trees I cannot encounter cowardice as a latent part, so the blend of "tree-coward" is not possible. The base for the coherence of material parts is thus the continuum of experience into which a judgment is submerged when it is desyntaxed and the judgmental consciousness gives way to the perceptual. In the other direction, the continuum of perceptual experience, with its potential parts, can become articulated into judgmental consciousness when the parts become actually recognized as parts and a fact is registered. Perceptual objects lend themselves to the registration of facts, but perceptual objects are not yet facts, just as perceptual consciousness is not judgmental consciousness. What comes out of perceptual experience as the material core in judgments then serves as a norm for making judgments in the absence of the objects, either in signitive reporting or in the mere framing of judgments, because the teleological sense of judgments is to return to the registered fact and ultimately to the objects in the process of verification.

The work of formal moments in a judgment is to link the parts of the judgment to one another in the many ways that morphology allows. They determine how the parts are to be articulated as parts. Formally consistent judgments are those whose parts are acceptably linked to make one whole; formally inconsistent judgments are not one whole of meaning but many. A distinct judgment must have good linkage to come to be as a unitary sense.

The work of stuff-moments in a judgment is not to link parts but to refer outside the judgment to what is intended through it. There is a "naming" dimension to all material cores; the expression of each could, in a limit case, be used just to name some object, attribute, or dimension, in pure perceptual recognition, apart from setting up what is named as a base for syntactic articulation. This is obvious for names which work as the subjects of sentences and refer to concrete objects; they are names par excellence. But it is also true of words that stand as predicates in sentences and thus express predicates in judgments, words whose unmodified, original use is adjectival and not nominative. "Red" can be used as a name in sheer perceptual recognition. If articulation were to set in, we would immediately recognize that the unmodified use of "red" is not referential but qualifying; our primitive judgment would be, "This X is red." But this recognition only arises within the judgmental consciousness, when such differences become actualized; in the perceptual consciousness they are only latent.

When the judgmental consciousness makes its articulation— let us say in a predicative form like the judgment "This car is red"—the immediate naming function of the judgment's subject remains; the subject is used to refer to an object and to set it up for attribution. But the predicate "red" no longer names immediately; it now exercises its objective reference through the subject's referring.[10] The predicate keeps its objective tendency. It does not become purely syncategorematic like the formal parts of the judgment; if it did, it would no longer serve to modify the object. But its objective tendency works in intending "car as red," not simply "red." The predicate's objective reference can work through that of the subject because the two are joined, by formal moments, into a single complex whole of meaning. So there are not two independent references in a judgment, but only one, which is complex, because what the judgment matches is the fact that the car is red, not just the car or even the red car.[11]

10. *FTL*, app. I, § 4. See J. Searle, *Speech Acts* (Cambridge: At the University Press, 1970), p. 118.

11. Tugendhat has an extensive criticism of Husserl in "Phänomenologie und Sprachanalyse," *Hermeneutik und Dialektik*, ed. R. Bubner, K. Cramer, and R. Wiehl (Tübingen: Mohr, 1970), II, 3–23. He complains that Husserl's concept of intentionality is dominated by the idea of having an object simply present to us (*Vorstellung*), as when we name something or have it visually given (pp. 19–22). This idea, he says, does not let Husserl develop sufficiently the notion of object as the subject given for predication; one of its bad effects is to force Husserl into conceiving predication as the synthesis of two objects, not as a rule-governed use of language (pp. 14–19). I do not think Husserl is vulnerable to these criticisms. The description Husserl gives of the emergence of predicates out of perception acknowledges that the predicate is latent in the thing perceived, and does not appear as another object yoked to the subject (*LI*, VI, § 48). And the categorial activity that actualizes this state of affairs is certainly a rule-governed performance. A rule can be either "emptily" or "intuitionally" exercised, and in this way Husserl allows us to reconcile cognitive fulfillment with the following of rules. Finally, Tugendhat claims that teaching the rule-governed use of words means showing the conditions under which statements involving the words are true (pp. 16–17). I admit this is a necessary condition for learning the rules, but in addition one must come to exercise the rule authentically and not languidly.

§ 80. TEMPORAL FACTORS WITHIN THE
STATES OF JUDGMENT

A JUDGMENT CAN BE BROUGHT from a state of vagueness to distinctness and clarity, but the three states do not simply succeed one another in time. The judgment is not moved from vagueness first to distinctness and then to clarity. Rather the motion is from vagueness on one side, to a state where the two moments of distinctness and clarity are brought about together. The two extremes, vagueness versus distinctness/clarity, cannot be simultaneous. A given judgment cannot be vague and also distinct/clear at the same time. But it does become distinct/clear simultaneously.

Since a judgment must exist in some state or other, an element of temporality is introduced into Husserl's theory of judgment, and an element of historicity into his theory of meaning. The effect a judgment has in human thinking, and in human affairs generally, depends on the state in which it subsists at a given time. It makes a difference whether it is vaguely possessed or authentically framed with distinctness and clarity. Even its effective logical implications depend on this.

§ 81. TWO KINDS OF JUDGMENT WITH DISTINCTNESS
BUT WITHOUT CLARITY

A. Judgment using metaphor

A JUDGMENT THAT REACHES DISTINCTNESS is one that is explicitly executed and obeys the laws of formal consistency. But no judgment that does not also enjoy clarity of anticipation would be executed by anyone who knows the language he is speaking. No one who knows English would say, literally, "Tall virtue sleeps furiously," or "Stones are quick-witted friends."

There are two kinds of judgment, both using language in nonordinary ways, in which a distinct and consistent judgment, seriously executed, may still lack clarity if taken literally. First, there are judgments using metaphor: "Red is a loud color," and "That is a friendly building," are formally consistent but materially incoherent if the words are taken literally. Of course they are not meant to be taken literally; they are distortions artfully made and are necessary for the life of the language. But their decidability and verification work in ways different from the ways of univocal speech.

Before we decide whether the judgment is acceptable, we have to let the metaphor sink in. We have to tolerate the manifest incoherence. The decidability of the judgment using metaphor is not settled by saturating the intention with a familiar perception; rather the metaphor is an attempt to make us perceive differently. It wants to provoke a new perception, to make us aware of differences and similarities that have not been institutionalized in univocal, accepted speech. A metaphor, with its surprising incoherence of meaning, with anticipations which lead into unfamiliar ways, makes things appear afresh to our shocked sensibility. Its "verification" consists in making truth, not matching it. It brings about an unfamiliar identity synthesis.

Therefore, the success or failure of a judgment with metaphor is not expressed by saying the judgment is true or false, but that it uses a good or bad metaphor. We cannot say that "Red is a loud color" is true, while "Red is a soft color" is false; if the propositions were so definitely decidable, they would not contain functioning metaphors. The metaphors would no longer be lively, but would have settled into established meanings. Instead we would say that the first judgment is better than the second in most circumstances, but there could be cases where the second metaphor is better to arouse the perception that is appropriate and desired.

To carry out its function, a judgment using metaphor must achieve distinctness. If it were formally contradictory it might serve to express a paradox (if we wished to retain it at all), but then its metaphorical disclosure would be subordinated to that purpose. Thus a judgment with metaphor lives on the difference between distinctness and clarity, for it possesses distinctness, being explicitly executed and formally consistent, while it defies clarity.

Metaphor rearranges the potentials of our sensibility and provokes a new way of perceiving. Perceiving is taken here in the wide sense Husserl gives it, meaning any unarticulated intuition at all, not just immediate seeing, hearing, smelling, tasting, and touching. I may perceive someone trying to make a decision, and this involves more than what my senses immediately report. It involves an extensive acquaintance with the person and the circumstances in which the decision is being prepared. Suppose that, at an exasperating moment, the man says, "I'm just treading water with this problem." The metaphor in this judgment articulates what I perceive and allows me to perceive the man and his situation as capable of being articulated in that way. Perhaps I never thought of deliberation in that way before: as an attempt to find a foothold against which one has leverage for one's choice.

Are all metaphors registrations when they are first formulated? Can't some be introduced as reports? If they can, perhaps metaphor is not as closely associated with perception as we have claimed. Obviously we do not need to be in the physical presence of what we are discussing in order to establish a metaphor. But simple reporting, the purely signitive consciousness, does not provide a proper context either. One's mind must be held in focus on the subject for the metaphor to have its effect, and it is so held, generally, by memorial or imaginative consciousness which, according to *Logical Investigations,* count as intuitive awareness as opposed to signitive intending. And sometimes, of course, a fresh metaphor does work in the actual perception of the object. Metaphors are put into reporting, however, only when they cease being lively.

Metaphors are enlightening precisely because they would be incoherent if taken literally. The fact that they don't literally fit what we are talking about makes us scrutinize the object more carefully than we have been accustomed to; we let it manifest itself in the new way. The initial incoherence of metaphor dissolves in the new intelligibility disclosed in what we perceive. The scrutiny a metaphor provokes makes each judgment using metaphor into a registration. If we have been carrying out a report in our discussion, the surprise of a metaphor makes us hold the object in focus once more—through memory, imagination, or perception—to let its new intelligibility be registered.

Aristotle observes that the formal structure operating within metaphor is often the analogy: A is to B as C is to D (*Poetics* 21). In the metaphor "Red is a loud color," the analogy at work is that a certain quality is to red as loudness is to sound. This quality, which has no name, is registered by the use of metaphor.

The formal structure of analogy is not expressly manifest in a metaphorical judgment; it is submerged, and some of the material components of the analogy are submerged as well. In our example, "sound" is not mentioned even though it must be understood by anyone who appreciates the metaphor. The formal structure of the analogy remains hidden, and the only explicit formal structure that lies on the surface of our example is the predicative form, "S is an x-ish p." But a metaphor requires the tension between this explicit formal structure and the submerged but working form of analogy; without the latter we would have an ordinary univocal statement like "Granite is a hard rock." We might say that the analogy in metaphor comes from superimposing one perceptual registration on another, in order to bring out fresh aspects of the object of metaphor.

The structure of analogy in metaphor is necessary for the life of a language, because it provides us with new categoriality to register perceptions that do not fall under standard, established univocal terms. Only a finite number of names have been developed in a language, but there are infinitely many ways in which objects lend themselves to registration. Use of analogy in metaphor lets us draw a categoriality from one domain into another and so bring out a new aspect of what we perceive. The "loudness" of red is an aspect that cannot be registered by an ordinary term.

To appreciate the metaphor we may need some patience and toleration of its incoherence before its sense dawns on us. Likewise we must trust the speaker of the metaphor. We tolerate the incoherence and hope to see it dissolved if the speaker is generally insightful; if he is not, our patience runs out quickly. We will brood over a good writer's difficult passages for a long time, but we will not spend much effort on a weak student's apparently incoherent examination.

In actual speech a measure of a speaker's effectiveness and of the interlocutor's ability to follow the argument is the swiftness with which a metaphor is registered and appreciated. The mind opens and closes without pause. And sometimes the speaker hears the metaphor for the first time when he expresses it himself; it is due not only to his wit, but also to the sympathetic context set by him and his interlocutors, the radioactive moment in which the object they discuss can be effectively registered.[12] There is one actuality for several minds.

The authority of the speaker is an important factor in metaphorical judging. At the very least he must have the linguistic capacity to make a metaphor, i.e., he must know the language well enough to realize the difference between speaking literally and not. On a more refined level, he must have the insight to

12. The metaphor is Hugh Kenner's, from *The Pound Era* (Berkeley: University of California Press, 1971), p. 60.

make enlightening metaphors, not just confused or trivial ones. This is a function of his ability to think, not merely of his linguistic skill.

A good metaphor stays and keeps alive the illumination and identity it brought about; a poor metaphor comes and goes, letting the mind return to old ways of thinking.

B. Unacceptable philosophic judgments

THE SECOND KIND OF JUDGMENT that someone who knows a language can seriously execute with distinctness while the judgment fails in clarity is that of pretended philosophic judgments, those that we wish to reject as being "wrong" philosophically. They may be protophilosophical maxims or proverbs, or the initial attempts of someone beginning to think philosophically, or even the fully articulated but unsuccessful judgments of an established philosopher—for instance Locke's judgments about abstract ideas as interpreted by Berkeley.[13] Judgments like "Things are just what I see with my eyes," or "Democracy is the best way of life," are formally consistent and can be explicitly executed and even preserved as permanent beliefs, but they contain latent incoherence. They fail in clarity. And unlike metaphors, their incoherence is not something we are conscious of when we accept such statements; therefore we are misled by what appears as philosophy. Success in achieving distinctness deludes us into believing we have clarity as well, when we do not. This is the kind of category mistake or confusion of language games that Wittgenstein and others have said is endemic to philosophic discourse whenever it tries to do anything more than discover and unravel such incoherences, that is, whenever it makes a positive truth claim of its own. Without agreeing that all philosophical judgments are incoherent, we can say that those we consider wrong are rejected primarily because they are said to be incoherent, meaningless, deficient in what

13. Sometimes speakers in ordinary situations can find the words too much to handle, and cute incoherence can result; here is a coach talking about players: "There are people with something extra. They have the facility for turning a game around, even on one play. And if they don't—if they never get that one play—that threat is still there and you have to respect them for that threat. These kind of people come around most infrequently and sometimes never" (*New Yorker*, February 19, 1972, p. 106).

Husserl calls clarity. Sometimes they may be rejected because of straight inconsistency, but this is uncommon and arises primarily when an interlocutor paraphrases a judgment he considers incoherent into terms which make it formally inconsistent, to make the incoherence more apparent. Philosophical polemic works in the element of incoherence and inconsistency.

Language goes on holiday in two ways in respect to the clarity of judgments: recreatively, when it enjoys the games, fancy, and disclosure of metaphor, and blindly, when it is on vacation but does not know it and keeps up the strain of work without pay; it labors "philosophically" with incoherence while convicted by its own beliefs.

In order to fashion or appreciate a metaphor, one must know the language in which it is made. Knowledge of the language is also a condition for philosophical judgments. The ordinary speaker of a language exercises a normative role over both metaphor and philosophical discourse. He recognizes that certain formulations are not to be taken literally, and it is his ordinary, nonphilosophical judgments about what is the case that must be respected by philosophical statements. The incoherence of wrong judgments that pretend to be philosophical is measured against the meanings established in ordinary use of the language. It is not an incoherence as measured against certain kinds of perceptions of things which only the philosopher has; there are no such privileged perceptions.

Philosophy's quarrel is not with the speaker of ordinary language but with his pretended philosophical judgments. Once a language is spoken there arises the tendency to speak about the conditions that allow such a language-permeated life to be lived: men begin to talk about the world as the whole which lends itself to opinion and speech, and about themselves and what they must do to lead this kind of life well. For the life with language, like all activities of living things, allows the difference between simply being done, and being done well. There arise then judgments about the world as a whole and judgments about the good life for man. Such judgments are not executed without ordinary language, because they talk about ordinary language and its conditions. They are attempts at philosophy. To the extent that philosophy wishes to argue or can argue with such positions, its strategy is to disclose incoherence in them and in their implications with ordinary discourse.

The beliefs expressed in ordinary language are repeated in philosophical discourse, but as neutralized or suspended, as

Husserl shows in his argument for the epochē. But the philosophical judgments themselves, into which ordinary discourse is assimilated, are not neutralized or suspended. They are expressed with conviction: not with a conviction based on the world-belief which supports ordinary language, but with one based on the being-belief which persists through both the natural and the philosophical attitude.

Philosophy requires as its conditions the activity of a life with language and the emergence of opinions about the world as a whole and about the good life. Part of its activity is the examination of such opinions, and where none exist there can be no philosophical life. Philosophy appreciates its own good by contrast with the opinions it examines.

Husserl's form of philosophy requires, in addition, the presence of the kind of science that Galileo initiated. Phenomenology is conditioned by modern mathematical science and its conception of the world as a whole, as well as by the rationalist conception of the good life. It is colored by these conditions and is therefore a distinctly modern philosophy. However, it is analogous to ancient philosophy, for Socrates himself had to distinguish his thinking from that of Anaxagoras and the physicists, and from their opinions about the world as a whole. But the differences between ancient and modern physics are sufficient to bring about a difference in the philosophy conditioned by each.

The discourse of science has been very much revered in modern times for what it has to say about the world as a whole and even about the good life. In some respects, and especially in regard to perceptual experience, the scientific image of the world has entered into conflict with the manifest image. Husserl's attempt to show the origins of science in the ordinary, lived world is an attempt to recover, in a critical and nonnaïve way, the coherence of ordinary discourse with science and philosophy.

The disconnection between the lived world and the world of science is analogous to the problem of a special language for philosophy. The fact that philosophy since the Greeks has been carried on with the help of translation—from Greek to Latin, from Greek to Arabic to Latin, from Latin to modern vernacular, from English to German and German to English, and so on—introduces a disconnection between ordinary language and what philosophy has to say. But unless philosophy is to be book learning or the transmission of fixed propositions, it has to be put into the idiom of a language actually involved in a way of life. Only this will allow it to illuminate phenomena and examine opinions.

9 / Verification in Philosophy

> "Know thyself" is not said to the mind . . . as it is said to a man, Behold thy own face; which he can only do in a looking-glass. For even our own face itself is out of the reach of our own seeing it; because it is not there where our look can be directed. But when it is said to the mind, Know thyself; then it knows itself by that very act by which it understands the word "thyself"; and this for no other reason than that it is present to itself. But if it does not understand what is said, then certainly it does not do as it is bid to do. And therefore it is bidden to do that thing which it does do, when it understands the very precept that binds it.
>
> —Saint Augustine, *De trinitate* (trans. A. Haddan) 10. 9

§ 82. JUDGMENTS BEFORE, DURING, AND AFTER VERIFICATION

HOW ARE JUDGMENTS VERIFIED? Verification, etymologically and in fact, is bringing about truth. There are two senses of truth. First, a judgment is matched to a registered fact and is shown to have the truth of correctness. Second, the registration of the fact is brought about, and we are not concerned with the correctness of any judgment verified thereby, but only with the sheer presence of what is registered. This is the truth of actual presence, and it founds the truth of correctness. Bringing about the truth of correctness must be distinguished from bringing about the truth of actual presence; Husserl calls these achievements two kinds of evidence, since evidence for him is the noetic process correlative to truth. It is the bringing about of truth (*FTL,* § 46). The term "verification," if used in a sufficiently wide sense and not restricted to the confirmation or dismissal of propositions within scientific theory, is also appropriate.

In discussing verification, we must distinguish three states of judgment in function of the time when verification happens: (1) Judgments framed simply as meanings or suppositions, *before* verification takes place. Before seeing Monticello or any pictures of it, I may be given the statement "Monticello is red with white trimmings." All I can do is entertain it as a supposition pending evidence. Years ago the judgment "The moon has a hard surface" had the same status. When there is no evidence yet, not even the assurance of other persons, such judgments are more properly questions than assertions. But they must be distinct and clear if they are to expect saturation. (2) Judgments made *during* saturation. They are part of registrations. Looking at Monticello I describe its color, or someone standing on the moon says it does indeed have a hard surface. (3) Judgments made *after* fulfillment. Once their truth is established we assert them as true even though we do not enjoy their evidence at the moment of assertion. They are made as reports. They have become our convictions, "habitualities" of our intentional life which Husserl compares to the habits that become part of our ordinary personal life. Judgments in this third category can be made in empty intentions; they can be executed in the absence of the objects they are about, but they are executed as true. I cannot remove the fact that in my conscious history they have been verified at some time, so even when I use them to report, I mean them with conviction.

In assimilating the common opinion within which I live, I accept as convictions many judgments which I have not verified myself. But most common beliefs do rest on someone's intuitions, and so are in class (3) in an intersubjective sense. Within common opinion there also are judgments floating around which rest on no fulfillments and belong to (1). It is up to one's own good judgment to determine which are which.

Although both judgments in (1) and those in (3) are exercised in signitive intentions (only those in (2) are intuitive registrations), they are different from one another. Those in (1) are not taken as reports, only as suppositions. They are left undecided.

Judgments in (1) might well be punctuated by "?", those in

(2) by "!", and those in (3) by ".". Such punctuation would express what cannot be expressed in a part of the terminology or syntax of a judgment's expression: the fulfillment or nonfulfillment of the intention whose meaning the judgment is.

Whenever a judgment is actualized it must be in one of these three states, and its truth status depends on which state it enjoys. The truth of a judgment, therefore, cannot be transtemporally asserted. It must be referred to the event of evidence or verification, which is achieved in acts positioned in the time-filled stream of consciousness. Truth logic involves reference to intentional acts that are events in the ego's history.

The standard state of a judgment is to be a report. Its status as a question is geared, teleologically, toward being answered by saturation or by someone else's report, and its status as a registration is exceptional and does not endure. The exclamation point does not express a long-term process; it is punctual. Judgments as reports are settled and rested.

§ 83. JUDGMENTS IN THE NATURAL ATTITUDE

THE SPATIAL CHARACTER of material being brings about gaps between states (1), (2), and (3) for all judgments made on the basis of the natural attitude and thus supported by world-belief.

We can bring a judgment to distinct and clear form as a question, and yet be utterly unable to answer it. We have to go places and do things to uncover its truth or falsity; in the meantime the judgment does subsist as a clear and distinct meaning. Spatial absence is a condition in being which prevents immediate resolution of such empty intending. It keeps (1) and (2) apart.

When registration of material things occurs, the open-ended perception that underlies it prevents each registration from being exhaustive and final.[1] Not only does it not say everything

---

1. ZB, no. 52, pp. 356–57: "The judgment is not evident when the perception that underlies it is incomplete." Husserl adds that all thing-perceptions are incomplete, then says, "On the other hand when you don't have a thing, but an object which is 'closed' in itself as the object of judgment, then the judgment is evident, if the perception of this object is there, and insofar as perception here can include nothing unfulfilled (that makes no sense in regard to such objects)."

that can be said about the object; what it does say is itself never free from possible revision or cancellation. It is always corrigible.

We have discussed the reasons Husserl gives for this. A registration asserts something about an object as it is in itself, but it does so on the basis of exposure to only some of the profiles of the object. There are always profiles that are absent. Exposure to them may adjust or negate the registration we have made.

A registration transcends the immediate profiles, just as perception does; perception is the presence not just of the series of profiles that actually occur, but of the identity of the object within the manifold of profiles, and this identity includes the aspects, sides, and apparitions which have not become actually present. Registration makes this identity intelligible, and so it takes the risk—as perception does—of believing in an identity beyond that of actual presence, and of implicitly asserting what its other presences will be like. This implicit prediction may turn out to be wrong, and the registration itself rejected.

This risk is not a fault of consciousness, as though we bite off more than we can chew. Our unclosed intentionality is based on the kind of object we know in the world. The material thing exists in such a way that it does not present itself fully at any time. It is not a question of getting around a thing more quickly in order to see all the sides at once; such an "ideal" of total presence would destroy the object we wish to experience. There is no other way for a thing to be manifest except through the mixture of presence and absence; its profiles are exclusive and disjunctive. The mind is distended in perceiving because the objects it knows are distended in being, not because of its epistemological greed.

To put it another way, each registration has implications. Other judgments can be made about the object as implications of the single registration. We believe the implications, but they are not registrations. It is always possible to try to verify them in registration, and they may, conceivably, turn out to be false. Their falsity reverberates along the implicational channels and makes us adjust or negate the registration we once experienced as positive. No registration of material things is free of this possibility. Implicational networks of judgments about a thing exist in the categorial domain and are the categorial equivalent of networks of profiles in the thing as perceived. The possibility and the need for implication in natural science are based on the spatiality of material being.

This does not mean that we should suspect our registrations. The correction of perceptual registration is a conceivability, not an imminent threat. It is asserted in reflective analysis of perception and registration. It does not make us "more careful" in what we say; in the natural attitude assurance is assurance, with sufficient force for the needs of the natural attitude. Philosophical reflection does not change that. But it does disclose the nature of this assurance.

When a judgment becomes a report, going from state (2) to (3), it is again separated from its registration. It floats on its own after being registered. It may subsequently be difficult or practically impossible to register it again and reconfirm it, because of the spatial absence of what it is about. As much effort may be needed to reconfirm as had to be used to register it originally.

The low density of saturation in judgments registered about things means that a judgment which is used as a report is always liable to be returned to the state of a question, or even negated as a conviction. So even though it has reached state (3), we cannot be absolutely certain it will remain there forever. And yet, because state (2) has actually intervened, state (3) is quite different from state (1). Judgments in (1) can't get to (3) without passing through (2), and when they do revert from (3) to (1) they do so only because of further occurrences in (2). Registrations keep questions and reports apart, but also bind them to one another. Registrations in the natural attitude, because of their matrix of spatial and material being, always keep open the flow between questions and reports.

We have developed these characteristics of judgment in a formal way. Let us illustrate them. We see a bird and register it as a robin looking for worms. The "robin" suddenly starts to expand and then to shrink, getting very large and very small! Or the "robin" suddenly explodes in a puff of smoke! Our reaction: "Whatever that is (was), it isn't (wasn't) a robin." We have a piece of wood in hand. We turn it around, and it is transparent from the other side! "This can't be wood after all." A cup of water is on the table. The water suddenly becomes blue and then starts changing color rapidly; it creeps out of the cup and congeals into a sphere on the table! "This is definitely not water."

We do not expect these things to happen. Even after my description of them, you will not expect water, wood, or robins to behave this way. There are standard series of profiles for these things, and we will trust them to behave as they have behaved, and continue to expect the registrations and confirmations we are accustomed to. Empirical universals are at work in our registration of things, and such universals are not to be changed unless our experience actually changes. Words cannot change them, nor can imagination.

Fantastic processes like these are often narrated in children's stories. For a child the empirical universals in the world are still not permanently settled, and the possibility of such wonders is not yet as implausible as it is for adults, who have gotten quite sure about what one can and cannot expect from things. Eidetic variation is a means of regaining the limits of conceivability which the child tests with his stories. Science fiction is another way in which imaginative variation is carried out: "One's first encounter with good science fiction is a mind-boggling event. It's like having the mind washed clean of everything taken for granted and suddenly seeing things in an entirely new way. Horizons expand to touch worlds that had never even existed before." [2] In science fiction we stay with the variation long enough and consistently enough to make a story out of it.

You did not take seriously the marvels I described, but you did understand them. They are conceivable. And despite some discomfort you agree that if these things did happen, you would have the reaction which I described: you would negate your original registration. Any registration based on the perception of spatial things is *conceivably* corrigible. There are, Husserl claims, certain other registrations for which such corrigibility is inconceivable. We will examine them as judgments made within the science of phenomenology.

In contrast to the examples just given, consider the following narration: "The first verse of the song having ended, the second verse is sung instantaneously. It takes no time to sing it." The rejoinder to this is not to say, "Well, it couldn't have been a song after all; it must have been something else." Rather the response is: "That makes no sense." In fact, it is inconceivable. The words shatter as a whole meaning.

In the first group of examples, a surprising registration forces us to adjust or negate our original registration about the

2. Samuel Mines, "Science Fiction Reaches Escape Velocity and Swings into a Wider Orbit," *Book World, Washington Post*, August 6, 1972, p. 9. See Richard Rorty's introduction to *The Linguistic Turn* (Chicago: University of Chicago Press, 1967), p. 38. And see Wittgenstein's use of imagination and conceivability in *On Certainty* (Oxford: Blackwell, 1969), § 4.

robin, wood, and water. In the second case, the initial registration of the song is followed by a string of words that are incoherent and cannot anticipate any registration at all, so no correction of the first is really proposed. In the first group, the "impossibility" of the fables is based on the overwhelming evidence behind empirical universals. In the second case, the "impossibility" is based on a violation of eidetic necessities. The first is conceivable but most improbable; the second is inconceivable. The first leaves us still anticipating further experience, however curious, of a "this"; the second leaves us with no "this" at all.

In philosophical analysis we get down to the bare bones of conceivability, and must say that all judgments that rest on world-belief and the perception of things are conceivably corrigible, so even when they are used as reports, it is not inconceivable that they could be turned back to questions or into negations by surprising new registrations. And of course, besides the conceivable but unlikely examples we have concocted, there are many ordinary cases. We register something as a man, then subsequent experience makes us doubt, and the report is turned back into a question. Still further evidence may show we were right the first time, or that we were wrong, that it is a tree or a mannequin.

§ 84. PHENOMENOLOGICAL JUDGMENTS ABOUT CONSCIOUSNESS

IF WE SUSTAIN the natural attitude and make judgments about consciousness, we consider consciousness as located within a certain body, and therefore spatially conditioned, and we take it as subject to causal interaction with things. If we perform the epoché and reduction, we are left with pure consciousness as the object of further judgment, and with reflective, immanent perception as the experience that grounds such judgment. How are phenomenological judgments about consciousness, its life, and its objects to be verified? How are they to exist in state (1) as questions, in state (2) as involved in registration, and in state (3) as used in reports?

For the moment we will speak only about judgments concerned with conscious life, acts, and sensations—those that make up "noetic" and "hyletic" phenomenology. Later we will also discuss the judgments in "noematic" phenomenology, about things as meant by consciousness, things as phenomena, the transcendences within pure immanence.

The experience that underlies phenomenological judgment is such that its manifolds of profiles are assimilative and not exclusive and disjunctive. The profiles in "immanent" perception are unlike the profiles at work in "transcendent" perception of material things. Spatial absence does not infect reflective perception; the consequences of spatial absence do not infect judgments based on reflective perception. Therefore, to verify phenomenological judgments it is not necessary to do the kind of work required for ordinary judgments. We do not have to go places and do things in order to discover whether phenomenological or philosophical questions are to be answered affirmatively or negatively. All the evidence is available.

The three temporal states of judgment, (1) before, (2) during, and (3) after registration, which are chronologically separate from one another in the natural attitude, lose their separateness in the transcendental focus. When doing phenomenology, once we bring a judgment to a clear and distinct existence as a meaning, once we bring it to state (1), we have all we need to decide its truth or falsity. Once we execute a phenomenological judgment distinctly and clearly in an empty intention, its truth or falsity dawns on us immediately. There is no obstacle between (1) and (2). Nothing can get in the way and hinder us from verifying the judgment. This is quite different from mundane judgment, where considerable effort may be needed to overcome obstacles between (1) and (2). A phenomenological judgment is decidable as soon as it is understood.

For example, consider the judgments Husserl makes in his description of noeses and hylē and their relationships, his analysis of simple intentions and categorial acts, the definitions of evidence, the contrast between privacy and intersubjectivity, the description of the temporal dimensions of impression, protention, and retention, the distinctions between memory, perception, and imagination, and so on. The judgments he makes in these analyses are such that when we understand them, we have all we need to decide if they are true. They must be executed distinctly and clearly, but if they satisfy these two requirements of understanding, no more needs to be done before they can be decided.

We are never in the position of having to say, "I clearly and distinctly understand what Husserl means, but now I must attempt to see whether it is true." We are never suspended in the interval between intention and verification. Once we understand the meaning we do not have to go anywhere to find its truth, because what he speaks of is constantly available to us. There is nowhere else to go. In the natural attitude it is quite common for us to be stuck between (1) and (2). In the phenomenological attitude the gap between (1) and (2) is closed.

Furthermore, once a judgment in phenomenology has been registered or verified, and thus enters into state (3) as a permanent, habitual conviction of ours, there is never any danger that what was once asserted in evidence will be put back into the state of a question. Phenomenological registrations do not run the risk, as all mundane registrations do, of being countermanded by subsequent registrations. There is no threat that they will fall back into state (1); indeed, it makes no sense to say they might fall back into (1), because, as we have seen, (1) is itself in immediate contact with (2), and would lead us right back into (3).

Thus in phenomenological judgment, all gaps between (1), (2), and (3) are closed. The three states are squeezed into direct contact with one another, and the move from one to the other is instantaneous. As soon as (1) is reached distinctly and clearly, the registration of (2) is immediately available, and established phenomenological judgments in state (3) never leave the accessibility of their evidences in (2), so there is never any fear that they will be subverted.

This self-registration of judgments made in phenomenology is illustrated by a remark of Husserl concerning the attempt to psychologize logical laws. He says in the "Prolegomena": "One might almost say that it is only inconsistency that keeps psychologism alive: to think it out to the end, is already to have given it up" (§ 25, p. 111).[3] The remark is incidental and is not intended to express the nature of phenomenological discourse, but its very casualness makes it a good example. Just "thinking through" the position of psychologism makes it destroy itself, for when we work it out rigorously, we find we have "already" registered its falsity. No further labor is needed.

3. Some other examples: *APS*, § 43, p. 200. "To raise the question is to deny it"; *EP II*, § 53b, p. 180: "To pose the question is already to answer it"; *Ideen III*, § 3, p. 12: "Whoever has followed our expositions has seen it with us." The apodictic statements in Husserl's phenomenology can be compared to what Strawson calls "root tautologies." See *Introduction to Logical Theory* (London: Methuen, 1952), pp. 225–26.

§ 85. ARE PHENOMENOLOGICAL JUDGMENTS TAUTOLOGIES?

DO WE THEN DETERMINE the truth or falsity of phenomenological judgments by inspecting the terms of the judgment? Are phenomenological judgments self-registering because they are tautologies, true or false *ex vi terminorum*?

We must distinguish three kinds of tautology. (*a*) Some complex judgments are inevitably true or false because of their formal or syncategorematic components. Husserl calls these "analytically" true or false. No matter what values are substituted for the variables of a form like "All S are *p* and some S are *p*," it will yield an analytically true judgment, and no matter what is inserted into "All S are *p* and some S are not *p*," it will be analytically false. Analytical truth simply means that the judgment is valid as a meaning.

(*b*) Other judgments are tautologies because of their stuff-moments or material cores, but the speaker or listener accepts them as self-evidently true because of the linguistic conventions in the language they use. "An elevator is a moving platform which brings goods or persons from one level to another." "A prodrome is a symptom that warns us before something occurs." "Fernsehen ist, was Sie 'Television' nennen." Such judgments are paraphrases, definitions, or translations of words. They too work in the domain of meaning.

In order to appreciate the validity or acceptability of these two kinds of tautologies, we do not have to think about the objects meant through them. We do not have to undergo thoughtful experience of elevators, prodromes, or television. Our concern must be not primarily with the thing, but with the words and the meaning expressed in the words. Such judgments are tautologies by the strength of their terms.

(*c*) In another kind of tautology, we must experience the object and register the moments that make it up. Our concern and attention is with the object, not directly with a meaning, term, or words. To appreciate the self-registration of such a tautology, one must be familiar with the object in question.

Such judgments either register parts of the eidos in the object, or—and this is more common—they apodictically speak of instances of the eidos, attributing characters to them which inhere by virtue of the eidos. Bodies interact with one another, melodies take time, language and politics involve obedience to rules, living things assimilate nourishment from their environment. These are tautologous judgments to anyone who is familiar with the objects discussed. They are not full-blown eidetic intuitions because imaginative variation is not played out on them, but their truth rests on the strength of what each object is.

There is some overlap between (*b*) and (*c*). After all, the conventional definitions in (*b*) are not made whimsically; they reflect ordinary experience of real things. And what we are to call things and how we are to break up perceptual continua may affect the possibilities available in (*c*). But the force that explains the necessity is different in each case: in (*b*) certain things are said because we talk this way and call this by that name; in (*c*) certain things are said because that is how things have to be, to be what they are.

The tautology of phenomenological judgments falls under (*c*). It is based on what it is to perceive, to sense, to judge, to remember, to imagine, to exist in temporality, to infer, to forget, to express, to reflect, and to live and perform in the various other ways that make up conscious life and being truthful. We must experience and be concerned with perceiving, sensing, judging, remembering, and the rest if we are to appreciate the judgments phenomenology makes about them. It is not enough simply to inspect the terms used in phenomenological judgments; we must be familiar with what is intended by them.

For this reason there is a difference between states (1) and (2) in phenomenological judgments. If the judgments were true merely *ex vi terminorum*, their validity would be assured within state (1). But they are true not by the strength of the terms, but because of what they are about. So although there is no space-conditioned gap between (1) and (2), the two states do not melt into one another. Phenomenological truth does not rest simply on how we want to define our terms.

The tautologous character of phenomenological judgments is reflected in Husserl's frequent admission that what he says is obvious, trivial, self-evident, and a matter of course; but his judgments are illuminating "trivialities," and are by no means clear to everyone: "Naturally, all these things are the most obvious of the obvious. Must one speak about them, and with so much ado? In life certainly not. But not as a philosopher either?" (*Crisis*, § 28, p. 110; see also p. 111).

§ 86. OBSCURITY IN PHILOSOPHICAL JUDGMENT

IF THERE IS NO GAP between framing a judgment in phenomenology and bringing it to registration, why is there any difficulty in doing phenomenology? Why don't we go from one easy illumination to another, touching truth the way the pre-existent Platonic soul views eternal ideas?

There may be no difficulty in getting from judgment as question to judgment as registration, but there remains the need to get to distinct and clear understanding. We have taken this for granted so far, but can do so no longer: the obstacle to be over-come in phenomenological and philosophical thinking is the move from vagueness to distinctness and clarity, to consistency and coherence. To formulate the question in appropriate terms is the difficulty. Once that is done, verification is no problem. When we let the question sink in, it answers itself.

When Husserl refers to problems still outstanding in his phe-nomenology, he situates them in areas that are still vague and confused, unexplored horizons, places about which we still speak in paradoxes, where contradictions are latent, and where new vocabulary must be established (*Ideas I*, §§ 66–70; § 150, p. 417). We can intend and experience these areas, but only vaguely at first, as horizons left over from registrations we have made. There is room for progression and work in phenomenol-ogy, but progress is not the successful verification of meanings we already have; the labor of phenomenology and philosophy is the constitution of these meanings themselves. As Husserl often says, the elaboration of univocal meanings, the excision of confu-sion and vagueness, is the first and most difficult task he faces.[4]

If framing judgments is the challenge for the phenomeno-logical thinker, understanding them is the challenge for his student. Once clearly and distinctly understood, the judgments will be appropriated, positively or negatively. The problem for someone reading one of Husserl's texts is not to find out if what he reads is true, but to understand what he reads. If he is able to frame the judgments himself, in the derivative way a reader

4. See *LI*, "Prolegomena," § 67; and Introduction to (German) Volume Two, § 2 (pp. 250–54 in Findlay's translation); see the remarks at the end of the introduction to *Ideas I*, pp. 46–47, and those on equivocation in *LI*, V, § 13.

or listener frames judgments, their truth or falsity will be immediately determinable.

In judgments made within the natural attitude there is chronological separation between states (1), (2), and (3). It is brought about by the spatial absence infecting the perception of things. This chronological separation is eliminated in phenomenological judgments because there are no spatial absences in phenomenological experiencing. Phenomenological judgments are "eternally" true or false; once distinctly and clearly articulated, their truth is attached to them immediately and stays attached perpetually. Nothing new can happen to disturb them.

But the catch is in the condition that they be distinctly and clearly articulated.[5] This does take time and effort, but effort of a kind different from that which mundane verification requires. And even when distinctness and clarity are achieved, there is no guarantee that the judgment will not slip back into vagueness, not only in the minds of those who repeat it secondhand, but also in the thinker who managed to frame it authentically. Philosophical thinking demands constant reappropriation; there is always the need to get clear on what we most take for granted.

The process of philosophy takes place in the interval between the vague possession of philosophical judgment and distinct and clear framing. The career of the individual philosopher lives here, and so does the history of philosophy. A philosophical discourse, as illustrated in one of Husserl's meditations, is a process of distinguishing and clarifying, removing confusion and penetrating unexamined horizons. None of it is hypothetical, awaiting further information to decide its truth, nor is any of it simply factual in the mundane sense, subject to the counter-registration of later experience. Phenomenology is apodictic as it proceeds (*CM*, § 9).

The self-evidencing of phenomenological discourse is shown by the way disputes are carried on within it. Since the only progression is from the vague to the distinct and clear, the only way of attacking other positions is by accusing them of being either contradictory (violating distinctness) or meaningless (violating clarity). For example, Husserl rejects skepticism, as well as the theory that evidence is an inner feeling, by claiming

5. *Die Idee der Phänomenologie,* ed. W. Biemel (The Hague: Nijhoff, 1958), p. 61: "Even absolute givenness can be vaguely talked about." See *EP II,* § 50, pp. 155–56; § 52, p. 165; *PP,* § 27, p. 149.

that such doctrines are contradictory or lead to contradictions, or that they are confused (*Ideas I*, §§ 20–21). His attack on some traditional concepts in logic is that the tradition does not distinguish logical structures from the acts that constitute them, and also confuses formal apophantics with formal ontology (*FTL*, § 26), and he observes that only "confused philosophers" could ever deny that perception presents the real material thing (*FTL*, § 106, p. 281). He is able to judge such vagueness and confusion because he has managed to get out of it. Husserl's frequent claim that other positions are absurd, nonsensical, or meaningless is not verbal abuse; it is an exact statement of what is wrong with them.[6]

In such polemics the issue always is: How are we to frame the judgment as question? It is never a matter of disagreement about verification of a judgment whose meaning we agree upon.

Even the stimulus to philosophy has to do with inconsistency and incoherence. A signal that a particular area needs philosophical clarification is the fact that paradoxes and enigmas arise in our talk about it.[7] These are apparent contradictions which are stirred up because we are vague and confused about what we mean. We are surreptitiously doing philosophy without getting clear on how to do it. The root of all such paradoxes, Husserl claims, is being unclear on the way man has a world, i.e., being unclear about the reduction; as long as we are confused about that we cannot move at all in the direction of phenomenology.[8] But once we do turn into the proper focus, and

6. Countless passages illustrate the fact that Husserl rejects opposing positions because they are contradictory, absurd, confused, or meaningless. Just to select a few from *Ideas I*, see his remarks in § 20; § 46, p. 143; § 55, p. 168, where he says, "If anyone objects . . . we can only answer that he has not grasped the meaning [*Sinn*] of these discussions"; § 79, pp. 227–32; and so on. The reader looking for examples could begin almost anywhere in Husserl and will run into instances within a few pages. "Root confusions" would be a good name for such unacceptable positions in philosophy; see Strawson, *Logical Theory*, p. 249.

7. *Crisis*, §§ 53, 58, 65 (pp. 225–26), 70 (p. 241), 57 (p. 202): "If this is supposed to be not an actual absurdity but a paradox that can be resolved. . . ." Husserl also thinks that the philosophical tradition is beset with opposing opinions which can be reconciled by phenomenology; see *PP*, pp. 299–302. And in talking about his analyses of time, he remarks, "Verbally this is contradictory talk, but it is clear that all this does have its absolute right" (Ms F I 29, 1922–23, p. 103).

8. *Crisis*, § 58, p. 204: It is "the enigma of all enigmas." See also § 53, p. 180, quoted above, Chapter 7, n. 15.

apply our minds to the issues at hand, we can turn the provocative paradoxes into illuminating tautologies. Philosophy lives on paradoxes the way medical science lives on the symptoms of illness; but the good of philosophy consists in more than just curing the paradoxes.

These characteristics of philosophical discourse help us understand why there can be no "summary" of someone's philosophy. In mundane science, where the main problem is to verify truth claims, it is possible to abbreviate judgments and give the collected results of investigation without demanding that everyone go through the process of verification that the investigator carried out. I can accept as true the results of a sociological survey or physical experiment without experiencing the survey or the experiment. But there are no "results" separate from the process of expressing philosophy, because the expression is the clarification of philosophical meaning, and the process of philosophy is this clarification. Its truth is immediate to its understanding. It is a gradual crystallization of intelligibility, and in order to understand and appreciate its truth one must go through the process oneself. For the same reason, a scientific fact may be discovered or a theory conceived at the same time by two men working separately, but the same philosophical achievement cannot be made by two men.

To say that one must go through the philosophical process in order to understand a philosophical judgment and appreciate its truth is to say that one must authentically execute the judgment; it must be judged distinctly. We must make it our own and take responsibility for it. This is implied in Husserl's insistence that phenomenology begins with each person's own subjectivity and his explicit reflection on it.[9]

A judgment that is not explicitly made our own is accepted associatively. It is entertained in vagueness, in a sort of "associative dreaming."[10] In contrast, a distinct phenomenological judgment is a "remembering of the forms," since it brings to clear and distinct awareness what is already possessed by us, but forgotten and obscured. Like the Platonic *anamnēsis*, Husserl's

9. *CM*, § 3, p. 7: "And so we make a new beginning, each for himself and in himself, with the decision of philosophers who begin radically." See also *FTL*, § 95.

10. Association is a degenerate state of mind when we pretend to judge; but in itself it has its own excellence, and the identities constituted in association are the basis for all higher identities. Also, in the matter of revealing a person's character and taste, the associations that come to his mind are most important.

process of making phenomenological judgments distinct is carried on in a dialectic with other philosophical positions, which he attacks by reducing them to the dilemmas of contradiction and incoherence. For it is in dialectic that we establish ourselves as speakers in the face of an interlocutor; we identify ourselves—find our identity—with a given philosophical position and strive to protect ourselves from the one weakness that can break our defenses and split us into disorganized pieces, the weakness of inner contradiction and incoherence. Such weakness can be ours if we have accepted a philosophical position by associative dreaming instead of authentic remembering, if we entertain it vaguely instead of distinctly articulating it as our own. Errors in philosophy are due to the precipitance with which we assume philosophical positions publicly as ours before we have thought them through as our own. They do not truly reflect ourselves. And someone who has not thought through his philosophical position has no philosophical persona and no voice; like the carrier of common opinion in public discourse, he is a blank in the conversation appropriate to philosophical thinking.[11] A philosophical voice has to be constituted by its own energy, just as a distinct voice in public conversation has to emerge, out of public doxa, through its own force; but both are supported by the tradition within which they arise.

Alas, no philosophical judgment can rid itself of all vagueness and confusion. There are always horizons to be explored, distinctions to be made.[12] In effect we are never totally clear about what we are saying in philosophy, even though we manage to overcome a lot of the obscurities which permeate the protophilosophy of ordinary discourse, or the confusions of wayward philosophy and sophistry. And we are never exhaustively distinct either: the philosophical voice always quivers a little, and the persona has shadowy parts. The career of philosophy is never finished.

To the extent that vagueness still dwells in our philosophical

11. The effort of phenomenology, Jacques Derrida has said, is to defend ourselves from confusion, forgetfulness, and irresponsibility. See the introduction to his translation of L'Origine de la géométrie (Paris: Presses universitaires de France, 1962), p. 38.

12. Crisis, § 53, p. 181: "[Phenomenology's] fate (understood subsequently, to be sure, as an essentially necessary one) is to become involved again and again in paradoxes, which, arising out of uninvestigated and even unnoticed horizons, remain functional and announce themselves as incomprehensibilities."

judgments, they are not decidable. Their meaning remains uncertain and open to further interrogation. To the extent that we do sweep away vagueness, the judgments are immediately decidable. Both decidability and uncertainty reside in philosophical judgments, and heightened decidability brings about a heightened degree of perplexity, because so many new horizons then appear. We may be most sure about things that get very undetermined: What is it to be in the world, to have a tradition, to perceive, to make a poem, to remember, to sympathize, to speak?

A "philosophical" judgment that makes a point but raises no further questions, putting the mind to sleep, is not what it appears to be. It does not touch the effective truth of things ("la verità effetuale della cosa"; Machiavelli, *The Prince*, ch. 15). Philosophical judgment makes the mind active in the extreme.

As we said above, the three states of judgment can be punctuated thus: (1) "?", (2) "!", (3) ".". Philosophical judgments are punctuated by "!?". If p is a judgment in phenomenology, it should be written "?!p!?" or "!?p?!" to indicate the immediate registration and permanent questioning that cohabit within it.

The state of being a report, which is the standard condition for judgments in the natural attitude, is the degenerate state for philosophical judgments. Philosophical judgments punctuated by "." are like rubber bands that have lost their elasticity. They seem without life, pointless and grotesque; why would anyone say such things? This is why "teaching" philosophy is so much more difficult than teaching other ways of thought, in which reports can be used and one is not constantly calling oneself into question; exercising philosophical discourse requires that one keep the tension of "!?" alive.

The tension in philosophical judgments is sustained when they are played off against judgments in natural language, which are supposed to be assimilated coherently into the philosophical discourse, and when they are put into conflict with unsuccessful attempts at philosophy, whether these occur in pretentious ordinary language, science, myth, sophistry, or wayward philosophy. A student of philosophy should find his ordinary experience and science refreshed by it, and his pseudophilosophical convictions shattered. This is what makes listening to philosophy or reading it so fascinating and yet so irritating. Philosophy brightens natural language and mundane experience, but dissolves sophistry and confused pseudophilosophical formulation.

§ 87. JUDGMENTS IN NOEMATIC PHENOMENOLOGY

WHAT WE HAVE SAID and the examples we have used in the last section deal chiefly with noetic or hyletic phenomenology, the description transcendental consciousness gives of its own states, structures, acts, and life. How do judgments work, and how are they verified, within noematic analysis?

The philosophical description of various regions of reality, the phenomenologies of living things, physical things, animals, society, art, sport, and so on, demand judgments that are not merely factual but apodictic and necessary, not subject to falsification by further perception. We have judgments that physical things occupy space, appear as figures against a background, are a mixture of spatial presences and absences, cause changes in one another, and have inner and outer horizons. Colors are said to exclude one another in a given place at a given time, physical motions require time, and other persons are experienced only through the mediation of bodily presence.[13] But isn't new experience needed to verify such philosophical judgments about various kinds of beings? Don't we have to find out what sports or games are like, in order to verify philosophical judgments about them?

We must have experienced the appropriate kind of being in order to understand philosophical discourse about it. Philosophical judgments are framed only after the natural experience —of sport, paintings, buildings, animals, tools, and also of science—has been actualized. Natural experience generates its own judgments in mundane language and achieves its own truth. Philosophy begins its experiencing and judging after ordinary experience and science have done their work. And once the philosophical judgments are understood, they are immediately decidable; there is no gap between states (1) and (2).

Noematic phenomenology examines objects as phenomena; but they must have been actualized in natural experiences and language for philosophy to begin. Phenomenology does not initiate the objects that appear. It takes them as granted by the conscious life that goes before it.

Question: Judgments about noetic and hyletic aspects of consciousness are not subject to corrigibility because the tem-

---

13. *Ideen II* is a collection of noematic analyses of many regions.

poral profiles in which inner objects are experienced are assimilative manifolds, not disjunctive and exclusive. In noematic phenomenology we speak about the objective correlates to consciousness; are these objects not spatial, and are their profiles not disjunctive and exclusive? Are phenomenological judgments about them not subject to the correction of further experience, because of this infection of spatiality?

Response: They are not, because the objects are experienced and judged as phenomena in noematic analysis. This twist of focus, from objects to objects as phenomena, makes the difference between ordinary thoughtful experiencing and phenomenological experience and thinking. In the natural attitude we enjoy the presences and try to overcome the absences of things, but we do not focus on the presence of presences and the presence of absences, nor do we think about them. So long as we stay in the natural attitude each present profile does exclude the absent profiles; they cannot be present while the first one is given. But when we make the transcendental turn we recognize the presence of what is present as involving the presence of absences; this is what we register in phenomenology. The profiles, when considered this way, are assimilative.

In the natural attitude I enjoy one view of the cube and assert the cube as having other views as well, which I can see later. In the phenomenological attitude—even if the eidetic reduction is not yet performed—I assert the presence of one view of the cube and the absence of the other views; I am concerned not with the other profiles, but with their way of being present, i.e., with their particular kind of absence. So all I assert as a phenomenologist is the presence of one view and the absence of the others, all of which is assimilatively—not disjunctively and exclusively—present to my phenomenological experience. Of course, as a phenomenologist, I must find words to describe the special kind of presence and absence appropriate to the kind of thing I am experiencing. To bring about the subsequent presence of the views I do not now enjoy is the work of mundane experiencing and registration, not the work of phenomenological experiencing and registration. Phenomenology cannot make up for the work of ordinary experience and science.

Phenomenological judging about consciousness only registers what is available within the assimilative temporal profiles that constitute an inner object. Phenomenological judging about noemata only registers the transcendences still flashing as correlative to the profiles, parts, and inner objects of consciousness. It does not go beyond them.

Each object has its own peculiar blend of parts which are to be present and absent in the perception of that object, and the articulation of these as noematic parts is the work of reflective philosophical thinking. The registrations of natural experience cannot simply be transported into phenomenology. There is a special phenomenological experiencing, in which the latent noematic parts are gradually brought to registration in judgment. A philosophical analysis of sport, for instance, is not just repetition of what ordinary language says about it.

Phenomenological experiencing is reflective because it can set in only after mundane experiencing and thinking and speaking have done their work. Philosophical experiencing attends to how the object has become experienced and registered and spoken about; it attends to the object as phenomenon. Phenomenological thinking registers the manifolds that are enjoyed, anonymously, by natural experiencing when such experiencing lets us register the identity within the manifolds.

§ 88. How Mundane Language Gets Drawn into Phenomenological Language

WE HAVE ON ONE HAND the language one speaks after one has made the transcendental turn; it is phenomenological language, or transcendentalese.[14] On the other hand we have the language one speaks while one remains in the natural, prephilosophical attitude; it is natural language, mundane language, or the vernacular. It includes both ordinary language and the language of science.

If phenomenological discourse is to brighten natural language, it must be continuous with it; but if phenomenological discourse speaks of objects as phenomena, there must be a break between it and mundane language, which just speaks about objects in the world. This continuity and discontinuity provide the

14. See *Crisis*, § 59, p. 210: "All the new sorts of apperceptions which are exclusively tied to the phenomenological reduction, together with the new sort of language (new even if I use ordinary language, as is unavoidable, though its meanings are also unavoidably transformed). . . ."

problem which the epochē tries to handle: the world and things are sustained within the epochē but in a neutralized way, as phenomena.

Since natural language actualizes objects for us, phenomenological language has to take natural language into itself in order to secure its own objects, i.e., the objects as phenomena. Transcendentalese has to quote the vernacular. We also quote within natural language, and we may even neutralize the belief we quote. We may assert "He says '*p*'," even though we don't believe that *p*. However, we keep our belief in the existence, as a mundane entity, of the speaker whom we quote, in the actuality of his speech and speaking as mundane realities, and in the world as a general backdrop for his speeches as well as ours. This belief is not neutralized, even when we neutralize our belief in what he says.

Phenomenological quoting of mundane discourse is more radical, for belief in the speaker and speech as mundane, and belief in the world, are put out of action. We do not put out of action our belief in the speaker as a transcendental consciousness, nor our belief in his speaking as an event in his transcendental conscious life. These are parts of what is left over as a residue of the epochē, for they belong to the domain of pure consciousness. In the Cartesian way to reduction the ordinary speaker whom I quote when I do phenomenology is I myself as a mundane man. In the psychological way to reduction I, as phenomenologist, can quote other men. Thus intersubjectivity is included right at the start in phenomenology when it is approached through the psychological way; it has to be brought in subsequently when we work through the Cartesian way.[15]

So transcendentalese quotes the vernacular. Does it do any more than repeat vernacular speeches? Does it have any words of its own? Does it give a new use or force or modality to vernacular terms and judgments?

In the vernacular we can say, "A cube has views we cannot see when we look at any one of its sides; but we can see them from elsewhere." What happens to this sentence when it is said in transcendentalese? The same question can be asked about sentences like "I have access to your thoughts and feelings only as manifest or expressed in some bodily way; I can't have your feelings as parts of my conscious life," and "In remembering,

15. See the stress on intersubjectivity in *Crisis*, §§ 71–72.

the past is present to me." In the vernacular, these judgments can even be registered as eidetic necessities, for the eidetic reduction can be carried out in the natural attitude.

Although we do talk about views of the cube in the vernacular, we cannot talk about them in their being at work in bringing about truth. We cannot talk about them in their presencing. We do bring about truth in the vernacular, but we don't systematically talk of bringing about truth.

But surely we sometimes talk about truth and presence in the vernacular, don't we?

We do, and such remarks are pseudopods the natural attitude projects into the phenomenological attitude. There are scraps of transcendentalese in the vernacular. The natural attitude verges on philosophical detachment, but only intermittently. And all such incipient philosophy is put back into the service of natural experiencing and the truth it tries to register, so the full move into transcendentalese is never made.

This intermittent tipping into philosophy is what provides continuity between natural experience and phenomenology. Natural experience and language already taste philosophy. That is why everyone who speaks thinks he should know what philosophers are talking about: everyone thinks he is an expert in truth, just as everyone thinks he knows what justice is. But failure to make the transcendental turn prevents one from speaking coherently about truth and presencing, because objects will always be intruding where the presence of objects should be discussed. The result will be either sophistry or wayward philosophy.

The phenomenological attitude is the rigorous, systematic execution of what is already germinating in natural experience and discourse.

Then does the vernacular suffice as a vocabulary for philosophy? No, because in philosophy we need words that distinctly register objects as phenomena, and cut us off from relapsing into the natural attitude and taking them just as objects. The word "noema" is such a term. So are "epochē" and "reduction." Such terms keep our minds propped away from the natural attitude. But in finding names for the parts of objects, there is no problem in using vernacular terms like "side," "aspect," "manifold," and "identity." And of course we need special, nonvernacular terms for the parts that arise in inner time-consciousness—"retention" and "protention," for instance—because these parts are not attended to in ordinary experience; "for

all this, names are lacking," says Husserl (ZB, § 36). And occasionally we may have to filter out a natural ambiguity which
certain words have in the vernacular, or even give a special
sense to a word like "apparition." But there is no reason why
"a series of aspects" should not have had a term in the vernacular. It was just an accident of linguistic history that it did not.
It was, however, not an accident of linguistic history that no
word like "noema" evolved spontaneously with the sense Husserl
gives it, for the reality named by that word requires a special
achievement in the history of mind in order to be registered: a
new kind of reflection has to come to pass.

Metaphor is helpful in phenomenological discourse.[16] It
brings out aspects of objects as phenomena, or aspects of the
conscious life that actualizes phenomena; the aspects may not
have regular names, and the metaphor can help in registration.
But phenomenological discourse cannot be all metaphor, for
metaphors make sense only when used in reasonable quantity
and as contrasted to literal discourse (Aristotle, *Poetics* 22).
And the metaphors only work if the reader has gotten the knack
of phenomenological reflection.

§ 89.   THE PHILOSOPHICAL VOICE

WHO IS THE SPEAKER of phenomenological discourse?
1. The voice of the speaker of natural language is constituted when he frames a judgment distinctly and thus emerges
out of the anonymity of common opinion. The framed judgment may be used as a registration ("The airplane is starting to
land") or as a report ("The car passed through the stop sign and
collided with the truck").

Emergence of a man with a voice is more than the emergence
of a man who can use a language as the carrier of ordinary
doxa. Not everyone who speaks English has a voice of his
own. Emergence of a man who knows English is, in turn, more
than the constitution of a man who has feelings and moods,
pleasures and pains, and can recognize some perceptual identities.

Along another direction there is the emergence of a man

16. See *Ideas I*, § 84, Note on Terminology; *Ideen III*, § 9, pp.
55–56.

with a special sort of character: courageous, temperate, honest, or cowardly, dissolute, and dishonest. Such a man becomes identifiable through the actions he has performed and by his capacity to perform further actions in keeping with his character. Although action is the primary issue in manifestation of character, language is also at work, because a man of good character is one whose opinion we estimate in questions about what is to be done in certain circumstances appropriate to his virtue. He can say what is right and what is wrong. Analogously, certain men become distinctive by having skills; they can say how certain things should be made or organized if there is a need for them.

2. On another level, the sentences made by a speaker may be used to register his registration or report: "I see that the airplane is starting to land" and "I am sure that the car ran into the truck." Such reflective discourse highlights the voice which had emerged in the original framing. It accentuates his conspicuousness, explicitly reaffirms the responsibility he takes for the judgment, and stresses his identification with this position. Judgments on this level—"I see (know, assert, am sure) that p"—mention the speaker who has emerged on level (1).

On level (1) it is essential that a factual registration or report that I make can be contradicted by you or by someone else, because the thing being registered or reported does lend itself to diverse interpretations. It does so because it is based on thing-perception, with its spatial infection, and thus legitimately admits a plurality of viewpoints. The material thing gives rise to many points of view and so to many speakers. "The box is gray." "That's because you see it from that angle and in that light; if you saw it from other viewpoints you would see that it is blue."

Since every mundane thing has an infinite manifold of exclusive and disjunctive profiles, it is possible for it to present only one part of this manifold to a given viewer, and he may quite honestly say "S is p" even though further experience would prompt him to say "S is not p but q." Because of the spatiality of mundane things, all the perceptual evidence is never in and any judgment is conceivably open to correction.

Still, within the limits of conceivability, we do arrive at empirically sufficient criteria for asserting that enough evidence is in to assure us that "S is p" for the purposes at hand. An empirical identification of the thing and its attributes can be made, though the standards of identity may vary in function of the purpose for which the identification is made: what counts as "the same house" may differ for the real estate agent and for the physicist (Ms F I 29, 1922–23, pp. 245–46; *APS*, § 4, pp. 23–24).

Husserl introduces a plurality of viewpoints and voiced minds because of the character of thing-perception and the world-belief that rests on it. If one were to begin philosophy by reflecting on political life, the diversity of public selves would be based on various appreciations of the good and the just. Husserl's philosophy needs supplementation along such a line, but a philosophy based on political life also needs cosmology as ingredient in itself.

The plurality of voiced minds is explicitly registered in judgments made on level (2): "I see (say) that *p*," "You see that *q*," "He sees that *t*." If it were not for the diversity of views permitted by things, we would not have different things to see and say, and would not have to distinguish different voices, unless we were to bring in the different things each of us wants; but this too would involve different perceptual viewpoints at least as a condition.

Your voice also can differ from mine because you have developed a different sensibility and a different categoriality from mine. We have each mastered different languages and have come to diversify our concrete experience in different ways. You have become a plumber or a violinist, I have become a bricklayer or physician; you have grown up speaking Japanese and I have grown up speaking English. Once again such differences are not reducible to diversity of spatial profiles, but they could not have come about without them.

The difference between your voice and mine, and our mutual emergence as users of a language and as voices with positions, makes possible quotation and allows it to become a factor in the attempt each of us makes to be truthful; for in my desire to verify what I claim—which is also the desire to make my view predominate over yours and theirs, and to make my voice rule, not by violence but by the evidence of things—I must take into account what your viewpoint allows you to say. I define my position against yours or theirs. I also acquire the fruit of the perceptual manifold you have undergone, and am able to expand the potential of my own perceptions, using your views as well as mine.

The plurality of speakers is expanded by the possibility of distinguishing between my speech now and my speech before or later, and between what I say here and what I say there. Changes in my own position need not be dishonest, because the new viewpoints of things may require that something else be said. Of course sometimes the viewpoints may not require a new statement, and then one may be dishonest in making it.

The multiplicity of voices and viewpoints makes it necessary for a language to have what Husserl calls "occasional expressions," which linguists call by the more pungent name of "shifters." [17] These are terms like "I," "you," "he," "now," "there," and "here." When used in framing a judgment they refer to the voice that takes responsibility for the judgment or to the situation within which the judgment is being made. Their "reference," of course, it not like the reference made with the subject of the judgment, in which we set up an object for attribution. Shifters identify the voice by which the judgment is made, or the stage within which it is made, but they do not make the voice or the stage ready for attribution. We do not register a fact about ourselves when we say "I see the house is on fire"; we simply confirm and explicitly appropriate the position we take.[18]

Question: How can you say that judgments with reference to the speaker don't register facts about the person who judges? Can't judgments like "I see the house is on fire," and "He sees the horse is running away," register me and him as seeing something? Isn't "seeing" an attribute we can be said to have?

Response: It depends on how you take the activity of seeing. If you take it as a nonphilosophical psychologist would, as an episode like any other in the world of living things, you might call it an ordinary fact, like the fact that my dog has bitten me or that I am sunburned. A statement like "He is watching the

17. On occasional expressions see *LI*, I, §§ 24–26; VI, § 5; *FTL*, § 80, including the footnote. See also R. Sokolowski, "The Structure and Content of Husserl's *Logical Investigations*," *Inquiry*, XIV (1971), 339. Otto Jespersen introduced the term "shifters"; see *Language, Its Nature, Development and Origin* (London: Allen and Unwin, 1922), p. 123.

18. The use of demonstratives as the subject of judgments is no exception to this. True, the "this" in a sentence like "This is delicious" is a shifter, but it does not suffice by itself to set up a reference for attribution. "This" or "that" is a formal moment; it needs supplementation by a term that identifies what is referred to. Explicitly or implicitly we say, "This tree, this block of stone, this proof, this idea, etc., is *p*." Furthermore, demonstratives also imply a reference to the speaker, for something is a "this" only to a certain point of view.

house burn down" would normally be taken just that way. Seeing can be taken that way too, but it can also be taken in its work of bringing about truth, and then it is not an ordinary fact. It enters into the process of bringing about ordinary facts. The appropriate attitude for us to take toward seeing as working in truth is not the natural attitude but the phenomenological one—the kind we are led to by the epochē. This attitude will let us do justice to shifters as well, for they work in the situated process of being truthful.

Notice that to realize the difference between a fact and the process of truthfully bringing about facts, we have to stand outside both level (1) and level (2). We have to reflect as incipient phenomenologists. Husserl tries to bring this attitude about in a systematic and permanent way, but we do wander into it occasionally even before we undertake philosophy. This is one of the anticipations of philosophy that exist in the natural attitude.

3. The discourse of modern science since Galileo and Newton calls for a special analysis. Some ancient science used registrations and reports like those mentioned in (1), and allowed the kinds of statements about registrations and reports, complete with shifters, which we described under (2). Aristotelian science, for example, is essentially situational, since cosmic space is considered qualitatively different; one "here" is not the same as any other "here." In particular, the earth, at the natural center of the cosmos, provides a base for shifters which cannot be repeated anywhere else.

With the modern mathematization of nature and the conception of absolute space and time, laws of nature are rendered indifferent to place and time, and the discourse of science, in principle, can exclude the use of shifters. Occasionally it may have to mention a place or a speaker, but this is only incidental, a reference to something subjective, and does not fall within the work or content of science as such.[19] Statements such as those we listed under (2) are not required as part of science.

Natural science is an attempt to speak of "the world as nature, that is, the world as it lies beyond any human involvement."[20] Obviously, natural science cannot give an account of how the world enters into human involvement, nor can it

19. *PP*, § 18, p. 123. Shifters are used when science moves into the life-world; see *Crisis*, § 33, pp. 122–23.
20. The formula is from Francis Slade; see above, Chapter 7, n. 6.

account for being human and having a world. Still less can it concern itself with the being-belief that supports having a world. Any attempt by scientific thinking to give an account of being human transforms humanness into a thing: an entity governed by natural laws, explained by causalities that originate outside itself, fully determinable in terms of empirical universals. Being human is turned into a mass of facts. Nonphilosophical psychology, sociology, linguistics, anthropology, and economics do this. The "man" they scrutinize is not humane.

Should such sciences reduce themselves, in principle, to physics, they could, in principle, do away with all shifters.[21] If they do not go so far, they may retain some shifters as demonstratives to single out particular bodies, living things and men, but unless they become philosophical they cannot account for shifters used to mention one's own voice and to confirm one's own registrations and reports, i.e., they cannot account for the use we describe under (2). Such sciences treat this use of shifters as no different from their use in (1); shifters are allowed to help register ordinary facts, but not to help register the registration and reporting of facts, because such registration and reporting is taken as no different from ordinary facts.

The whole that science examines is the whole with the humanness of being truthful flushed out. And in eliminating the humanness of judgment, science also eliminates the judger as a rhetorical person and as the man who can decide what is right in a situation calling for action. Left to itself, science aims at the well-managed world in which contingency is mastered and no need remains for good practical judgment, nor for intelligent persuasion in predicaments that can develop in diverse ways. Ignoring the judger as witness, it also ignores political society and questions about what is good. Natural science does not need shifters because what it registers and reports does not provide alternative points of view. Science speaks in a chorus and everyone says—or aims at saying—the same thing. This is why it is so easy to overlook the work of judging which is a condition for science.

4. Philosophical discourse differs from science because it examines the work of judging and the whole of conscious life, private and intersubjective, and all the way down to inner time,

21. *Crisis*, § 11, pp. 63–65. If pure science eliminates shifters, it recovers in this respect the status of general opinion, which has no identifiable speaker either.

that goes into judgment.[22] It scrutinizes what science overlooks and does so in a way that does justice to the humanness of thinking. The philosophical approach recognizes the difference between authentic, distinct judging and the vague entertainment of what "they" say. The whole that philosophy discusses includes the world of science and the human dimension. It includes the scientific world as constituted by consciousness.

In order to do justice to the humanness of thinking, philosophy has to come after both (1) registration and reporting of facts and (2) confirmation of registration and reports, expressed in the forms "I see that *p*" and "I say that *p*." Philosophy does not just reiterate such confirmation. It thinks about registration and reporting—i.e., about judging—and thinks about them in their humanness, as actions that can be confirmed and appropriated, freely and responsibly, by men. It thinks about level (1) as subject to level (2). It thinks about being truthful.

Since philosophy scrutinizes what is on level (2), its viewpoint is different from the point of view available at (2). It recognizes necessities and impossibilities that are not visible to someone at levels (1) and (2). But it is on level (2) that shifters come into their own, as an expression of the multiplicity of viewpoints and speakers engendered by the nature of thing-perception. Do shifters have any place in philosophy? Is there a multiplicity of viewpoints in philosophy, like a multitude of world-views? Is the "I" that I use in philosophy different from the "I" that you use? More radically, is the "I" that Husserl uses in philosophy the same as or different from the "I" used by Plato, Kant, Descartes, Aristotle, or Augustine?

Shifters, Husserl's "occasional expressions," are not just used occasionally in phenomenology (*Crisis*, § 54b). They are used all the time, since the transcendental ego is the subject for phenomenological analysis. In phenomenology the shifter becomes universal, but does it then keep its status as an occasional expression? This is one of those "provocative paradoxes," which Husserl claims are signs of philosophical problems, and the resolution is not to show that the shifter is not really universal in philosophy, but to show that philosophical

---

22. Problems of logic reach down into the level of association and into inner time-consciousness; the lectures edited in *Husserliana* as *Analysen zur Passiven Synthesis* were actually delivered under the titles *Logik* and *Grundprobleme der Logik*. See the editor's introduction, APS, pp. xiii–xvii.

thinking is such that the occasional and the universal need not exclude each other within it.

Husserl says that the philosopher is drawn into philosophical thinking primarily by

> the philosophical world [Umwelt] he has at work around him, the world of philosophers and their thoughts even from the remotest past. This world, which stretches back to the foundation of philosophy and philosophical productivity, is his living present [lebendige Gegenwart]. In this enclosure he has his coworkers, his partners, he deals with Aristotle, with Plato, with Descartes, with Kant, etc. Except that the deceased can no longer be transformed in their philosophical existence by those who follow them, as the latter can by the deceased. The development of the future is a matter for the living.[23]

We should take seriously Husserl's claim that contemporary philosophy and the history of philosophy are the "living present" for the philosopher at work; when someone does philosophy, the thought of philosophers who lived in the past is activated, not as something that is being called back from oblivion, but as something that has never gone out of its appropriate kind of actuality.

Husserl's remarks can be compared to Machiavelli's famous description of reading the writers of the past, with its intimation of a kind of life which is immortal and not subject to either bodily necessity or the contingencies of the world:

> When evening has come I return home and enter my study; and at the threshold I take off those everyday clothes, full of mud and of mire, and I put on garments regal and courtly; and reclothed appropriately I enter the ancient courts of ancient men, where, received by them with affection, I feed on that food which alone is mine, and for which I was born; where I am not ashamed to speak with them, and I ask them the reason for their actions, and they in their humanity answer me; and for four hours of time I do not feel any boredom, I forget every trouble, I do not fear poverty, death does not terrify me: I transmit myself entirely to them.[24]

23. *Crisis*, app. XXIV, p. 489 (*Husserliana* ed.). Appendices XXIV–XXVII, not included in Carr's translation, have excellent remarks on the history of philosophy.

24. Letter No. 137, to Francesco Vettori, December 10, 1513. I have used the translation by Allan Gilbert in his volume, *The Letters of Machiavelli* (New York: Capricorn, 1961), but have modified it somewhat. The last sentence is particularly hard to translate ("tutto mi trasferisco in loro"), and J. R. Hale catches the sense quite well

Both Husserl and Machiavelli make us think of Socrates' wish to be able to talk with Orpheus, Musaeus, Hesiod, Homer, and the heroes of the ancient world (*Apology* 41A–C). They also make us think of a condition analogous to what Aristotle calls the state of mind set apart, when it exists just as it is. For in this state there is no remembering either, only the enjoyment of a living present. Furthermore, without this kind of mind "nothing thinks," for without the completion brought about in philosophy all other discourse falls short of what it truly is (*De anima* 3. 5.430a22–25).

Aristotle and Husserl seem to differ from Machiavelli and Socrates in that the latter are concerned with remembering, philosophically, what men in the past have *done*, while the former are not. Of course, it is not the task of philosophy to recall the acts of men; that is entrusted to the ordinary doxa and world-belief of the Athenians, the Spartans, and the other communities. Philosophy recalls events and actions only as instances of what it wishes to say, and this is certainly the way both Machiavelli and Socrates (or Plato) read history.

But does Husserl not concede a kind of eternity to all ideal meanings? If we repeat a judgment that involves no shifters—in the purest case, a mathematical theorem—do we not have the very same ideal entity that someone else might have actualized a hundred years ago? (*Crisis*, app. VI, p. 357; *ZB*, § 45). Do that person and I not share in the same actuality of mind? So isn't philosophy just another case of a science dealing with ideal meanings?

This sort of indifference to temporality is not the same as the actuality of philosophical thinking, for the mathematical proposition is the same at different living presents, which are separated from one another. In philosophy only one living present is actualized. Philosophy is actualized as having been operating all along, though perhaps in a vague way. For the living present, whether we consider it at work in philosophy or in any other kind of experience, is stretched and can contain within itself fluctuations between vagueness and distinctness/clarity. It can have these differences even without the interstices of absolute forgetfulness. Important philosophers are those who are able to heighten the distinctness and clarity in philosophical judgment.

---

in his loose version: "I pass indeed into their world" (*The Literary Works of Machiavelli* [London: Oxford University Press, 1961], p. 139).

Even if the history of philosophy lives in a single living present, are shifters eliminated? Certainly Plato is different from Husserl, and when each says "I" must we not take into account who is speaking?

The living present as a structure in temporality need not be solipsistic. It is not limited to being a moment in a solitary stream of consciousness. In his Cartesian way to reduction Husserl does stress the solitariness of consciousness, but in the other ways to reduction he brings out the presence of other minds as a necessary condition for my having my own mind. Even in the Cartesian way he must account for intersubjectivity. And intersubjectivity does not get constituted only subsequently to the living present; there must be a sense of contemporaneity, of the presence of other minds who share the same temporal present, within the living present.[25] Multiplicity in the direction of contemporaries accompanies the multiplicity of elapsed and coming phases within the living present. For example, my action of framing a judgment for an interlocutor takes place in the present, but the actuality of my present involves the actuality of my interlocutor's appreciating my judgment. No one teaches unless someone is learning. This contemporaneity is not built up on levels of consciousness beyond the living present, levels like remembering, within which the present is only an ingredient; it happens in the present itself.

So philosophy as permanently present does not exclude shifters, but the shifters are not the same as those used on level (2), because the colleagues in philosophy do not really have different points of view; not because they are kindred spirits, but because what they talk about—being and being truthful and being human—does not lend itself to many irreducible viewpoints, as material things do. The philosophical conversation is like a discussion among good friends who have things in common; what Plato says can be appropriated by Husserl, what Aristotle says can be appropriated by Heidegger. Plato's philosophical discourse belongs originally to Plato, but it can also become "mine" if I appreciate it clearly and distinctly. So there are shifters in philosophical discourse, but they are not as irreducible as those in ordinary discourse where, because of the perspectives of things, they may express absolutely different points of view, or in politics, where they may express factions that remain permanently hostile.

25. See Ms C 17 I, 1931, pp. 1–8; Held, *Lebendige Gegenwart*, (The Hague: Nijhoff, 1966) pp. 156–60.

The problem of the use of shifters in philosophical discourse is, of course, the problem of how the transcendental ego is identified with the empirical or mundane ego. No metaphysical alchemy is needed to fuse these two egos into one another. The mundane ego is actualized through sensation, perception, memory, judging, and the confirmation of judgment. He lives in the element of common opinion and distinguishes himself and his positions from common doxa. The transcendental ego is fully actualized when he does phenomenology and reflects on the other actualizations and the world that he has through them; the mundane ego wanders into this actualization sporadically, but does not do it in a thorough way and finds it hard to get the right kind of reflection going, so he often goes awry. But in all this it is the same "I" who is actualized to different degrees. The transcendental ego is not an inner ghost who watches the mundane ego and has a hard time getting to know anyone else.

When the transcendental ego relaxes his philosophical activity and engages in ordinary life, discourse, and verification, he behaves according to the rules everyone else obeys, except that he does not entirely forget the philosophical activity he once engaged in.[26] Although he submits to world-belief, he is marginally aware of the possibility of suspending it, so it does not cast the same spell over him that it does over others.

Don't philosophers often criticize one another? Doesn't Husserl criticize Kant and Descartes on certain points? Aren't philosophical shifters necessary to express and quote philosophical viewpoints we do not wish to identify ourselves with?

There are different philosophical positions, but their difference rests on diversities allowed in the domain between vagueness and distinctness/clarity. An opposing philosophical view is refused because it is a partial view, has not actualized all the relevant horizons, and remains vague on points that must be made distinct.

A successful argument against another philosophical position must not only show its inadequacy, but must also explain why this inadequacy has come about. It must make the judgments and distinctions the opposition fails to make, and show what, in the logic of the argument, kept the opposition from

26. *Crisis*, § 59, p. 210: "I can, as before, be active as a father, a citizen, an official, as a 'good European,' etc., that is, as a human being in my human community, in my world. As before—and yet not quite as before. For I can never again achieve the old naïveté; I can only understand it. My transcendental insights and purposes have become merely inactive, but they continue to be my own."

making them. It must show which parts of the argument were overwhelmed and kept vague by other parts. No matter how hostile such a process may sound in its actual execution, its logic is always sympathetic and friendly, for it tries to preserve what is good in the opposition and to protect it from its own inadequacies.

Argument in philosophy turns into warfare when both opponents are seriously deficient in distinctness and clarity on important issues and are unable to provide an adequate possession of the whole. The grasp each has on the whole is so confused that it solidifies into a piece which excludes the other true parts of the whole. The combatants engage in a war of ideologies; each is unable to preserve what is good in the other, and aims at eliminating the adversary instead of preserving him as an interlocutor. This may be necessary in other levels of discussion and activity, but it is not part of philosophical conversation; to the extent that it exists, the argument is not philosophical.

Why must a successful philosophical argument account for the inadequacies of its opponent? Why is it not enough to point them out? We can never explain everything people do or say.

The inadequacies are to be explained insofar as they are inadequacies of argument. The philosophical conversation touches only on what the interlocutor puts forward in speech. Inadequacies are not explained in terms of the person's character, history, or pathologies; inadequacies on that level may prevent him from making a philosophical speech at all, and may be recognized by the philosopher insofar as he, as a citizen and ordinary person, may also be a good judge of people. But such areas are conditions for the philosophical argument as such, which deals primarily with what the interlocutors can actualize in discourse. The philosopher must address himself to inadequacies in the discourse which his adversary presents as giving an account of being and being truthful.

The philosopher must not only point out deficiencies but also explain them, because deficiency in philosophy is mistaking one thing for another—taking perception for intuition, for example, or taking rhetorical objects for aesthetic ones, or saying that remembering is constructing the past out of the present—and such mistaking occurs because of a state of vagueness. To make the appropriate distinction is also to dissolve the mistake, since the two that were once inertly accepted as one are now differentiated from one another. So in making the deficiency clear one also accounts for it.

Philosophical argument is not an attempt to impose a new world-view on someone else, but an attempt to disclose the parts ingredient in having a world and being truthful. It might be appropriate to appeal to someone's character, history, or pathologies to explain his resistance to accepting one's world-view, but the appeal is insufficient in philosophical discourse.

So there may be shifters in philosophical conversation to set apart positions that differ in their degree of vagueness, but these differences can be reconciled as the positions are made more distinct and clear, and in principle each position, if it is really philosophical, should be capable of being appropriated by all the conversants.

The historical situation within which one does philosophy is another parameter for philosophy. At certain times certain ingredients may predominate—in our time, the presence of technē is more dominant than in other ages—and human customs change, so certain parts of philosophy may more easily come into prominence while others fall into confusion; but the theme of philosophy, being and being truthful and man having a world, does not change. Distortions of philosophy brought about by the force of historical circumstances and the inability of thinkers to master them can have deleterious effects on human life and expectations, especially through education which may have become sophistic.

There are many people who are not interested in doing philosophy but sustain the ordinary opinion within which the world is present to us. They too provide a parameter for philosophy. Besides conversing with figures in the history of philosophy, does philosophical thinking carry on exchanges with them?

It is true that most people are not concerned with carrying on the philosophical life, but practically everyone has an inclination toward philosophical issues and finds philosophical judgments, if they are appropriately articulated, enlightening and pleasant; most people are fond of repeating them as a kind of maxim. Not being able or interested enough to generate philosophical judgments consistently and on their own, they don't care to carry on a philosophical controversy in the strict sense, and unfortunately are not always able to ferret out the sophistries that float around in general opinion along with authentic reports and maxims. One of the major functions of philosophy is to disclose sophistry for what it is.

Part of the work of philosophy is to let things be what they are; sophistries and confusion establish binds in ordinary experience and natural science, with one kind of thing being mistaken for another and the natural evidences of things not being allowed to assert themselves. Philosophy cannot carry out the ordinary registration of things, but it can break the bind that hinders registration in particular cases, and release the differences in things and in experience.

In contemporary life, the central confusion philosophy must handle is the rejection, in principle, of the truthfulness of ordinary perceptions and common sense. The claim is made that the manifest world must give way to the idealized or constructed world of science in matters of truth and being. Husserl's argument against the double-thing or double-world is an attempt to restore the acceptability of ordinary experience and still do justice to the place of science in human affairs.

Does everyone have to be a philosopher to handle the problem of sophistry? It would be folly to expect everyone to want to carry on the philosophical life, but the presence of philosophy is not only realized in men like Plato and Kant and Husserl; there is an appreciation of philosophy in the form of right opinion which, distributed in the commonplaces of a society, can do its part in keeping sophistry at bay. And philosophers are not the only sources of such *topoi;* they arise also from the exercise of ordinary experience if it is energetic and confident enough in its registration of being. In fact, vigorous ordinary experience and opinion are a condition for the emergence of philosophical thinking in its pure form. Trying to have philosophy without such conditions is like trying to have a flame without fuel.

Some writers in the phenomenological tradition have seen a great problem in bridging the gap between strict phenomenological discourse and mundane discourse.[27] The change between the natural attitude and the phenomenological attitude seems to erect a barrier between the two ways of life. It appears impossible to disclose the meaning of phenomenological terms to those who have not carried out the epoché and reduction.

It is true that the problems of how phenomenology can quote ordinary discourse and how the ego that does phenomenology is

27. See Eugen Fink, "The Phenomenological Philosophy of Edmund Husserl and Contemporary Criticism," in *The Phenomenology of Husserl,* ed. and trans. R. O. Elveton (Chicago: Quadrangle, 1970), pp. 104–6, 142–45; also Thomas Seebohm, *Die Bedingungen der Möglichkeit der Transzendental-Philosophie* (Bonn: Bouvier, 1962), pp. 48–49.

identified with the ego in the world are provocative philosophical issues. But they are not insuperable dilemmas; the break between the two domains is not entirely clean. There are anticipations of philosophy in the natural attitude.

The appropriate form of discourse philosophy uses when it addresses those who think within the scope of the natural attitude is rhetoric.[28] Rhetoric is used both to encourage those who have a natural inclination toward philosophy, and to establish the philosophical commonplaces which should have their say in ordinary opinion. Rhetoric is an attempt to bring about conviction in regard to judgments that cannot be made apodictically certain, either because of what is said in the judgment, or because of the state of mind of the audience. In philosophical rhetoric, if an auditor gradually becomes an interlocutor, he becomes capable of appreciating the self-registering character of what is said in philosophy and the need for rhetoric evaporates; but until that occurs, no other form of discourse can present philosophy's case.

In Husserl's philosophy there is a dilemma as to whether philosophical discourse can straddle the natural attitude and the phenomenological attitude, because Husserl considers the proper form of philosophical speech to be that of rigorous, apodictic science. It may acquire this form in a community of philosophers, and Husserl's rationalistic prejudices do make him expect that the general good of all men requires that practically everyone become a philosopher. He dramatizes the turn to philosophy as an act which should occur in the conscious life of the solitary ego, as though it could take place in the soul of everyman—a philosophical *Pilgrim's Progress* or *Paradise Lost*. But the human good that philosophy achieves can be reached without forcing everyone to make the transcendental turn; and if this is recognized a corresponding form of discourse must be admitted for philosophy to retain its public presence. This is the protreptic, the form of philosophical rhetoric.

By helping remove the factional power of sophistry and confusion, philosophy brings about an equality of men—including the philosopher, when he acts within the natural attitude—in regard to mundane registrations and reports. For things can be recognized for what they are, and anyone who manages to

28. See R. Sokolowski, "Husserl's Protreptic," in *Life-World and Consciousness,* ed. L. Embree (Evanston, Ill.: Northwestern University Press, 1972), pp. 55–82.

recognize them should have his voice heard. Because we are made clear on what it is to be truthful, actual exercises of truth can be acknowledged, and each man counts as a registrar of what is; he does not have his voice just because of social status, wealth, power, or strength.

Philosophy accomplishes for the life of perception and thinking what a good conception of laws accomplishes for social and public life (Plato, *Republic* 9. 592A–B). It brings about the possibilty of justice, peace, and prosperity in thinking: justice because each voice is acknowledged according to its own worth in being truthful; peace because the factional forces of sophistry and confusion are kept at bay; and prosperity because things can be appreciated and discovered as what they are. Each man can plan his future and count on preserving his identity of mind to a worthy old age, since what he says, if it is a true registration of what things are, will continue to be recognized. It should be one of the greatest concerns of those who work in the sciences and in other ways of knowledge that they live within a city of the mind which is just, that is, founded on a good conception of what it is to be truthful, and that they do not labor under sophistic convictions.

Philosophy alone cannot bring about a healthy intellectual and human life, no more than a man who conceives a good constitution can alone bring about a good and prosperous city. Good citizens, good habits and models for imitation, and appropriate material conditions are also necessary. But just as a misconceived constitution can prevent all the other public and private goods from happening, a confused attempt at philosophy can cripple attempts to think and see things as they are.

Besides acting defensively by warding off confusion and sophistry, philosophy works in a positive way by disclosing dimensions not appreciated in nonphilosophical life. Mundane experience possesses and enjoys things in all their variety, but philosophy as phenomenology enjoys the disclosure of things. It delights in all the things that are delightful, but enjoys them specifically in their being manifest. It further appreciates the human process of being truthful, which allows things to be recognized for what they are. And when philosophy moves beyond phenomenology it also delights in the being that supports the truthfulness of things and of men.

Appendix / Logic and Mathematics in *Formal and Transcendental Logic*

§ 1. THE TEXT AND THE ISSUE

THE DISTINCTION between judgment and registered fact provides the setting in which the concepts of formal logic and mathematics can be clarified. Husserl examines this problem in *Formal and Transcendental Logic*. Treatment of the problem requires an exegesis of the text, because the steps in Husserl's argument are not just devices of exposition, but arrange his definition of logic and mathematics.[1]

Formal and Transcendental Logic is as organic and independent as a written composition can be. It engenders its own parts, incorporates them, adjusts them when its growth demands, and finally subsists in a completeness of its own making. Of course, like an organism, no philosophical writing can live in sheer autonomy; Husserl's *Logic* must absorb words and meanings from its context, ordinary language, and the tradition of philosophy and science, but it leaves none unchanged. The book builds itself in assimilating them; it is the assimilation and reactivation of sedimented tradition. In comments on his methodology Husserl says he intends to accept "intellectual formations" from the tradition and radically investigate their sense by bringing them to original clarification. Radical

1. This Appendix should be read as a continuation of Chapter 2. The sense of logic and mathematics, and also of formal ontology, is defined in the context of empty and filled judgmental intentions. I am grateful to Martinus Nijhoff of The Hague for permission to reprint this essay, which appeared originally in *Explorations in Phenomenology*, ed. D. Carr and E. Casey, 1973.

investigation and original clarification mean "shaping the sense anew," bringing it to clarity and understanding it has never enjoyed.[2] The completed book is a constellation of such clarified senses, each determined in function of the others and brought to its definitive philosophical exposition.

We will follow part of the organic growth of the *Logic* to see how Husserl accepts traditional senses of logic and mathematics and refreshes their meaning in his phenomenology. Two assumptions govern our study. First, we shall deal with judgment *forms* and the *forms* of categorial objects.[3] Judgments are formalized when we substitute "the moment 'anything whatever' for each materially filled 'core' in the judgments, while the remaining judgment-moments [are] held fast as moments of form" (§ 12, pp. 48–49; see also § 6). Second, our judgments must be brought to the state of distinctness, where the judgment is explicitly framed (as opposed to being languidly or vaguely performed) and where the criterion of noncontradiction comes into play. We go beyond the morphology of judgment forms that is possible even with vague and confused judgments. Our entire study will be within the domain of distinctness.[4]

Husserl makes two parallel moves to establish the fundamental difference between logic and mathematics, first in §§ 23–25, in Chapter 2 of Part I, and second in §§ 42–45, in Chapter 4 of Part I. The second move exists only as a corrective to the first. It "originally clarifies" the sedimented tradition described in the first move.

2. *FTL*, p. 10. There are remarks on Husserl's "hermeneutics" on pp. 8–10; § 23b, p. 75; § 24, p. 76; and § 70, pp. 180–81. These passages clarify what it means to bring something latent in sedimented tradition to intuitive givenness in the present.

3. In keeping with *FTL*, § 39, we will always use "judgment" in the broad sense, covering anything that can be asserted or posited, whether predicatively formed or not.

4. *FTL*, § 16, describes the move from vagueness to distinctness in regard to judgments; § 17 shows that the genus "distinct judgment" is the theme of "pure analytics," the discipline governed exclusively by noncontradiction as a criterion of validity (§§ 18–19). See § 14 for a description of the "consequence logic" governing this domain. The level prior to the distinct judgment and pure analytics of noncontradiction is the domain of vague or confused judgments, and on this level we can carry out a morphology of judgment forms even though noncontradiction does not come into question; see §§ 13, 22.

§ 2. THE FIRST APPROACH: APOPHANTIC LOGIC AND MATHEMATICS IN THE TRADITION

IN § 23 HUSSERL ACCEPTS two philosophical traditions, one from Aristotle and one from Leibniz and nineteenth-century British mathematics. Traditional Aristotelian logic provides a discipline that examines judgment forms and relations among them. Husserl calls such classical formal logic "apophantic" analysis, to stress its orientation toward the judgmental domain.

Leibniz introduced another tradition. He considers scholastic logic as part of a larger whole, the *mathēsis universalis,* the task of which is to discover and classify formal elements and arrangements like those determined by classical logic, those found in the formal science of quantity (mathematics), and those present in any other argumentation that holds strictly because of its form. Husserl's treatment of Leibniz is brief in *Formal and Transcendental Logic;* a fuller discussion is given in the "Prolegomena" (§ 60, pp. 218–20). There Husserl distinguishes narrow, wider, and widest senses of *mathēsis universalis.* The narrow universal mathematics is the usual formal science of quantities, concerned with more and less, equal and unequal, large and small. It is sometimes called algebra. The wider sense comprises Leibniz' *ars combinatoria,* the formal qualitative science dealing with the similar and dissimilar. It examines arrangements of logical formulas in general, and since algebra sometimes uses these rules it is subordinated to the wider *mathēsis universalis,* although its strictly quantitative formulas are not part of it. The widest sense of *mathēsis universalis* is a formal calculus that includes both the quantitative and the qualitative sciences, and formulas and rules either common to both or extending to other kinds of *argumens en forme.* At this level "mathematics and logic form a single science," and scholastic logic is enlarged into "a universal mathematic in the highest and most comprehensive sense" (p. 218).[5]

This new tradition had another beginning, with no explicit influence from Leibniz, in the work of Boole and De Morgan, who express syllogistic reasoning and traditional logic algebraically

5. There is a significant misprint on p. 219, l. 20, of Findlay's translation: "qualitative" should be "quantitative."

and interpret them primarily from an extensional viewpoint. Their extensional interpretation leads to paradoxes which provoke contrived attempts at removal, notes Husserl. He admits that it is in some way legitimate to unify logic and algebra, but these mathematical logicians do not have the perspective within which it can be done. They even lack the appropriate interest, he claims, for they are motivated "not by philosophic reflections on the fundamental sense and the necessity of a *mathēsis universalis,* but by the needs of the deductive theoretical technique of mathematical sciences" (*FTL,* § 23b, p. 74). In this respect they lag behind Leibniz, but even he cannot properly explain how the science of quantities and the science of logical formulas can constitute a single formal *mathēsis.* It is not enough just to subordinate one to the other, as the mathematicians do, nor simply to put them together, as Leibniz does.

In an attempt to explain this unity Husserl interprets the new mathematical logic, the algebra of classes and relations, as "formal ontology." [6] Formal ontology is defined in contrast to formal apophantics. The domain of formal apophantics is the region of judgments, with all the parts, combinations, and procedures appropriate to them. This discipline uses categories that refer to meanings (*Bedeutungskategorien*), such as judgment, predicate, subject, proposition, and syllogism (*FTL,* § 27b, p. 88; "Prolegomena," § 67). The domain of formal ontology contains not judgments and meanings, but objects in their formal relationships and arrangements. It uses categories that refer to objects (*Gegenstandskategorien*), such as object, sets, numbers, states of affairs, facts, relations, property, combination, whole, and parts (*FTL,* § 27b, p. 88; §§ 24–25, pp. 77–79).

Formal ontology and formal apophantics are defined against one another, but they are inseparable because all the forms of objects "have being for us . . . only as making their appearance in judgments" (§ 25, p. 79). The structures examined by formal ontology are there only in correlation to judgments. The unity

---

6. *FTL* § 24 is entitled: "The New Problem of a Formal Ontology. Characterization of Traditional Formal Mathematics as Formal Ontology." Formal ontology must also be distinguished from material or regional ontologies, which examine eidetic necessities proper to certain regions of being, such as the spatial, the animated, the personal, etc. Regional ontologies are the result of generalization, not formalization. See *Ideas I,* §§ 8–10. The term "formal ontology" is original with Husserl; see S. Bachelard, *A Study of Husserl's Formal and Transcendental Logic,* trans. L. Embree (Evanston, Ill.: Northwestern University Press, 1968), p. 37; and *FTL,* § 27, p. 86.

between formal ontology and formal apophantics is a unity of correlation, not one in which either is deduced from or absorbed into the other. A judgment is correlated to a registered or reported fact, because there are facts only when there are judgments; still, to talk about facts is not to talk about judgments, and vice versa; and to formalize systematically facts and their relationships, in formal ontology, is not to formalize systematically judgments and their interconnections, in formal apophantics. The two domains are distinct but correlative.

Husserl has inherited two philosophical traditions, the Aristotelian and the Liebnizian-mathematical, and has purified the sense of each by contrasting them to one another. Formal apophantics is his acceptance of scholastic logic, formal ontology his appreciation of mathematical logic.[7] So far his exposition has been controlled by the tradition he receives. He has not yet attempted to disclose the "original presence" of these things by a direct analysis of the phenomena. He does so in his second assault on the problem, in Chapter 4, §§ 42–45. For the moment we omit consideration of Chapter 3.

§ 3. The Second Approach: Apophantic Logic and Formal Ontology in Their Intuitive Presence

In § 37 Husserl asks, "Is it already clear what this properly signifies: to be focused sometimes on judgments as such and sometimes on objectivity as such?" (p. 105). The problem is this: since the objects and structures examined in formal ontology arise only when we frame judgments, i.e., only when we bring about the elements and structures examined by formal apophantics, is there truly a difference between formal ontology and formal apophantics? Formal ontology studies objects only insofar as they have become objects of judgment; "how then have we gone beyond a formal judgment-theory?" (§ 38, p. 107).[8] Is there really a difference of focus in the two inquiries? Can we explicitly recognize the difference?

7. In *FTL*, § 11, Husserl gives a formulation of the sense of logic which is even more primitive historically than the one he achieves by contrasting apophantics to formal ontology. This early appreciation of logic has some positive aspects that will be retained by Husserl, but it contains many confusions as well, as he shows.

8. The question is raised two more times in § 38, at the end of the first and second paragraphs. It is repeated in § 41.

Husserl introduces a new factor to answer his question. In § 40 he begins to talk about "the interest in cognizing." What we have hitherto described is now put into a new context: the concern with knowing. Apophantic and ontological forms will now be examined in regard to the work they do for knowledge. This horizon was not made explicit in §§ 23–25, and so the treatment of formal ontology and formal apophantics had to remain incomplete.

The horizon of interest in knowledge or truth interest is the same as that of interest in identity synthesis or recognition. The apophantic and the ontological domains will now be shown to be two moments within the whole of identification or fulfillment. In the first approach they were treated "abstractly," as two separate pieces; now they are to be treated within their proper whole.

With the new context of truth interest formulated, Husserl repeats his question once again in § 41 and starts answering it in § 42.

When we wish to know a certain object, we are concerned with the object itself. We make judgments about the thing, not about our minds or about our judgments. We register more and more facts about our object as we get to know more about it. We say, "The animal is brown, and it is small, and it runs fast, and it barks." We can complicate the process further by registering facts not directly about the object, but about a fact concerning the object: "The dog is brown because all his ancestors were the same color." "It is too bad he is that shade of brown." Or we can register facts about something that originally arose as part of a fact; we can compare attributes ("this shade of brown is darker than that") or we can speak about "brownness" as such, thematizing a property and registering more about it.

Throughout these elaborations the underlying object of our concern, "this animal," remains the same. Moreover, facts and parts of facts remain the same when we go on building on them. Husserl says that syntactical operations have a dual function: they create the syntactic state for their underlying object, they are form-creating; and they preserve the identity of the created form when they build still further syntactic forms on it (§ 42d, pp. 114–15). A fact is registered as such when we judge, and it is preserved as a fact when it becomes a part of a still higher syntactic structure, when, for instance, we give reasons for it, declare it to be regrettable or good, or register facts about facts. Facts can become ingredient into higher facts.

Husserl describes the syntactic elaboration of an object in

§ 42. The major point is that all such operations take place without a change of focus. We are constantly busy with the object or with facts about the object; we never turn our attention to our minds or to our judgments. All structures are fashioned in the objective focus; we never need to leave that focus, turn to judgments and fetch a category or structure, and impose it on objects or facts. Now keeping this focus on objects, we can formalize, eliminate any content in what we are busy with. We are then left with the skeleton of formal structures, the grid left as a residue of our categorial activity. We still have the empty forms of facts, relations, reasons for facts, relations between facts and relations, groups of objects, sets and subsets of them, and so on, all taken formally. Even in this move we do not abandon our objective focus. The formal science we obtain when we try to elaborate systematically what formal structures, relations, and operations can be carried out in this focus is formal ontology, the science we naïvely inherited from Leibniz, Boole, and De Morgan in § 24. We now have read it off the work of knowing and have presented it originally, phenomenologically.[9]

We never turn away from objects during the process we have described. How and when do we make this turn? In § 44a Husserl once again raises the question he repeated so often in §§ 37, 38, and 41; in § 44b he "phenomenologically clarifies" the change of focus.

As we keep learning more about the object of our concern, our registration goes along harmoniously. The object and its facts remain there for us as we frame further judgments about it. But sometimes the harmony is broken and some facts change modality, becoming doubtful, for instance, or questionable, or just probable "facts." Registrations begin to conflict with earlier registrations. Every fact is subject to such perturbation, but such disturbances need not change our focus.[10] We are still concerned with objects and facts, but now we also have to contend with some purported facts that are not simply accepted as the case.

9. *FTL.* § 42a, p. 111. "Originaliter" or "original clarification" has a technical sense for Husserl: the subject of analysis is brought to its original way of being present, its original way of differentiating itself from what is different. This is not a tautology, but rather expresses the aim of phenomenological description: to make us aware of the identity and sameness of a phenomenon over against that "other" which is proper to it.

10. We do not go below the level of facts here. Objects are also subject to perturbation, but that is on the level of prejudgmental perceptual experience and calls for a separate analysis.

But a new mode of consciousness is possible in which we become concerned with verification. Having ceased to accept all facts as simply real, we now can take steps to make a decision in regard to those that have become disturbing; we now focus on what we have meant *as supposed* by ourselves. We are no longer absorbed in objects and facts; we now focus on some objects and facts as supposed. We lose the naïveté of consciousness and become aware that there are not only objects and facts, but also facts and objects as meant, as supposed; besides being, there is also the opined.

This disturbance of the naïve harmony of consciousness, and the rise of an initial critical attitude, can develop in two ways. We can become aware of what we supposed as supposed, and then find that things are indeed as we opined, so the harmony of thoughtful experience is reestablished. Our conscious life has suffered a distention, but no break (§ 44b/β, ⊄ 2). Or we can find that what we supposed is not the way things are, that in further experience the registered facts falsify what we meant earlier. Then we abandon our earlier supposition. This break is much more radical. We now focus on what we supposed merely as supposed, as definitely canceled and disqualified from stating what is the case, as only an opinion and a wrong one (§ 44b/β, ⊄ 3). At this point we have a full-blown reflection on our opinion, our meaning. We are now completely disconnected from objects and facts. We are in the sheer apophantic focus as opposed to the objective focus. The shift from the objective domain to the apophantic domain is reflection.

Strictly speaking, Husserl does not have to go as far as complete cancellation of an opinion to bring out the apophantic focus. In the less radical case, when we consider a supposed sense as supposed and then find it to be correct, we already have a focus on the apophantic domain and a difference from the objective focus. But the move is much clearer when we cancel the position entirely, so the extra step is not without value.

A consciousness that is not critical will not fully appreciate the difference between facts and facts as meant. It will generally live in the objective focus, captivated by facts, and its awareness of the supposed as such will be only marginal. People often do not appreciate the difference between what is and what is meant as meant, between being and opinion; in areas in which they have not been educated, it may be impossible for them to distinguish, so they may take all opinions as stating what is the case. But a scientific consciousness is one that takes a professional interest in this difference (§ 44b/γ). Scientific obsession with verification is precisely the explicit awareness that there is a difference between what is and what is meant. It lives first in concern with things and elaborates facts pertinent to its objects, but then it sharply changes focus and considers what it has meant as a mere supposition, to be purified and tested against further experience of things and registration of facts. The scientist, says Husserl, lives in such zigzag motion between supposition and facts; this awareness and motion defines him as a scientist. And because he is aware of this verifying dimension, he is also aware of varieties and degrees within it; he is sensitive to the differences among necessity, probability, factuality, guesses, clues, and the like, an awareness that is by no means shared by everybody.[11]

Through § 44 Husserl makes us aware how we focus on judgments. He discloses the origins and the primitive presence of the apophantic domain. This provides a phenomenologically justified access to the domain we had naïvely accepted from the Aristotelian tradition in § 23. The sense of logic is being shaped anew.

The primitive, authentic presence of the apophantic domain is brought about by showing that this doman differentiates itself from the domain of objects in three respects: it initially comes to light when disturbances in the validity of objects and facts arise; it comes more radically to light when certain purported objects or purported facts are totally disconnected from the world and its objects, when they are canceled as not acceptable, as having been merely supposed at one time; finally, apophantic structures are teleologically oriented to being brought back to the domain of objects and facts, they are meant to match registered things and facts, and even when they are canceled and abandoned they have this sense of abandonment because they fail to match the way things are.[12] In its origins and in its finality, the domain of meaning is derivative from the domain of objects.

Since judgments are disclosed only *as different* from objects and facts, we are sure that focusing on judgments is different

11. Proof of this in ordinary experience is the way scientific hints, clues, or hypotheses are often presented as established truths by commentators.

12. Strawson, "Truth," in *Logico-Linguistic Papers* (London: Methuen, 1971), p. 197: "Of course, statements and facts fit. They were made for each other."

from focusing on objects and facts. The judgment has been disclosed and defined precisely as that which, in the truth interest and the enterprise of knowing, differentiates itself from objects and facts.

It should be clear now why Husserl takes such great pains in § 42 to show that facts, relations, and other syntactic transformations of an object do not depart from the domain of objects and do not involve a change from the objective focus; such objective syntactic structures are often mistaken for judgments by philosophers and logicians.[13] When this mistake is made, all hope is lost of keeping the two domains distinct and of revealing the true status and original presence of the apophantic sphere.

In the objective focus we are concerned with objects and facts. In the apophantic focus we are concerned with supposed objects and facts as supposed. If we were to state the last two sentences in the context of Husserl's first approach to the problem of formal ontology and formal apophantics, the approach given in §§ 23–25, they would appear contradictory, and so would the following sentence which occurs in § 45: "*Judgments, in the sense proper to apophantic logic, are* supposed predicatively formed *facts* as supposed" (p. 126).[14] In this sentence we are told that judgments are facts—as supposed.

Such statements appear contradictory because, in the initial formulation of §§ 23–25, facts are relegated exclusively to the objective sphere while judgments are in the apophantic sphere. In the new formulation, facts as supposed are in the apophantic sphere and are equated with judgments.[15] The new formulation

13. I find it hard to see how Bachelard avoids this difficulty in *A Study of Husserl's Logic*, p. 34, where she also seems to say that the process of nominalization moves categories belonging to the objective sphere into the apophantic sphere of propositions: "Ultimately all categories of the object in formal ontology . . . exist only insofar as they play a role in judgments. What is more, the operation of 'nominalization' . . . makes these categories of the object appear as constitutive elements of the proposition."

14. Italics mine. I replace "affair-complexes" in Cairns's translation with "facts." See above, § 10. It is true that "affair-complexes" are not the same as "states of affairs," but we do not wish to develop that difference here.

15. A similar statement occurs in § 49, p. 134, where Husserl equates "the proposition as a sense, the supposed categorial objectivity as supposed." On p. 83 of *A Study of Husserl's Logic*, Bachelard distinguishes the objective focus from the apophantic focus by attributing to the former an interest in possible adequation while

is more acceptable philosophically because it shows how each focus is possible and intrinsically relates the two domains within the whole of truth interest. The first formulation merely accepts both from the tradition and places them over against each other.

Husserl's new understanding of the apophantic domain and its relationship to the objective domain is made possible because he now sets both domains within a horizon which is unmentioned in his first formulation, but which gives both domains their sense: the horizon or context of the concern to know. There is an objective domain, and there is an apophantic domain, only for a consciousness concerned with knowing. The consciousness that undergoes pleasure or pain, the artistic consciousness, the consciousness rapt in fantasy, do not recognize these domains. To understand the sense of the domain of objects and that of the apophantic domain, we have to consider them at work in the knowing consciousness. We would get no help at all by discovering more and more formal structures within either domain; we must move into a new dimension and start talking about intentionalities. This is why Husserl introduces the theme of concern with knowledge in § 40 and why he returns to it in § 46, immediately after distinguishing the two domains. In § 46 he proceeds to analyze truth and evidence, which are exercises of intentionality and not properties of formal systems, whether apophantic or ontological.

The two notions of truth Husserl distinguishes in § 46 are merely refinements of what we have already encountered. First, truth is the correctness of a judgment which is found to match registered facts; it occurs after we have reflected on a judgment —a supposed fact as supposed—and then experienced its adequation to intuited facts. Second, truth is the actual presence of the fact or object as that which saturates our supposition when the latter is brought to the things themselves. This second truth allows the first truth, correctness, to occur. Husserl then gives corresponding definitions of evidence as the noetic performance

---

denying it to the latter. In focusing on judgments the following prevails, in her opinion: "Then I consider the judgment as a simple sense without focusing upon the objects which this sense intends, hence without placing myself in the situation of possible adequation." But it seems to me the apophantic focus can well involve interest in adequation. Also, she puts "categorial objectivity grasped qua sense" into the objective focus, but shouldn't it be apophantic if it is grasped as a sense?

proper to each kind of truth: the experience of correctness, and the experience of actual presence as saturating.

Husserl stresses the relevance that the distinction between objective and apophantic domains has for scientific consciousness. However, his principles can be put to work in the wider sphere of political life. The possibility of political life depends on the capacity to speak. Speech makes possible a kind of agreement which excludes physical violence; Aristotle says that the man who is by nature an outcast from political life is a "lover of war," like an "isolated piece at draughts," obeying neither grammatical rules of language nor legal rules of politics (*Politics* 1. 2. 1253a3–7).

Nature gives us speech to express the expedient and inexpedient, the just and the unjust, and this use of language suffices for political life (1253a14–18). But if there is to be the kind of political life where opinions can be subject to criticism, a further exercise of speech is necessary: one in which it becomes possible to focus on what is said, distinguish it from what is, and match it against facts. It must be possible to adopt the apophantic focus—now, of course, in regard to judgments or suppositions that are not formalized. When we critically examine our own past opinions, we reflect on our own judgments in this way; this is what Husserl has described. But if we are to examine other speakers' judgments, it must be possible for us to be apophantically oriented toward them as well. We must be able to detach what they say from them and accept it as supposed, then to decide its truth according to the facts and not by reason of the character of the one who has held the opinion. The apophantic focus is the condition allowing critical toleration of another's opinion. Here, as in so many other instances, Husserl uses our awareness of our own past as an analogue for our experience of other persons: "If it is a matter of another's judging, then, in case I do not believe too, I have the 'mere idea' of the other's belief that has such and such a content: I have a presentation analogous to a memory of some past belief of my own 'in which I no longer join' but which I nevertheless accept now, in memory, as my previously exercised believing" (*FTL*, § 16a, p. 59). Such detachment of judgments either from our own past or from other speakers is also a function of the "ideality of meaning" which Husserl describes earlier in *Formal and Transcendental Logic* (§ 2).[16] A judgment or any

16. Compare this to Augustine's *Confessions* (trans. F. Sheed) 10. 9: "In memory also are all such things as we have learned of the

other sense can appear as identically the same throughout many repetitions and in many speakers.

The apophantic focus allows that level of political life which is carried on in debate or dialectic, a form of controversy proper to man living under the order of law; debate does not take place in transpolitical or prepolitical initiatives or violence. Sciences like physics are one form of this critical but tolerant conscious life. Husserl acknowledges a debt to Leibniz in regard to the *mathēsis universalis,* but Leibniz' hope of reconciling conflicting points of view, in science and in politics, may also be at work in phenomenology, with similar deep-seated limitations.[17]

§ 4. Formal Logic and Pure Mathematics

WE HAVE BEEN WORKING with three dimensions: the objective domain, the apophantic domain, and the concern with knowledge. We have been able to clarify the objective focus and the apophantic focus. Logic has traditionally been exercised in the apophantic focus and its attitude has been critical. It tests apophantic formulations for consistency, with a view to their service in knowledge. Logic does not focus on the objective domain, but the apophantic structures it examines are apprehended as geared toward objects, facts, and the world. So it does have ontological reference indirectly. Logic carries on its activity while the truth interest, the concern with knowledge, is kept alive; its apophantic themes are kept within the horizon of knowledge. We now move to distinguish pure mathematics from logic, and will do so in two steps.

1. Pure formal mathematics, the "mathematics of mathematicians," is defined against formal logic by disengaging the concern with knowledge or application. Like formal logic it is apophantically oriented and so it focuses on facts or states of

---

liberal sciences and have not forgotten, lying there as if in a more inward place, which yet is no place; and of these I have not the images but the things themselves." See also 10. 10.

17. On Leibniz' program of intellectual pacification see D. Mahnke, *Leibnizens Synthese von Universalmathematik und Individualmetaphysik* (Stuttgart: Fromann, 1964), Introduction, § 3, pp. 9–14; this study originally appeared in 1925 in Husserl's *Jahrbuch.* Probably the greatest weakness in Leibniz' hope is the conviction that agreement of minds pacifies human affairs.

affairs as supposed, objects as supposed, relations as supposed; it is a "science that has to do with nothing but apophantic senses" (*FTL*, § 52, p. 141). But it disconnects the teleology of what it examines. It studies these formal structures as ends in themselves.

Apart from this, pure mathematics may be just like formal logic. Both are essentially concerned with consistency, but pure mathematics stops with consistency while logic sees consistency as a condition for truth. "Mathematical existence" of a certain form means simply that the form is consistent in a theory within which it can be derived.[18] The actual formulas articulated in a logical deduction may appear exactly the same as those in a mathematical deduction; even the symbolism may be the same. The difference between the two appears neither in the symbolism nor in the deduction, but in the sense each has: one is done with truth interest operative, the other with truth interest shut off.

This simple difference—which could be recognized only after we introduced the horizon of a concern with knowledge—allows Husserl to make the bold claim that "in this manner the proper sense of 'formal mathematics' . . . at last becomes fundamentally clarified. Here lies the sole legitimate distinction between formal logic and mere formal mathematics" (§ 52, p. 141).

2. There is another dimension, a fourth to the three we mentioned at the beginning of § 4, which we have been using implicitly: the process of deduction. Husserl introduces deduction in Chapter 3, §§ 28–36. We skipped this section when we moved from (*a*) the early formulation of formal ontology and formal apophantics in Chapter 2 to (*b*) the later formulation in Chapter 4; we must now fill this gap in order to round out our understanding of pure mathematics.

Chapter 3 deals with the theory of theory forms and its correlate, the theory of multiplicities.[19] A theory is a series of judgments or propositions in which some are derived deductively from others. If we formalize such a concatenation of judgments we are left with a theory form; for instance, if we take Euclidean

18. *FTL*, § 52, p. 140: "Thus it is understandable that, for a . . . 'pure' formal mathematics, there can be no cognitional considerations other than those of 'non-contradiction,' of immediate or mediate analytic consequence or inconsistency, which manifestly include all questions of mathematical 'existence'."

19. In his translation of the *Logical Investigations*, Findlay uses "manifold" for *Mannigfaltigkeit* (see "Prolegomena," §§ 69–70), while Cairns employs "multiplicity."

geometry and disregard its "content," the spatial sense of the judgments comprising it, we have the theory form of this deductive science. If we do the same for other theories we acquire many theory forms; let us name them A, B, C, etc. Husserl then introduces the notion of a theory that will examine theory forms; it will articulate possible theory forms, show relations among them (for instance, that theory form A includes theory form Q), show how certain ones can be transformed into others (for instance, that Q and R can be combined to yield theory form M), and so on. This highest formal science will be the theory of theory forms.[20]

A theory form is correlated to a multiplicity. This is a group of objects determined only by the characteristic of being governed by that theory form. All the x's and the y's governed by theory form A make up the multiplicity A; all those governed by theory form B make up the multiplicity B, etc. In analogy to the theory of theory forms, Husserl proposes a theory of multiplicities which will elaborate the various possible multiplicities and show the relationships and transformations holding among them, for instance, that multiplicity B can be included within multiplicity A, or that multiplicities Q and P combine to produce T. A theory form is made up of judgmental or propositional forms; a multiplicity is made up of objects.

In Chapter 3 Husserl places theory forms within the apophantic domain and multiplicities within the objective

20. Is the theory of theory forms itself a deductive theory? No, for there are no "axiomatic theories" from which all the others can be derived.

It would be helpful to clarify Husserl's use of "levels" and "strata" in *FTL*, §§ 51–52. (1) First paragraph of § 51: Analytics has two lower strata, morphology of judgment forms and analysis of noncontradiction. Then a third level of analytics is added, the theory forms and theory of multiplicities (p. 138). We now have three layers. (2) Second paragraph of § 51: Cutting across these layers is another distinction between two strata: analysis as mere concern with senses, and analysis with the truth interest active, as a concern with possible truth. This duality is possible on each of the three layers including the highest one, where it will yield a pure *mathēsis* of noncontradiction and a *mathēsis* of possible truth. A pure mathematician can, of course, exclude any concern with possible truth. (3) The "three levels" of analytics mentioned at the beginning of § 52 are the three layers noted above in (1). (4) But the "essential stratification" mentioned later in § 52 refers to the option between mere noncontradiction and possible truth as noted in (2) above. I believe this interpretation agrees with Bachelard, *A Study of Husserl's Logic*, pp. 40–42.

domain. A theory form would then be placed over against its multiplicity. Husserl has to do this because of the rough way he sets the apophantic domain over against the objective domain in Chapter 2, where he simply accepts traditional positions and does not phenomenologically differentiate the two domains.

In Chapter 4 Husserl presents his new, phenomenologically legitimate differentiation of the apophantic from the objective. The apophantic domain of senses receives its senses from the objective domain, but interprets them as supposed. A judgment is a supposed fact or state of affairs as supposed. Hence a theory is now a concatenation of supposed facts or states of affairs as supposed.

A multiplicity can also be peeled off the objective domain, and then it becomes a group of supposed *objects* as supposed. When treated apophantically, it is a group of object-senses, while a theory is a concatenation of judgment-senses.[21] In this new formulation the theory form and its multiplicity collapse into the same domain: they are both within the apophantic sphere, no longer set over against each other as in Chapter 3. This "reconciliation" is possible because of the new definition of the apophantic domain in terms of interest in knowledge.

When the pure mathematician restricts himself to the apophantic domain and disconnects the truth interest, he has within his scope both theory forms and multiplicities; multiplicities are still those objects as supposed, the object-senses, which are governed by a system of states of affairs or facts as supposed, or relations as supposed. The pure mathematician thus has two possible areas of study: he can work on the theory forms and engender propositional forms or even new theory forms, and he can work on the multiplicities and engender classes whose laws and relations he can examine. He can do both algebra and set theory. But he does all this without concern for the application of his theory forms in the actual exercise of knowing the world. The multiplicities he discusses need not be

21. See *FTL*, § 53, p. 142: "As the correlate of a possible systematic theory, we have a possible multiplicity, a possible object-province that it theorizes systematically. When this possibility is left out of account, its place is taken by a multiplicity, not of objects *simpliciter,* but of supposed objects as supposed—that is to say, object-senses, as substrate-senses, that are adapted to function harmoniously in a judgment-system as substrates of predications. The substrate-senses, however, are only fundamental object-senses belonging to that theory, which has itself been reduced to the pure theory-sense."

thought of as possible multiplicities, as groups that somehow can be active, formally, in the thoughtful experience of things, facts, and the world. "It becomes apparent that, when questions about possible truth are consistently excluded in this manner, and the truth-concept itself is similarly excluded, one has not actually lost any of this logical mathesis; one still has the whole of it: as 'purely' formal mathematics." [22]

§ 5. FORMAL ONTOLOGY VERSUS APOPHANTIC LOGIC AND PURE MATHEMATICS

IT ONLY REMAINS to show where formal ontology fits into the new formulation of apophantics and mathematics. Pure mathematics is defined by disconnecting the concern with knowledge; we now activate that concern again, and the mathematical system we have elaborated "becomes related to any possible objectivity whatever." Husserl says mathematics now "lies once more within the theory of science, where it exercises functions pertaining to criticism" (*FTL*, § 54a, p. 143). But although it has indirect relevance to objectivities, this science is still apophantically oriented and does not turn to direct contemplation of objects in their syntactical formations. As long as we are concerned with judgments, our attitude is not "formal ontological" (§ 54b, p. 145).

We now take an intermediate step. Suppose we recognize the teleology of the apophantic forms we study; we appreciate their tension toward objectivities, their aim at fulfillment in objective formal structures. We follow that teleology and contemplate the objective formal structures that fulfill apophantic meanings; let us contemplate them *as* fulfilling such meanings. For instance, we examine the formal structure of facts as that which saturates formal structures of judgments. We are now using the two senses of evidence Husserl discussed earlier: evidence as having objects or facts themselves, and evidence as experiencing the correctness of judgments that are adequately fulfilled. At this point we are still not doing formal ontology, because the

22. *FTL*, § 52, p. 140. Husserl adds that in practice the mathematician may well "contaminate" his thinking with concern for application, but this is accidental and he is not defined by this, any more than a greedy physician is defined as physician by his concern with gain; cf. Plato's *Republic* 1. 341c.

scope of our interest includes both the apophantic and the objective domains. We examine the objective domain as fulfilling the apophantic. This contamination of our concern by the apophantic has to be removed.

It is removed when we simply contemplate the objective domain without co-meaning the apophantic. We activate only one sense of evidence: having objectivities and facts themselves.[23] If we explore the categorial formations that can be carried out here, we will be doing formal ontology. We have recovered the purely ontological focus by eliminating the interest in the apophantic sphere that was introduced in § 44. We have critically returned to the place from which we naïvely began. The whole journey was made within the horizon of truth interest, the concern with knowledge: apophantic logic is the critical testing of categorial formulations with a view toward having them given in immediate presence; pure mathematics is the disconnection of any concern with knowledge; formal ontology is the sheer absorption in given categorial objectivities themselves, without explicit concern with the critical apophantic domain. All these disciplines remain purely formal and limit themselves to questions of consistency.[24]

HUSSERL DOES NOT DISCOVER new deductive techniques or formal systems; the old mathematical and logical "phenomena" remain the same, but they are viewed from a new perspective. To handle the foundations of mathematics and the relation between logic and mathematics, we cannot stay with either discipline but must move to higher ground for a new, phenomenological viewpoint. We appreciate formal sciences in their place within intentionalities. Differences then appear which are not manifest to the mathematician: "In his positivity, living entirely with a view to discovering new theoretical results, he is not in the least interested in changes of attitude or focus that convert an equivalent into an equivalent. Transitions from one

23. Facts and objectivities can be given only as saturating empty intentions, but we may abstractly thematize them simply as given, not as saturating.

24. All apophantic structures can be mapped onto the ontological domain; even complete theories can be so projected. Husserl speaks of the case when "a deductive theory is understood to be, not a system of judgments, but a system of possible, predicatively formed, affair-complexes and, in its entirety, a distinctively formed unity belonging to a categorial objectivity" (*FTL*, § 54b, p. 147).

thing to another that is evidently its perfect correlate yield 'the same,' in his sense of the phrase" (*FTL*, § 54c, p. 147; see also *Ideas I*, § 134 last ⊄). The moves made by Husserl seem pointless to the mathematician—they are moves that do not go anywhere—because they work within differences he cannot recognize in his professional perspective.

Apophantic logic deals with the formal structures of facts as supposed. Formal ontology deals with the formal structures of facts as registered or reported. Husserl's *mathēsis universalis* is simply the articulation of pure formal structures, on the level of theory, but in abstraction from their role in either facts as supposed or facts as registered or reported. Apophantic logic is a condition for truth because it provides the rules which a supposition must obey if there is to be any hope of bringing it to registration of what is. Pure mathematics deals with the formal structures of facts as supposed and is subject to the rules of consistency, but it shuts off the concern with knowledge and truth as adequation; its truth is exhausted in consistency.

Index

[291]